Bowhunting Modern Elk

Patrick Meitin

Petersen's Bowhunting Magazine
7819 Highland Scenic Drive
Baxter, MN 56425
www.bowhuntingmag.com

Bowhunting Modern Elk

Editor: Jay Michael Strangis
Associate Editor: Tony Peterson
Associate Editor: Daniel Beraldo
Production Coordinator: Carolyn Olson
Interior Design: Jill Voges
Art Director: Nicole Mahany
Publisher: Petersen's Bowhunting

Most of the photographs in the chapters to follow were taken by the author, Patrick Meitin. The author also wishes to thank Petersen's Bowhunting's Jay Strangis (Editor), Tony Peterson (Associate Editor) and Daniel Beraldo (Associate Editor), plus Randy Ulmer, G5 Outdoors' Garret Armstrong and Sitka Gear's Jonathan Hart, who also contributed photographs for this book.

Second Printing 2011

Library of Congress Cataloging-in-Publication Data
ISBN (10) = 1-892947-99-4
ISBN (13) = 978-1-892947-99-4

To my Gwyn, who even after suffering through the writing of this book agreed to marry me.

And to Petersen's Bowhunting editor, and my good friend, Jay Strangis, who believed in me when so many did not.

Contents

Introduction

I've been an awfully lucky boy, overall. Residing "Out West" all my life—the years that count anyway—allowed handy access to mountains and foothills where deer, wild turkeys, pronghorn, bears and elk roam. My folks are decided non-hunters to this day. When I was young they fretted endlessly over my hunting obsessions because they were sure it would be the ruin of any formal education. It's interesting to note that my biological father, a man I grew up not knowing, who I've only recently established a close relationship with, is an avid hunter and outdoorsman. That pretty much settles the "nurture verses nature" question in my mind, because my burning desire to hunt was viewed as strange by those who raised me. I'm lucky to have had neighbors willing to tolerate a smart-aleck kid, making me part of annual family deer hunting expeditions; and eventually forays for elk. I guess my folks reckoned it kept me out of mischief, because in time I pretty much kept my own schedule, coming and going at the odd hours hunting often dictates. In any case, I got a pretty early start in this hunting thing.

My elk-hunting memories begin with a six-hour drive to northwestern New Mexico with the father of a hunting buddy seven years my senior. My buddy's father, Lonnie Harper, and I were meeting a camp of his relatives for my first ever December late-season rifle elk hunt. I was somehow sure I'd punch my tag, rambling on about information contained in innumerable magazine articles I'd studied carefully over the past several months, the sum total elk knowledge I'd absorbed and believed in. Mr. Harper found this nothing short of amusing, having returned from far too many elk hunts empty-handed. I also recall the pointed campfire ribbing I endured as the youngest in the party. I received the most abuse regarding my .243 Winchester "pea-shooter." It wasn't up to the task was the general consensus.

"I guess I'll just have to shoot 'em in the ear," I answered innocently. Which is exactly what I did (from 150 yards) on opening morning, collecting an eating-fat five-by-five bull after tracking him through snow some nine miles. I was 12 years old. I rifle-killed another small bull two years later (With the same .243, this one shot through the lungs. It worked just fine). A nicer bull fell to my .50-caliber Hawkins muzzleloading kit rifle two years after (New Mexico allotted firearms elk tags only every other year back then, though you could hunt with archery gear every year).

But I was an archery hunter at heart from the get-go; chasing vacant-lot bunnies with bow and arrow from the age of nine (it took me a year to successfully bag my first). I somehow managed to arrow my first deer, a desert muley doe, with a recurve at the tender age of 13. As I remember it, I'd hounded my older buddy Perry Harper, (who owned the four-wheel-drive vehicle required to access remote elk country) to apply for archery elk tags the year before we'd tried the Mountain Man bit. He hadn't gotten completely over the rifle bug, so I was forced to follow suit. After we'd successfully graduated from muzzle-loader elk, we went on our first elk archery hunt the following September. It would be a short three-day weekend (the single additional day stolen from formal education) in which I stalked a nice six-by-six bull, delaminated under the pressure and shot over his back at something like 40 yards. It didn't dampen my enthusiasm a wit.

My rotted '68 Nova was packed and ready to roll, awaiting completion of high school commencement ceremonies. Thus initiated my career as a big game guide, a late spring and early summer filled with chasing hounds over high, rough mountains in pursuit of black bears, cleaning up after and feeding those hounds and the horses we used to pursue them. That fall I guided my first elk hunters, most of them suspicious of this youngster in braces. We had some great times and I arrowed my first archery elk on the final day of a 24-day archery season, a matriarch cow taken at 50 yards, *running*. I was guiding a client who'd first urged me to bring my bow to "back him up" and then insisted I shoot after he'd missed the same cow standing at 30 yards. The following year I took my first bull, a six-by-six that just passed Pope & Young minimums. You'll be reading about that bull shortly.

In the twenty-something years since that first bow elk (when you advance to full-fledged archery hunter, everything taken with firearms ceases to exist) I've guided many more archery hunters, taken something like 12 P&Y-quality bulls, most of them by stealing a day here and there between stints of guiding. I finally abandoned the full-time outfitting business because my personal hunting time had become rare indeed. I still guided elk hunters occasionally, when I needed extra cash for some financial emergency, or an outfitter friend desperately needed help and most importantly when I'd failed to draw my own elk tag and these scenarios converged. There were some hard times to be sure, because getting established in the outdoor-writing dodge includes mighty slim pickings, but I think back and understand I was living the life of Riley, that I got to archery hunt more than the average guy earning much more money. I've been very lucky.

For the past 15 years I've lived within an hour's drive of quality elk herds. I've drawn a good archery elk tag here and there and have taken a couple bulls I'm not too humble to brag about because I'm as proud of them as anything I've accomplished in life. My best bull scores about 386, a seven-by-eight non-typical that's really something to look at. *Petersen's Bowhunting* editor Jay Strangis was there, in fact, and the first thing I said to him after arrowing that bull and meeting with him again at the truck well after black dark was, "I'm the luckiest man on earth."

Like the open-range cattleman of old, who moved on when a country "played out," I'll soon be leaving New Mexico (where drawing quality elk tags has become nearly impossible), moving on to the elk country in Idaho or Montana. My new wife and I haven't found the perfect house yet, but we're headed north, sure as taxes. I'll have plenty of new country to explore and commit to memory, after a quarter century of intimate familiarity with the elk haunts of New Mexico's Gila country. This is a little scary, to be quite honest, but also very exciting. I've still got enough gumption left (at 43) to learn one more very large "backyard" so that I'll always "know a place;" dependent on current weather conditions and hunting pressure and summer precipitation. I'll doubtless have new lessons to learn about those Gem State or Big Sky bulls, whatever the case may be, but that's what elk hunting today is all about; being open to new lessons, flexibility, keeping an open mind.

If I get nothing else across in this book, I hope it will be that. Modern elk hunting requires an open mind. The wider your spectrum of elk-hunting skills, the more willing you are to deviate from a preferred method or one popularly adhered to, the closer you are to making the latter point reality. Please don't mistake this as an ego-driven need to "score" every time. It's simply about making the best of hard-won tags and time afield, maximizing our enjoyment of what is the best big game animal on earth, bar none. I'll stand by that.

Have your whitetails; make mine elk!

Patrick Meitin
Hillsboro, New Mexico
February 2008

Chapter 1

The Changing Elk Dodge

The bull bugled as I waited in my battered Land Cruiser, the window rolled to half-mast in hopes of just such a revelation. He bugled again as I departed the Cruiser in the icy silvering of a fresh New Mexico morning. It was a bugle I could feel reverberating deep in my chest. He was that close, a distance best measured in hundreds of yards, but he was on the move, heading deeper into roadless forest. Coyotes yodeled in the middle distance and there was the barely perceivable whistle of yet another randy bull well removed, betraying his position across the lifeless morning air. It stopped me cold, momentarily straining my ears, information against later hours. I shifted my back quiver for a better ride and hurried through knee-deep blue gamma whispering with dislodged frost. Inside 50 yards my camouflage pants were soaked to the waist—the thin, much-patched WWII outfit I had been wearing since I killed my first archery mule deer six years before. My lucky bowhunting duds. I was painfully superstitious. My bull bugled again, then was answered by a third bull farther up the drainage.

This is how it all started; Author Patrick Meitin's first archery-killed elk, an eating-fat cow taken on the run.

After a half mile of featureless juniper flats I reached foothills, live-oak motes skirting jumbles of abrupt points and isolated humps held in place by towering ponderosa pine. It was a maze of erosion cuts and sharp crests with grassy benches

Opposite page: Archery hunting for elk is considered by many to be the ultimate pursuit. Success is often hard won and extremely rewarding.

between. It was perfect stalking country. I tested the wind with a dried puffball mushroom secreted in a shirt pocket yesterday before evening rains arrived. I watched the dust-like spores drift languidly in the direction of the parked Cruiser, knowing I was in good shape before this test, simply releasing nervous energy. I slipped along quickly but silently, mentally encouraging my bull to sound off once more, to let me know how I was doing. Soon he obliged. I was closing the gap.

I pussyfooted around one of those walls of cover, created by a sharp slant of earth capped by thronged oak, hearing the bull cough, one of those involuntary grunts like a man talking to himself when he thinks he is alone. My bull was close now and I took a chance and pushed in a fast, running squat, cutting the distance across an open swatch of wet grass.

I saw his warm breath first, bellowing like wood smoke on a cold winter morning. I risked a few more steps before turning my left foot toward him and waiting. His antlers were beginning to emerge from the roll of dewy land, growing taller with each ticking second. An arrow had somehow materialized on my string. I had to take my eyes off him to find the bowstring with dead-numb fingers, fingers covered in surplus olive wool that served multipurpose duty as camouflage, insulation and shooting glove. I wrapped unresponsive fingers around the mono serving and turned my attention to the advancing bull.

The mud-splotched six-by-six cleared brush, pausing to rake an oak as if the entire episode had been scripted. My mind raced to form a solid range, grappled with myriad numbers. I settled on 45 yards while tugging on the string, looking at the entire animal, sweeping my single pin a fist's-width above his spine. The lovingly crafted Port Orford cedar, crested bright white and wearing real barred feathers, streaked toward the target, arching up and passing four inches over the bull's back. He hopped three steps and turned to regard me blankly.

The miss elicited a muttered oath that was not Great Caesar's Ghost. Tomorrow I would be guiding paying clients. My hunting opportunity would suddenly cease. This morning was my last chance. My anger erased earlier fumbling, created a calculated concen-

Author Patrick Meitin earned his elk-hunting stripes by guiding elk hunters professionally, a vocation started in 1983.

tration. I somehow fished an arrow from my Catquiver, looked down to find the string, knowing all too well the bull would have vanished by the time I looked up again. Seconds dragged. I looked up to find the bull still taking stock, quartering toward me slightly for a better look. I drew ever so gingerly, the mantra looping in my head something like, please hold, please hold, please hold, please hold...

This time I snugged the single pin low on his chest, finding an interesting piece of mud between his shoulder point and neck base that held all of my hopes and dreams. And the arrow slipped away. While that arrow flew empires were created and crumbled, stars flared and grew dormant, new galaxies formed. The hand-stropped, hair-splitting Zwickey Black Diamond arrived, missing the mud by inches, but close enough to do its deadly work. And everything whirled abruptly into real time. The bull vanished like smoke driven before wind.

SUCCESS AT LAST

I stood momentarily, listening to pounding hooves, breaking oak brush, then to nothing at all. The bull up the drainage bugled long and hard, chuckling out a series of deep grunts. I stole ahead, senses whetted, reaching the place where the bull had received my arrow. A couple steps further along half my cedar arrow lay atop wet grass, blood soaking the splintered end. I heard a strange gurgling groan and stalked to the edge of one of those sharp drops in the twisted topography. My bull struggled to get his legs under him a good distance away, rolled on his side again then righted himself once more. I invested a ranging shot at some ridiculous range, grabbed another arrow from my quiver with frantic hands and imbedded this one into his broadside ribs.

I had taken a cow elk with archery gear before this bull. That was the year before, taken at the insistent urging of a client, a lucky, 50-yard running shot as she sought safer pastures on the last day of the season after said client had missed an easy shot. I now had a bull. It was September 3, 1983. I was 18 years old. Among that year's sundry highlights I'd only recently shed my torturous braces to reveal miraculously straight teeth. A month before I'd lost my virginity. Those two seminal events were distant seconds to that first archery bull. He would better Pope & Young's 260-inch minimums by a safe margin that allowed for inches of shrinkage.

It's difficult to comprehend that this event took place nearly 24 years ago. It seems like only yesterday. But as they say: My, how things have changed. Those were different times. To ponder the equipment of those days alone never fails to bring on a chuckle.

PONDERING EARLY EQUIPMENT

Though I shot a compound bow I still clung tightly to my Zwickeys, a traditional, glue-on head still worthy and widely available and one that has never failed me to this day. The serious hunters who formed my early bowhunting opinions considered replaceable-blade broadheads untrustworthy, a suspicion well grounded in bad experiences. New equipment technology always receives the rap when events turn out badly, but beginning replaceable-blade broadhead models were certainly prone to sheared-off blades and bent-over tips.

I bought thousand-shaft lots of raw, "premium-grade" Acme Port Orford cedars (at $130 per thousand!), staying up late into the night spine testing them individually, bundling them into matched lots for staining, finishing and careful cresting. I held stubbornly to cedars because choosing aluminum meant adding a heavy screw-in adaptor to my traditional-style heads that boosted head weight to 180 grains and resulted in looping trajectory from the 2117 or 2216 aluminum arrows popular at the time. Only having recently (and quite reluctantly) abandoned my recurve bows, arrow speed was abruptly and very much on my mind. I wasn't alone in that regard. I killed plenty of critters with those cedars, though. I was an athletic boy who emerged from bed at 3:30 a.m. winter mornings to run 10-mile trap-lines before 8:15 first-period high school role call and easily handled 75-pound compound bows by age 16. The PSE Vector I favored at the time of that first bull was the fastest bow of its day, causing "oohs" and "awes" as it spun 215 fps (!) out of the chronograph down at the local bow shop with a full-length, 550-grain arrow. Never mind that its limbs exploded every few months (something unheard of today), once even removing a chunk of flesh from my right ear.

My traditional roots meant I preferred to keep things simple. A single brass pin was strategically drilled and tapped through the magnesium riser and secured with lock washers and dual brass nuts. That pin was sighted right on at 40 yards and used like pistol sights on longer and shorter ranges, holding high or low according to a guessed range. There was still a certain amount of instinctive shooting involved in each shot. It was merely a reference point. None of us at the time could have fathomed such science-fiction concepts as laser range finders, carbon arrows, mechanical broadheads or 300 feet per second!

BOWHUNTING'S HEYDAY

Nearly every aspect of elk hunting, as you might well imagine, was different then as well. You received an elk tag every single year for the asking, even in New Mexico's coveted Gila National Forest region (they were actually state-wide tags and we might bounce from one unit to the next during a single week). You might see another hunter occasionally, but there was plenty of room for everyone and it wasn't uncommon to go days between human sightings. A vehicle breakdown or getting stuck in the mud initiated a long hike to a distant ranch house. Odds are no one would be along for days to offer assistance.

Consequently, elk were calm, blissfully ignorant creatures when I started bowhunting them. It wasn't uncommon, as I have illustrated, to receive follow-up shots at bulls that had been recently and narrowly missed. I actually recall a client a couple years after my first bull missing the same 427-inch bull—antlers that would still make a world record—four times straight before the bull got the gist and fled the scene. I know that behemoth six-by-six scored 427 inches (typi-

Opposite page: Much has changed in elk hunting in the past 20 years; our equipment most of all. Today's gear is better in every way compared to that of only 20 years ago.

Elk have begun to reclaim the open prairies they were forced from with the arrival of hungry, westward-bound settlers.

cal, net) because another client killed him during rifle season a month later; a well-traveled client who passed 370 bulls to make that happen. He never even officially entered that bull, something difficult to grasp today.

Another memory comes quickly to mind, the morning with the heart surgeon from Indianapolis. The final morning of the 1984 season arrived with slashing, horizontal rain and everyone was understandably reluctant to venture forth, anyway worn down and tired and contemplating an evening flight and packing in preparation for the sad journey home. "Doc" said he'd do it if I would. He was always crazy like that, one of the good clients you'll always remember. We parked on the very spot from which I had first heard my bull bugle the year before (it was close to camp) and we waited in the clammy Cruiser awaiting a break in weather as the windows steamed. That break came at 10 a.m. and we alighted to hear bugling from all quarters. We dashed to a point a mile away and set up. I produced a three-noted whistle from a foot-long length of PVC tubing with a carved wooden plug wedged into one angled end. The bull came on the run, a 350ish six-by-six on a beeline course. He came straight on and he was still advancing when he crossed the 10-yard mark. I urged Doc to do something. He tugged on his bow, the arrow producing a violin screech as it dragged across wet rest arms. The bull simply stopped. The arrow sailed 20 feet high due to nerves or some such.

We got on that bull 15 minutes later and Doc missed him again, broadside at 35 yards. Another real-life bugle lured us deeper into dripping forest, more rain beginning to filter down. Our standard-issue cotton camo duds where soaked through and we where chilled to the bone but the siren's song of lovesick bulls made our discomfort easy to ignore. We blundered into that herd a few miles later. Blunder is the only correct term, because we simply rounded a ground-hugging cedar and were standing face-to-face with a raghorn bull, regarding us with a small amount of concern at maybe 25 yards. Not knowing what else to do I "mooed" like a beef cow, loud and belligerently. The bull resumed his morning feed. After he wandered out of sight (we recovered from our laughing fit) I quickly produced my PVC elk flute. Doc wanted that raghorn bad. I produced a pretty three-noted trilling. Instead of the raghorn, a 380-inch bull emerged, fighting mad and standing broadside in an opening between junipers and piñon.

Doc queried in a hiss for an eyeball range estimate, something I was pretty good at in those days. I offered 40 yards as a best guess. Doc's arrow flew eight inches high. That bull did not give him a second shot. I stepped it off after we regained our composure. Thirty-nine steps. We turned reluctantly toward the truck so Doc could pack and make his evening flight. The big boy was still bugling.

THE GOOD OLD DAYS?

The good old days I might be tempted to say. But is this actually true? The New Mexico state record at the time was something like 350 inches, and stood for years. A good bull even by today's standards, no doubt, but still only average-big (borrowing from guide parlance) in the scheme of things. Archery hunters somewhere take bulls in the 350s every year today. The success rate was 20-percent in the early 1980s when I started bowhunting and guiding for elk in New Mexico's Gila region. These days the state record is in the 400s and seems to be bettered every other year by some lucky archer. The 20-percent success rate continues to apply today in the

Not too long ago archery hunters might receive more shots at elk, but missed more often. Today that trend has been reversed.

Once thought of as strictly alpine game, spreading elk herds are often found in open deserts and prairies today.

very units that produced those numbers 20 years ago (once due to better hunting, today via better equipment). Elk numbers seem to still be on the rise, herds spreading each year into unprecedented areas. The one thing that has changed most of all is that quality elk tags are harder won than ever. Where I once received a tag every season, I might now "win" one every sixth or seventh year. Of course, some extremely lucky archery hunters draw every other year...

INEVITABLE CHANGE

Elk hunting has fundamentally changed, without a doubt. The popularity of elk hunting has grown at a meteoric rate. Hunters from around the world have been infected with elk fever. This isn't the handful of well-heeled, globe trotting archers I once guided while still a kid. Average, workingman citizens who once hunted only backyard whitetail and wild turkey now think little of piling gear into a pickup and trundling out West to try their hand at what is arguably North America's most majestic, thrilling, awe-inspiring big game animal. Annually groups of Eastern archery hunters make the pilgrimage into elk country. Lessons learned the hard way stick most thoroughly and some of these guys, and gals, become extremely proficient elk hunters. Resident archers no longer squander the days stretched between weekends when a coveted elk tag comes their way. They save precious vacation time, strain marriages, forsake families, risk permanent employment, to spend as much time as possible in their

It is no longer novel for hunters to travel from afar to enjoy the challenging sport of elk hunting.

quest for a trophy bull. The same faces appear in outfitter camps year after year despite past successes.

Though elk numbers have, for the most part, risen across the West, there are also more hunters in elk woods during a given season than ever before, all seemingly owning annoying ATVs and a willingness to take them places they should not be. Taken as an average, today's elk hunter is hunting longer and harder, and most importantly, (mostly) smarter, than ever before. They better understand elk habits and bowhunting, even if they reside in the far-removed state of Michigan or New Jersey or Georgia. As a consequence elk are pressured like never before. They have evolved into a different animal than those I bowhunted as a kid. Public-lands bulls that aggressively respond to even the most realistic bugles, or cow calls for that matter, are quickly culled from the genetic pool. Odds are the average trophy-class, public-lands bull has received a hard education via several close calls with archery hunters, perhaps even the painful reminder of a broadhead lodged in a shoulder blade or vertebra. They continue to survive by playing it safe, becoming increasingly neurotic, by traveling to areas where most hunters dare not venture.

A SAVVIER BRAND OF ARCHER

It must also be remembered that the modern elk hunter is also much better armed than years past. I would say as well that a given archer, on the average, due in large part to improved equipment, but also due to more diligent practice, shoots far better than those I guided in the early to late '80s. We live in an information

Despite increased hunting pressure, elk thrive and archery hunters in nearly every western state take big bulls.

age. If you own the penchant, you can shoot better, shoot farther. With today's modern equipment, like dead-nuts broadheads and fiber-optic sights, drop-away arrow rests, high-precision, more efficient bows, straighter, faster carbon arrows and especially drop-dead accurate laser range finders, I have automatically added 30 yards to my absolute maximum range. When I killed my first bull at 35 yards it was a long stab, one I'd practiced long and hard for. The last truly big bull I killed was taken confidently at 60 yards. Complete penetration. Never found the arrow. Bull down in 30 yards.

I once earned bowhunting clients nearly daily shots, and fully expected them to miss. More recently I expose archery hunters to far fewer shots, but now expect them to connect. At least half the time they will.

GUIDING LESSONS

In a relative world, archers continue to kill bigger bulls every year, success rates remain stable, but elk hunting is not the same. Many hunters apparently do not understand this, continuing to ply outdated hunting ploys that only makes hunting more difficult for those around them, stirring up elk and letting them know it's time to run for cover. These are the hunters who go home empty handed. After nearly 24 years of guiding elk hunters I have witnessed the changes, how elk have reacted, and what elk hunting has become. Outfitting is an unforgiving pastime. Paying clients still demand a certain degree of success. They pay dearly for this expectation. In the occupation of guiding elk hunters you keep the pace or are

Hunters are living in a dawn of a new elk hunting era. Elk are abundant but hunting is more difficult than ever.

soon out of a job. This requires an open mind and a willingness to change, to adapt, to abandon the old ways and try all things new. This is modern elk hunting.

Of course it is always dangerous to speak in generalizations. Each elk is an individual, and as an individual may act in a manner, on a specific day, that does not bear out my overall observations. I may point out that the average trophy-sized bull on public land can no longer be counted on to charge headlong into man-made bugles, or even subtle cow calls, when several readers might turn right around and rattle off several examples of how they, or acquaintances, have experienced just that. I may state dogmatically that today's bull elk never allow a second shot after a miss, or that the average elk will no longer pause for a confirming glance when spooked, when it has happened just like that for you last season. There are exceptions to any rule and the experienced hand seldom offers definitive answers to questions regarding wildlife behavior.

And, too, every hunting area is exposed to different degrees of pressure by various styles and classes of archers. Sure, you might arrive in a heavily pressured area and blow on your garden-variety elk bugle just enough times and in enough locations to finally discover that single behemoth bull who somehow missed his survival lessons and strides in blithely. These things happen, obviously. It is what keeps hopes alive, and archery hunters adhering to worn-out ploys.

Bowhunting modern elk successfully is about playing the odds. The odds dictate that you aren't going to wander into a public-lands area a week behind a dozen other desperate hunters and make something outlandish happen. You don't want to depend on the spectacular. Luck only gets you so far in today's elk woods. This can also mean playing it safe; never letting a big bull know he's being hunted, not giving him cause to turn taciturn, to go nocturnal or quit the country completely. Playing the odds might entail bowhunting where others won't or can't due to remoteness, difficulty, or hard-won lottery tags; or financial considerations or family ties. The latter is important to keep in mind when observing the average bowhunting television show or video. You must occasionally stop and ask yourself; "Does this seem logical in relation to the elk hunting I have experienced?"

Today's elk hunting is better than ever, yet today's elk hunting is worse than ever. It depends entirely on your perspective, your temperament, and your expectations. A world record bull still lives out there somewhere, somewhere on public lands open to all of us. World records aside, elk-hunting success is still a high-odds proposition, even when the object is only an archery record-book bull. I still enjoy nearly 50-percent success while guiding clients in units normally bearing only 20-percent to the masses (still good numbers when archery gear is involved). I still manage a good bull every time I secure a quality tag, or at least most of the time, even after winning a marginal "third-choice" consolation. Elk can be taken with bow and arrow on a regular basis, it just means playing by a different set of rules, getting out of the rut of age-old assumptions. Hunting long and hard has always been a huge part of successfully bowhunting elk, but today the archer must also hunt smart; very smart.

Today's elk are smarter than ever. But they are not smarter than we are. At least I like to think so…

Chapter 2

The Lottery Game

t's a sad commentary to the times we live in that what most often separates a successful hunting season from an unsuccessful one is frequently determined by lottery drawings or available funds (which is another subject entirely). Highly coveted, limited-drawing tags have become a hard reality for nearly all-western big game today, especially so for the very best public-lands elk hunting. In the West, if you wish to hunt elk in prime public areas, those places with the consistently biggest antlers or the highest odds of success, you must play the application game.

Increasingly, this has become the rule in areas where trophy quality has been solidly established, but has also begun to apply to particular western states as a whole. Submitting an early application, with guaranteed funds attached, has become a large and all-important portion of planning for the modern elk hunt, prerequisite to taking to the field at all. Even when draw odds are even or sure this still entails carefully filling out tedious application forms, abiding by strict deadlines, but first and foremost, making hard decisions. It's a game most of us willingly play, dropping our hopes and dreams into the mail box or pecking them out via the World Wide Web and waiting months with crossed fingers, hoping against hope that our name will be plucked from the pot.

ESTABLISHING EXPECTATIONS

The prospective elk hunter must first decide where they wish to hunt, but only after establishing realistic expectations, determining what they really want from their elk-hunting experience and, finally, what area or region is best suited to those ideals. Not all elk hunts are created equal. Not every elk hunter has parallel expectations. In the most basic of terms, elk hunting decisions most often revolve around quality versus quantity.

Opposite page: Realistic hunter expectations are the most important aspect of playing the elk lottery game.

Well established expectations lead to more rewarding hunts. The smiles say it all after the harvest of this respectable Montana bull.

The devil is in the details. Some areas have high elk numbers, high success rates, but few record-class bulls. Other areas might provide low elk populations but account for some of the biggest antlers in the nation. Still other areas might appear appealing on paper, but require extra effort by way of wilderness backpacking or assembling a pack-string, though those undaunted by these prospects are assured plenty of trophy bulls to work with. Certain premier units offer a rare combination of both quantity and quality.

GUARANTEED TAGS

An example of the first case might include many high-country, over-the-counter archery elk hunts found in central or northern Colorado or portions of Idaho. Tags are guaranteed, elk numbers high, but tagging a bull bettering Pope & Young minimums can be quite challenging indeed. My buddy Tavis Rogers lives in central Colorado high country and bowhunts elk every year without fail. Every September provides a steady stream of evening telephone calls from Tavis, keeping me abreast of daily sightings, bulls called in close with no shot offered. Eventually the call comes in to let me know he has scored with his traditional longbow yet again. From the sounds of things he has an absolute riot of a good time, but none of the six or so bulls I can remember him tagging have come even close to making book. He couldn't care less.

These guaranteed Colorado and Idaho hunts can require a healthy dose of Shank's Mare, accommodating only those in the best physical conditioning and owning plenty of wilderness know-how. And this isn't to say these states don't produce trophy-class bulls, because they certainly do. When trophy quality becomes a regular occurrence, you can rest assured limited tags and a lottery drawing complete with preference-point requirements are involved (more later).

PLAYING THE ODDS

Even in many established trophy states, New Mexico for example, it's possible to pinpoint areas offering sure-thing draw odds. Many northern New Mexico units have healthy numbers of elk and easy-to-draw tags, but trophy genetics closely mirror those of bordering Colorado unlimited-tag units and will never match better western and southern New Mexico units. On the other hand, "fringe" habitat, so-called expansion units made of atypical "desert" or prairie country, have accounted for some of the biggest bulls in Arizona, New Mexico and Montana, as examples, but hunters may go days between sightings. This kind of hunting forecast can dictate better-than-average draw odds.

If you are equipped or willing to pay to trek into deep wilderness, fine hunting can certainly be had in remote areas where elk receive light hunting pressure and less of an education to the evil ways of man, in addition to a good chance of regularly drawing a tag. Wilderness hunting may be easier on the back end, but it is the effort required to get there that detours most hunters. Of course, there are also prime units that provide easy access to lots of big bulls. These are scattered up and down the Rocky Mountain West and seldom go unnoticed, often accounting for draw odds to rival the average bighorn sheep tag.

DESK JOCKEY RESEARCH

Word of mouth, record-book research, magazine articles or even Internet bowhunting chat rooms all factor when narrowing down your search for the right elk hunt to suit your needs (more in Chapter 3). Smart archery hunters can then proceed by pouring over game proclamations or department web sites to learn more about hunt areas that hold interest. Of utmost importance initially is determining how many tags or licenses are available for a particular date and hunt area verses the number of archers who also wish to hunt there, translating directly into the odds of winning a tag. This is where the hard decisions come into play.

Most states provide the number of available tags in game proclamations or on web sites, followed by how many applications were received the previous year. High success rates—or huge antlers—typically go hand-in-hand with steep draw odds. There are few sleeper areas in elk hunting today, news of the latest hotspots spreading like juicy gossip in a small town. Remember, too, draw odds often change drastically from year to year. A particular unit may have offered decent draw odds last year, but other hunters see those very numbers and quickly get the same idea as you. Some states actually separate non-resident draw odds from resident chances, but don't count on it.

Don't be dismayed, or surprised, to find that most western states hold the percentage of non-resident elk tags to a low percentage. Take heart, this might even work to your advantage. A common number allotted to non-residents is 20-percent of available tags per unit. For the sake of argument, let's say the unit you are interested in has 200 tags. That's 40 tags available for you as a non-resident. There are simply areas where 40 out-of-state hunters hold no interest, or more importantly, cannot swallow the price of admission. I made several bowhunting friends while attending a large Texas university. Today they draw elk tags more often than I do in the same units I annually apply for. There are simply many more residents willing to pony up $69 than there are visiting archery hunters willing to shell out $756. This certainly won't apply to obvious, headline-grabbing units heralded by the nation's outdoor writing community, but in lesser-known areas, or those generally less in demand, it can prove highly common.

Today regular bowhunting success in elk woods includes a willingness to venture into remote places others will not.

Hiring a local cowboy or outfitter with pack animals to take you into remote country is a great alternative to backpacking.

TOO GOOD TO BE TRUE?

The hunter new to a particular state's lottery process must adopt a buyer-beware stance as well. If it seems too good to be true, this just may be the case. I am aware of limited areas in Montana, for instance, where draw odds are good, trophy quality top-notch, but access to what small amount of public lands are involved is tightly controlled by surrounding private holdings. Many expansion units, such as I have mentioned in relation to New Mexico, border world-class trophy ground, provide high or sure draw odds, but harbor very few elk. Just because a state game and fish department conducts a hunt in an area does not mean there are actually elk there. Oftentimes game managers simply don't want elk pioneering new areas and make tags available to all in way of assuring this does not occur.

I made this mistake in 2006, placing a sure-bet unit as a third choice on a New Mexico application. The draw odds were 100-percent. Apparently a good number of archery hunters made the same deduction. Elk hunting in that unit was marginal at best, something I had known all too well going into the hunt. What I hadn't counted on is the complication of attempting to hunt a unit abruptly tenanted by more hunters than elk. It turned into a frustrating waste of time. In eight days I discovered and stalked six bull elk, a couple sure-enough behemoths. The wind betrayed me on one of those stalks (fair enough). Other hunters foiled all of the remaining five encounters; hunters approaching enthusiastically from upwind, blowing incessantly on bugles to bulls that wanted no part of all the fun. There wasn't a single road, officially closed or otherwise, that had not been tread by an ATV tire by season's end.

High-odds elk hunts may simply prove weather dependant or offer regularly low success because they fall well outside the rut, in most cases before the festivities really kick off, while some states also offer late-season dates. It's important when draw odds appear higher than average to query state game biologists familiar with the unit and its present state. I will use another third-choice tag as an example of how a couple phone calls might have helped me avoid a bad hunt: I once killed a 386 bull in a fringe unit, habitat with highly-scattered elk populations and highly-inaccessible escape cover created by extremely rough wilderness. An early hunt date promised little if any bugling. I knew this going in, but was prepared to invest the extra effort required of the place, which to my way of thinking was better than not hunting at all. What I didn't know, and should have investigated, was that in the three years since I had hunted there last, the unit had been opened to unlimited rifle tags. The New Mexico Department of Game and Fish wanted to thin elk numbers to create breathing room for a nose-diving mule deer herd.

DON'T DISCOUNT COWS

If meat and a quality hunting experience are your only concerns, cow-elk hunts are often shoe-ins, with some actually going undersubscribed each season. One of my best friends regularly purchases leftover tags well after the regular drawing in order to accompany me in camp when I have been lucky enough to draw a bull tag. He has never had a problem securing a last-minute tag under these circumstances. Elk meat is awful tasty; a freezer filled with chops and burger certainly a welcome relief to most hunters' monthly grocery budget. These hunt types make a highly viable third-choice option.

Elk meat is good stuff. Don't discount an easily-drawn cow tag when looking into elk-hunting possibilities.

Areas with plenty of "average" bulls can be easier to draw—but don't be fooled—many of these units still require plenty of scouting and homework.

CHOICE ELK HUNTS

All this third-choice talk might need additional explanation. Most state elk applications now allow multiple hunt choices—first, second, and third choice, for instance. States generally have two methods for dealing with these options. Some go through every application, looking at only first-choice applications before moving on. In other words, only when they have run out of first-choice options do they return to have a look at second-choice options, and so forth. If your form is drawn late in the process, odds are high that first-choice applicants have accounted for all the tags in the state, or at least any decent tags you might have opted for, making a second choice moot. The other common method is to simply draw your application number, and then go down through your various choices to see if a tag is still available from one of your several choices. This is why it is important to learn how a chosen state operates and fill out your form accordingly.

First-choice spots should be reserved for only the very best hunts, those with traditionally steep draw odds. If the drawing procedure looks only at all first-choice applications until all forms are exhausted, second- and third-choice spots are seldom drawn if odds exceed 50-percent, except in rare instances when your form is plucked from the hopper early in the drawing procedure. If your chosen state uses this procedure, use follow-up slots for hunt codes with even to sure draw odds to make the best of your application. If the state uses the actual lottery numbers and looks at all hunt choices after pulling it, anything can happen, especially if you are pulled early in the process. Remember, too, you're not required to fill in all your hunt choices. If you'll only be satisfied hunting the very best unit, or have particular plans for only one place, put your pen away after filling in a first choice. Overall, the odds are against you drawing a great tag on second or third choice.

Petersen's Bowhunting editor Jay Strangis found elk-hunting success during an over-the-counter Colorado hunt.

Dead-honest expectations are important when making decisions about hunt choices. Everyone dreams of huge antlers, of course. In reality, though, even those with big-antler aspirations are normally hard pressed to pass a shot at any legal animal, even if simply collecting the delicious meat of a cow. There's no shame in this. Hunt elk for yourself, not your peers. These decisions weigh heavily when making application choices. If nothing but the very best trophy quality will do, you're simply going to sit out more seasons than you hunt.

PREFERRED STATUS

Preference- and bonus-point systems increase your odds of drawing after each unsuccessful application, giving you some hope of bowhunting in the future. Many states exhort the price of a hunting license as prerequisite to winning your

Opposite page: Before the hunt, luck played a role in author Meitin's success, his biggest bull coming after drawing a tag in one of New Mexico's better elk units.

Over-The-Counter Licenses: Many Colorado and Idaho units, eastern Montana, portions of Oregon, Utah and Washington are all places where you can purchase a Rocky Mountain elk tag without beating draw odds. Oregon and Washington Roosevelt elk tags are nearly all part of this system.

Select Colorado and Utah units and most of Washington allow you to simply show up and buy a tag. You won't be alone on these hunts, and you better have done your homework if you expect to beat crowds and earn bowhunting success. Not all of these state's hunt areas are included in this system, with better areas on a limited drawing. Montana elk hunters must apply for a hunting license before purchasing an unlimited elk license. Check regulations for options, www.wildlife.state.co.us/ (Colorado), www.fwp.state.mt.us/, (Montana), www.wildlife.utah.gov/ (Utah), www.wdfw.wa.gov/ (Washington).

Oregon requires that you purchase your general archery elk tag before season opener, normally mid-August. Not all areas apply, better trophy units involving a limited drawing. Check details on line at www.dfw.state.or.us/.

Idaho issues licenses on a first-come-first-serve basis, so you must make decisions early, say by early April. Otherwise licenses are there for the taking, and there are sometimes leftover tags. Check out the details at www.state.id.us/fishgame/.

Easy-Draw Options: The best elk areas are no longer a secret, so you will have to scan game and fish department web sites and draw odds to find a hunt with better than 50-percent draw odds. These aren't that rare, but buyer beware, as some of these areas are true wilderness and accessing worthwhile hunting can require backpacking or pack animals, or private-land issues can complicate access. Note that non-residents must hire an outfitter to hunt in Wyoming's designated wilderness areas. Drop-camp options are often available through an outfitter, a real bargain when wilderness is involved. My top picks would be Montana (www.fwp.state.mt.us/), New Mexico (www.wildlife.state.nm.us/) and Wyoming (http://gf.state.wy.us/).

If you are after only meat (and elk meat is fine stuff) and a good time, check out cow-only hunts in nearly any western state, because most hunters want antlers and these hunts can be easy draws.

Going For Broke: If you are looking for only the biggest antlers in the business and are willing to sit the bench for many years before drawing a public-lands tag, the best places are no secret. Arizona (www.gf.state.az.us/) automatically goes to the top of the list, with areas such as unit 9, 10, 1, and 27 the best bets. New Mexico (www.wildlife.state.nm.us/) also has proven trophy ground, units 15 and all the 16s. Nevada and certain Utah and eastern Oregon areas are real sleepers, with record-book bulls common, but non-resident tags very limited. To try your luck see their web sites at www.ndow.org/ (Nevada), www.wildlife.utah.gov/ (Utah) or www.dfw.state.or.us/ (Oregon).

point (Arizona and Oregon come to mind), while other states don't. In Arizona you may apply without buying a hunting license, be included in the drawing, but receive no bonus point by doing so. In Oregon you may not apply at all without first purchasing a hunting license; though those licenses are less expensive than many western states. Not all states have point systems (New Mexico). Learn how your state's system works and use it to your best advantage.

For example, Colorado's system selects tags only from the highest preference-point pool. Those without the correct number of points simply aren't included in the drawing. Your application serves only to purchase a point. Colorado also awards a point if you don't draw first choice. This allows you to mark first choice with a hunt that you know you'll never draw, or more pointedly don't have the correct number of points for, but apply for a second- or third-choice hunt that assures a reasonable hunt. Arizona's and Nevada's (used as examples) system of bonus points simply increases your odds of drawing, but doesn't guarantee a tag even after a certain number are accumulated. Bonus points are akin to tossing additional raffle tickets into the pot, but also mean a single "raffle ticket" can win the big prize with luck on your side.

UNDER THE WIRE

Application deadlines are the first major stumbling block in this business. Miss the deadline and you're guaranteed not to hunt. This requires vigilance. State deadline dates aren't etched in stone, often changing from year to year. New Mex-

More elk hunts than not begin with a strict deadline and properly filled-out application form.

ico, for instance, seems to set its application deadline ahead with each passing year. I've nearly missed application deadline several times by assuming it would remain the same as the previous year—and I live here! A U.S. Postal Service postmark is normally required for acceptance of your application (Wyoming requires that your application arrives in their hands on time, despite post mark). Without the proper postmark you're automatically out of the running with no exceptions. Deadlines can be as early as February (Wyoming and Nevada), around April (New Mexico and Colorado), or as late as May or June (Arizona and Idaho).

PLASTIC FANTASTIC

On-line applications have streamlined the process, but also include credit-card payment. This is an inexpensive avenue for applying for several low-odds tags at once, because most states bill you only for an application fee, say $6, adding the full cost of the tag to your card only after you have actually pulled a tag. Care must be taken to assure that should you actually draw a coveted tag there will be enough available credit to cover the license cost. Come up short and, again, you're out of luck and will not be bowhunting elk this season.

Also, you might need to inform your credit-card provider of the possible charge, because some will place a block on perceived unauthorized use.

If you're like me you get a bunch of credit card applications in the mail every month. To assure a domestic emergency doesn't unintentionally burn up my line of credit at the wrong time I've secured a single card used for nothing other than hunt-license applications. This is welcome insurance should I happen to draw a $1,200-plus Nevada non-resident elk tag (Yea, right!), or, say, two coveted elk tags in a single year (Less likely!). I don't have to worry if recent spending habits have put me over my credit limit.

A LEG UP

For those with deep pockets, landowner tags have become a viable option for securing a guaranteed elk tag. States such as New Mexico, Utah and Colorado (Ranching For Wildlife), as examples, compensate ranchers for harboring wildlife by giving them tags that they in turn are allowed to sell at their discretion. In more coveted areas, New Mexico's Gila region as an example, outfitters normally contract for these guaranteed tags years in advance to provide for their high-roller clients who have failed to draw during the regular lottery process. Prices have reached enormous proportions in proven trophy ground, upwards of $3,000. In still other areas, especially for cow elk or where trophy quality is only average, tags can often be found on-line only days before season opener at a reasonable price. Occasionally bargains surface via landowners desperate to unload unclaimed tags. States such as Montana give guided clients an outfitter preference, while Wyoming offers better odds by paying more for your tag (more in Chapter 3).

High draw odds combined with low success rates are not the end of the world. You must simply approach such hunts willing to go the extra mile, sometimes even backpacking or pack stringing into remote country or true wilderness. Diehard elk hunters who are willing to do their homework can certainly enjoy better hunt-

No matter what tax bracket you find yourself in, elk hunting opportunities in one form or another are available to everyone.

ing success rates than those posted by the masses. High-odds tags may also require paying trespass fees for access on or through private holdings. If you can justify the added cost, this isn't really a bad deal, especially if this includes higher trophy quality for your investment. If you're undaunted by such situations, you can increase your odds of a quality hunt for elk this season.

I hate the fact that bowhunting public-land elk has come to this, but I play the game like everyone else because I live to hunt bugling bulls. Approach your western elk applications only after careful study. Weigh expectations with available options and you just might find a combination that allows you to hunt every year. When only the best trophy quality will do, work the system to your advantage to make that happen, but know that missed seasons will outnumber successful draws.

Chapter 3

Trophy Ground

I n regards to elk habitat as a whole, much has changed during the past 20 years. Hunters once thought of elk country strictly in terms of steeply-falling canyons ringed in golden quaking aspen, ragged peaks supporting patches of rotten snow, foreboding black timber and sundry alpine environments thought of collectively as Elk Country.

These images are well interspersed with visions of puffing pack-strings of heavily-burdened mules or horses winding up treacherous mountainous trails, white-canvas wall tents tucked into quiet meadows and stock wranglers sporting 10-gallon hats, saucer-sized rodeo belt buckles and well-used denim jackets. Elk hunting is still filled with these classic portraits, but ever-increasingly a different kind of trophy ground is emerging.

Today when the largest elk are discussed the mind is more likely to conjure scenes of piñon-juniper (PJ in western vernacular) canyons spilling intermittently from sudden mesa edges, sandy environs dominated by sage and cedar, perhaps even cactus "desert" or rolling grass prairie where it's easy to see into tomorrow. In fact, once a happy denizen of sprawling prairie habitat, Yellowstone or American elk were forced to retreat ever deeper into classic alpine settings only after the arrival of hungry explorers, settlers, miners and cattle drives into the West's uncharted hinterlands.

Ever-more careful game management, paid for nearly without exception by hunters' dollars, has initiated a reversal of historic trends. Elk have begun to reclaim the prairies and lowland foothills from where they formally originated. In many areas elk have pioneered completely new areas. Some of this "migration" has been intentional, artificially induced by the whims of man, state game agencies reintroducing elk into areas once void of these majestic animals. This is good news for the elk hunter, translating into increased opportunity and new hunting ground to explore. Still, many don't see this hunting boon as something deserving of celebration.

Opposite page: The face of western elk hunting is quickly changing. What was once thought of collectively as prime elk habitat could now include any number of atypical locations.

Bowhunting great Randy Ulmer took this monster bull in Arizona, considered one of the best trophy elk states in the West.

DEPREDATION CONCERNS

Expanding elk populations have caused some amount of dismay among many livestock ranchers, seeing the reestablishment or introduction of elk as a negative; competition for grass and land-management they alone have controlled for so long. The Western cowman is understandably suspicious of any endeavor carried out by big government that might, in turn, result in an erosion of their lifestyle and control of the land. On the same note, many farmers are suddenly faced with real and costly crop damage at the mouths and trampling hooves of wintering or permanent elk herds. Elk managers are increasingly busied by these potentially ticklish political scenarios.

Ever increasingly, though, landowners have come to treat pioneering elk as an economic Godsend in an era of plummeting commodities prices and escalating operating costs. For many landowners, elk literally keep their ranching lifestyle afloat, oftentimes through direct sales of elk-hunting tags, but also via trespass fees or providing various services to visiting elk hunters.

ELK COUNTRY

A long and rich elk-hunting history continues to thrive in the high-country elk habitat found up and down the Rocky Mountains, from New Mexico's northern Sangre de Cristos Mountains, through Colorado's Rio Grande, Gunnison, White River and Routt National Forests, north into Wyoming's Yellowstone Country and Montana's Beartooths, Absaroka Range, Flathead and mighty Bob Marshall Wilderness, to as far north as Alberta's Banff and British Columbia's Kamloops wild-lands. These are places where hunters still flock to experience the classic romance of elk hunting known by hunters of old.

Widely scattered mountain ranges throughout this region and farther west, in eastern Oregon and Washington State (not to mention coastal Roosevelt strongholds), through concerted game management by schooled biologists, have also become trophy elk ground. These are places where the four-by-four pickup or SUV, and more recently the dreaded ATV, replaces the horse and mule as the common mode of hunting transportation. No longer are long hours or days required to backpack or pack-string into the most productive elk ground. Many elk hunters today may actually lodge in a convenient motel, bed and breakfast, or their own home, and commute as little as an hour daily to reach fruitful elk pastures! So it often is today.

Southwest elk habitat accounts for some of the biggest bulls in bowhunting, habitat that's normally much drier and open.

Increasingly, though, trophy elk ground has come to embody the "Southwest." The Southwest as a geographic entity owns elastic limits, trussed by southern New Mexico and Arizona deserts at its lower reaches and stretching northward into Utah and Nevada canyon-lands. These relative lowlands are generally and commonly very dry and warm, but altitude takes place of latitude in forming climate and high-flung mountain ranges catch moisture from lofty clouds. Trophy hunters lucky enough to haunt these regions often forsake alpine habitat, seeking bulls in broken deserts and sprawling mesa country far from aspens and firs and spruce, roaming instead rimrock canyons of mountain mahogany, twisted PJ, sage and hardy varieties of gnarled oak.

Elk hunters no longer balk at hunting elk in isolated swatches of riparian habitat far removed from mountain ranges, foothill areas crowded by encroaching suburbia or even dominated by thorn and cactus spine. These are places where a good portion of the masses, steeped in long-held elk-hunting traditions, overlook or refuse to consider, and where some of the largest antlers in the nation now emerge.

But these are very wide-sweeping terms indeed. To learn more, it's important to query game managers from key western states about the best bets for trophy potential, as well as delving into available record books, seeking trends in the most recent entries.

CANADA & US PRAIRIE STATES

While record-book bulls commonly come from regions of Alberta, British Columbia, Manitoba and Saskatchewan, including the Boone & Crockett world record non-typical elk of 465 ⅞ inches from British Columbia in 1994, visiting hunters must contract the services of an outfitter in order to hunt these places. In any case, no single province has accounted for more than five B&C bulls and the do-it-yourself alien non-resident is left out of the loop. (FYI; Alberta has produced 23 archery record-book bulls, British Columbia 12, Saskatchewan nine, Manitoba seven). States such as California (with three archery record-book Yellowstone bulls), North Dakota (one), South Dakota (13), Kentucky (one), Oklahoma (one), Kansas (one) and even Pennsylvania (one), have produced B&C bulls, but these tags are so limited they have little bearing on public-lands elk hunting today.

ARIZONA

The Grand Canyon State has come to symbolize what trophy-elk fever is all about. Though it only accounts (currently) for the fifth largest take of archery record-book bulls, it also continues to produce some of the West's biggest. The state not only produces a high number of the nation's biggest bulls but does so with a relatively low overall number of tags and only 26,000 estimated head of elk in the entire state. This has not passed unnoticed. Serious archers consider drawing an Arizona archery elk tag the highest form of good fortune. Consequently, tags for the best areas are hard-won, even residents privy to the lion's share of available tags often going five to 10 years between tags. Preference points offer hope, but no single area offers draw odds that assure hunting the state's elk regularly.

Don't discount "fringe" habitat when seeking the West's biggest bulls; places where they often go unmolested by the masses.

Arizona is a bonus-point state. Bonus points may be purchased each year, or each time you are unsuccessful in drawing you accumulate a point automatically, increasing your odds of drawing in the future. Twenty-percent of Arizona tags are reserved for those with the most bonus points, but first-time applicants do hold some hope of drawing. Applicants must choose a specific unit and weapon choice. The application deadline has traditionally fallen around the third week in June, with results posted by late July. Internet applications are accepted and you must purchase a hunting license to apply for or purchase a bonus point. On a positive note, this hunting license also allows you to hunt over-the-counter archery deer (with the purchase of a $232.75 tag good for Coues whitetail or mule deer) during productive December and January rut hunts. As of 2007, a non-resident hunting license costs $151.25, an elk tag $595 (including $7.50 application fee).

Two hundred forty-one Grand Canyon State archers have entered record-book elk in the past 10 years; 24 of these scoring better than 350 inches, about 60-percent of these bulls scoring better than 300 state wide. About 75-percent of the bulls entered in archery records from Coconino, Navajo and Apache counties have scored better than 300 inches. Boone & Crockett records show that the Grand Canyon State's top end remains stable. Of 166 total typical and non-typical B&C entries (360 inches minimum awards, 375 all-time), 89 of these have appeared in the past 10 years; or roughly 54-percent. See "Arizona" chart for county specifics.

County	P&Y total	P&Y 350+	P&Y>300	P&Y>260	P&Y N/T	B&C total	B&C N/T
Coconino	152	16	79	52	5	13	8
Apache	34	3	23	8		16	
Navajo	20	1	7	8	4	19	
Gleelee	16	3	5	7	1	4	
Gila	8		2	6		15	
Yavapai	5		3	1	1	3	
Mohave	2	1	1			1	
Graham	1			1		2	
Statewide Totals	**241**					**89**	

ARIZONA - 10 Year Time Frame from 1997-2007

As records show, Arizona is one of the best states for top-end bulls. Sixty-percent of the Arizona bulls registered in Pope & Young scored 300 inches or better.

COLORADO

The most recent surveys reveal that the Rocky Mountain State harbors about 300,000 elk within its borders, the largest population of any single state. Colorado manages for quantity and not quality for the most part, so while archery record-book bulls are taken every year, Boone & Crockett bulls prove quite rare, even in strictly-regulated, limited-draw areas where hunting pressure is lightest. Oddly, a high number of Colorado's 350-plus bulls are taken in its most heavily populated areas; namely the Denver/Colorado Springs metropolitan area. Colorado's more remote elk country can also be good for big bulls, most often translating into over-the-counter bull tags, something that is becoming more rare in modern times. Overall bowhunting success runs about 15-percent.

Colorado offers both limited-entry elk licenses (which must be drawn) and unlimited over-the-counter archery elk tags. Unlimited tags offer the option of hunting every year, in areas with plenty of elk and public lands, but for the most part, lesser trophy quality. Prime public-lands areas include areas west of Fort Collins, and National Forest areas near Grand Junction, Montrose, Durango, Aspen, Pagosa Springs, Steamboat Springs and Gunnison.

Colorado offers applicants preference-points. In 2006 the ratio of limited-entry licenses allotted to residents and non-residents changed. In game management units requiring a minimum of five or more preference points for a Colorado resident to draw, 80-percent are reserved for residents, up to 20-percent for non-residents. Applicants may either purchase a point or are awarded a point automatically each time they fail to draw. Applicants must enter the drawing at least every three years to retain acquired preference points. In limited-entry areas licenses are reserved for only those with the highest number of points. The best trophy units

Opposite page: Petersen's Bowhunting columnist Bill Winke waited five years to draw his Arizona elk tag; rewarded by this 330ish bull.

Colorado offers a plethora of guaranteed elk tags, but also some of the roughest elk ground in the entire west.

(like Moffat County, unit 201) most often require seven to 10 years to draw. You must apply for a specific unit and weapon choice. Colorado's application deadline has traditionally fallen on the first week of April, with results available by late May. Internet applications are accepted. In 2007 the cost of a non-resident Colorado elk license was $501 for Bull and Either Sex tags (including a $3 application fee; a $5 habitat stamp also required), and $251 for a Limited Cow tag, with over-the-counter licenses on sale after mid July.

During the past 10 years Colorado has produced 273 archery record-book bulls, only nine of these scoring better than 350, but nearly 40-percent of these scoring better than 300 inches state wide. This puts Colorado in a solid number-four spot as a producer of overall archery record-book bulls. Of Colorado's 71 total typical and non-typical Booner bulls to date, only 20 of them have appeared in the past 10 years (28-percent), showing a slight slip in trophy quality in recent years. These have shown up in no single isolated region, though Douglas County has produced the most 360-plus bulls, with four in the past 10 years, though access is a real issue in this land of high-dollar subdivisions. See "Colorado" chart for county specifics.

COLORADO - 10 Year Time Frame from 1997-2007							
County	P&Y total	P&Y 350+	P&Y> 300	P&Y> 260	P&Y N/T	B&C total	B&C N/T
Larimer	25	2	9	14		2	
Moffat	20	1	14	5		3	
Mesa	18		7	11		2	
Routt	17		3	14			
Las Animas	15		6	9		1	1
Douglas						4	
Jefferson						2	
Boulder						2	
Dolores						1	
San Miguel						1	
Saguache						1	
Rio Grande						1	
Garfield	11						
Montrose	12						
Rio Blanco	12						
Archuleta	12						
Statewide Totals	273					20	

Colorado's archery record-book elk are available statewide, but most are found in the north, with 40-percent of the bulls registered with P&Y besting 300 inches.

IDAHO

Idaho provides a better-than-average chance of arrowing a record-book bull, with an estimated 100,000 head of elk, but only a scattering of antlers scoring better than 350 inches have surfaced in the state. Boone & Crockett bulls have proven historically rare. Over-the-counter elk tags sold on a first-come-first-serve basis during December of the year before they are valid makes the top-end issue worth ignoring. Idaho offers a wide variety of elk-hunting experiences, from classic wilderness pack trips, to wide-open lowland hunts.

Idaho makes a great back-up state, because many times elk tags remain available well after other states have completed lottery drawings. Also unique, unsold licenses may be purchased at the end of August for the non-resident fee, allowing archers to hold two elk tags during a single season, and kill two elk. Look to units in the Caribou National Forest (Diamond Creek Zone), Clearwater Forest (Lolo Zone), Nez Perce Forest (Selway Zone) and the Targhee Forest (Island Park Zone) for the best bowhunting opportunities. About 50-percent of the state's record book bulls taken in these areas score better than 300 inches. The Panhandle Zone and Boise River Zone also offer unique late-season bowhunting opportunities.

Internet and phone applications are accepted in Idaho. Both a hunting license and elk tag are required to hunt. In 2007 the cost of a non-resident hunting license was $141.50 (must be purchased before applying for elk tag), an elk tag $372.50; $380.25 for a Controlled Hunt. An $18.25 "archery validation" is also required to bowhunt.

In the past 10 years Caribou, Lemhi, Valley, Idaho and Custer counties (in that

Mike Andrews was fortunate enough to take this massive 408-inch bull in New Mexico.

order) have given up the highest number of trophy bulls out of 294 archery record-book bulls recorded during that period. These listings have helped Idaho elevate itself to the number three spot in total archery record-book entries during the past

IDAHO – 10 Year Time Frame from 1997-2007

County	P&Y total	P&Y 350+	P&Y> 300	P&Y> 260	P&Y N/T	B&C total	B&C N/T
Caribou	38	1	13	24			
Lemhi	35		12	23			
Valley	34		12	20	2		
Idaho	30	1	11	18		2	
Custer	23	2	5	16			
Blaine						2	
Freemont						1	
Benewah						1	
Butte						1	
Bear Lake						1	
Elmore						1	
Owyhee						1	
Cassia						1	
Statewide Totals	**294**					**11**	

Idaho ranks third overall in total archery record-book elk, but shows a low-scoring top end with only 42-percent of the bulls registered in P & Y topping 300 inches.

10 years. During that same period only eight 350-plus archery bulls have appeared, though nearly 42-percent of those bulls statewide scored better than 300 inches. Of the Gem State's 59 Boone & Crockett qualifying bulls (typical and non-typical combined) only 11 (19 percent) have surfaced in the past 10 years, showing a perceivable downward trend in trophy quality that many residents attribute to over hunting. Idaho simply doesn't produce a great deal of B&C genetics. Consult the chart on the previous page to learn more about the best trophy counties.

MONTANA

Montana's archery elk opportunities are a proverbial mixed bag. Hunts are broken into unlimited, limited draw and Outfitter Sponsored. Big Sky Country accounts for a large number of monstrous bull elk, including Pope & Young's second largest typical bull. Many of these bulls come from classic high-country habitat, but the state's biggest have began to appear in eastern prairie country. Yet, only eight-percent of Montana archery elk hunters are successful each year during the long six-week season. The state's estimated herd size is 140,000.

Montana's unlimited elk licenses are allocated in the Missouri River Breaks area west of Fort Peck Reservoir. Prospective archery hunters must still apply for a license before purchasing one of these permits, which means meeting a deadline. These units have produced a large number of Montana's record-book bulls, as well as some of the top scorers. Hunting pressure is intense, so getting well away from roads is key, or gaining access to private lands. Montana also offers about 11,500 limited-entry elk licenses to non-residents. A Big Game Combination License ($643 in 2007, including a $15 application fee) allows archery hunters to take both a deer and an elk. An Elk Combination License ($593 in 2007) allows only an elk. Both are taken from the 11,500-quota. Outfitter

Montana grows some big bulls yet only eight-percent of Montana archery elk hunters enjoy success. The best are taken in the eastern portion of the state.

Montana's elk habitat is as highly varied as the state is large; from high western mountains to eastern "plains" elk.

Sponsored Licenses are also offered ($995 and $895 in 2007); though require contracting an outfitter before application. A second antlerless tag may also be purchased for $275 for those who have already drawn.

Other Montana trophy-bull bets include areas in southwestern Montana, west of Anaconda, and northwest Montana north of Missoula and west of Kalispell. The largest bulls of these options traditionally appear from northwest units.

Montana has an optional bonus-point program priced at $20 extra per application. Those hunting the Missouri Breaks can skip the drawing and bonus-point procedures and purchase an unlimited tag. Montana's application deadline has traditionally been mid March, with drawing results posted by mid April. Internet applications are accepted. Unlimited licenses must be purchased by June 1.

With 408 archery record-book bulls to its name in the past 10 years, Montana currently ranks number one in archery record-book entries, with 44 of those bulls scoring better than 350, and a bit better than 50-percent scoring more than 300 inches. It's also interesting to note that Chuck Adams' 2000 former world's record, from Rosebud County, came from an area producing only eight archery record book bulls in the past 10 years, but six of these scoring better than 350 inches. It only goes to show that any unit in Montana can produce big bulls. Boone & Crockett shows that Big Sky's top-end trophy quality has slipped slightly in recent years. Of 129 total bulls scoring better than 360 taken since record keeping began, only 37 (29-percent) of these have appeared in the past 10 years (29 typical, eight nontypical). Like archery records, these bulls come from no single location. See the "Montana" chart for county harvest details.

County	P&Y total	P&Y 350+	P&Y>300	P&Y>260	P&Y N/T	B&C total	B&C N/T
Fergus	62	7	23	22	10		3
Pertroeum	45	3	22	19	1		2
Garfield	32	6	14	12			3
Gallatin	26	1	13	11	1		2
Beaverhead	44	2	22	19	1		2
Park	8			3	5	5	
Power River	2		1	1		5	
Phillips	27	1	10	15	1		
Rosebud*	8	6	1	1			1
Statewide Totals	408					37	

*including former world's record

Montana is the West's number one producer of archery record-book elk, with 50-percent of the Pope & Young entries better than 300 inches.

NEVADA

Nevada has emerged suddenly as a top-place trophy-elk producer, with several 400-inch-plus archery bulls appearing in recent years. Be that as it may, elk tags, non-resident tags in particular, are extremely limited and draw odds astronomical. In fact, only four non-resident archery tags are offered annually, at a budget-busting $1,200 a pop in 2007. A limited number of private-landowner tags are available, but the going price has settled in the $10,000 to $15,000 range. Competition for public tags is intense due to extremely good trophy quality and a 60-percent archery-hunt success rate.

In recent years, only three Nevada elk-hunting options were offered to non-residents, though in years to come growing herds could change this situation. Units 111-115, 221 and 222 offer two non-resident tags, located in White Pine County, which has accounted for most of Nevada's record-book entries, as well the highest number of 350-inch-plus bulls. Units 161-164, Nye County, and units 231, 241 and 242, Lincoln County, each offer one non-resident tag. Elko County archery elk hunts are not available to non-residents. Any has the potential for an outstanding bull.

Nevada is a bonus-point state. Applicants can purchase a point each year or gain one each time they fail to draw, increasing their odds of drawing with each application. Bonus points are squared each year to reward persistent applicants. In order to gain these preference points you must purchase a hunting license ($142); non-refundable in the event your application is unsuccessful, which is likely for many years. Nevada's application deadline has traditionally fallen around the third week in April, with results in by late June. Internet applications are accepted.

Any archery elk tag in Nevada has the potential for netting a monstrous bull, but Boone & Crockett records really give the best picture of the phenomenal trophy potential of the Silver State. Of 53 total B&C bulls taken in Nevada, 45 have been taken in the past decade. That's impressive for a state that issues so few tags. The "Nevada" chart provides the rundown per county.

NEVADA - 10 Year Time Frame from 1997-2007							
County	P&Y total	P&Y 350+	P&Y> 300	P&Y> 260	P&Y N/T	B&C total	B&C N/T
White Pine	15	6	1	3	*5	15	6
Elko	8	1	3	3	1	15	
Lincoln	2	2	1		2	6	
Nye						3	
Statewide Totals	31*					39	

* one better than 425 inches

Nevada currently produces a huge number of top-end record-book bulls, but drawing a tag is extremely difficult.

NEW MEXICO

It will be interesting to see what the future holds for New Mexico elk hunting. Land of Enchantment game managers threaten to squander an invaluable resource to placate aggressive, politically-connected ranching interests, and out of simple greed; continuing extremely heavy cow-elk harvest, aggressive depredation programs and issuing liberal landowner tags. Newly introduced Mexican gray wolves also pose a new threat to wildlife populations. New Mexico elk hunting is still some of the best to be found in the Southwest, but has quickly lost ground to Arizona as a consistent top-end trophy producer. Outfitters and longtime residents of traditional trophy ground in the southwestern and western portions of the state, especially the Gila region, have noted a heavy downturn in top-end quality, even as numbers continue to remain relatively stable overall (New Mexico game managers quote 80,000 head as their best-guess herd-number estimate). Statewide archery success rates run about 20-percent.

While Gila region trophy areas receive all the press (and much of the application attention, resulting in slim odds), units found in the northern portion of the state offer better draw odds and plenty of elk. Trophy potential is not as good, but a quality elk hunt can be had.

New Mexico has no bonus- or preference-point system. Ten-percent of elk tags are reserved for non-residents on their own; another 12-percent for non-residents contracting the services of an outfitter. Applications must include specific unit and weapons choices. Application deadline has most recently been about the second week of April, with results available by late June. Internet applications are accepted. The cost for a non-resident license in 2007 was $541 for less-desirable tags, $766 for "high demand" or "quality" units and hunt dates, and $331 for an antlerless tag. A scattering of late-season, over-the-counter elk licenses around the state were offered in 2007, with a six-point restriction in place.

New Mexico has produced 351 archery record-book entries during the past 10

Lee Hetrick backpacked into designated wilderness and hunted nine straight days to find this New Mexico behemoth.

years, 39 of those scoring better than 350, about 42-percent scoring better than 300 inches, making it the second best archery record-book producer in the West, though the state's Gila region has accounted for most of these. Boone & Crockett numbers solidify these findings: Of 73 total typical and non-typical book heads, about half, or 35, have appeared in the past 10 years. County details appear on the chart below.

NEW MEXICO – 10 Year Time Frame from 1997–2007

County	P&Y total	P&Y 350+	P&Y > 300	P&Y > 260	P&Y N/T	B&C total	B&C N/T
Catron	172	17	75	70	10	17	
Rio Arriba	37	3	13	20	1	1	
Socorro	23	*5	14	3	1	8	
Otero	23	2	6	14	1	4	
Cibola	18	8	6	3	1	10	
Sierra						3	
Colfax	19		9	10		1	
Lincoln	11		3	8		1	
Grant	10	2	6	1	1	1	
Statewide Totals	**241**					**89**	

* one scoring better than 400 inches

With 42-percent of the bulls registered in P & Y better than 300 inches, New Mexico currently ranks as the second-best producer of archery record-book bulls.

Oregon includes both Rocky Mountain and Roosevelt elk, their habitats normally highly defined west to east.

OREGON

Oregon remains relatively productive archery elk ground, though the best tags come from areas with limited lottery tags that are extremely difficult to draw, and Boone & Crockett top-end is nearly nonexistent. Much of the state includes general archery elk tags that can be purchased over the counter, making it a good back-up state for those who have failed to draw a tag in a lottery system.

With a general license, hunters can hunt various areas for Yellowstone or Roosevelt elk. For Roosevelt elk areas around Saddle Mountain, the Wilson or

OREGON - ROCKY MOUNTAIN ELK - 10 Year Time Frame from 1997-2007							
County	P&Y total	P&Y 350+	P&Y>300	P&Y>260	P&Y N/T	B&C total	B&C N/T
Grant	36	10	26				
Wallowa	25	1	13	11		1	
Umatilla	17						
Union	17						
Statewide Totals	175					1	

* Only 3 B&C bulls in the past decade. Found in the Multnomah, Crook and Wallowa counties.

Oregon is a great place to hunt elk, but generally not the best state to find a top-end Rocky Mountain bull.

OREGON - ROOSEVELT ELK - 10 Year Time Frame from 1997-2007				
County	P&Y total	P&Y 275+	P&Y 220-275	B&C total
Benton	3	1	2	9
Coos	13	5	8	9
Clatsop	13	4	9	5
Columbia	12	2	10	5
Lincoln	6	2	4	4
Douglas	8	5	3	3
Yamhill	3	3		3
Tillamook	13	3	10	2
Polk	1	1		1
Lane	4	1	3	1
Josephone	2	1	1	
Linn	1	1		
Curry	4	1	3	
Washington	1	1		
Statewide Totals	**84**			**44**

When it comes to Roosevelt elk, Oregon is the top destination. It produces both the most and biggest Rosey bulls.

Trask units in Clatsop and Tillamook counties, have proven excellent. Yellowstone elk hotspots in Oregon include those in the northeast portion of the state, as well as the Cascade Mountains. The best controlled-hunt areas seem to be the Starkey, Wenaha and Walla Walla units, with good trophy quality but poor draw odds.

Oregon is a bonus-point state. You can either purchase a point each year without applying, or accumulate them each year you fail to draw. In order to earn these preference points applicants must purchase a hunting license ($76.50 in 2007). Seventy-five percent of controlled-hunt tags are reserved for those with the highest number of preference points. This can mean up to five years or more between tags in better units, though first-time applicants do have a small chance of drawing. Applications are unit and weapon specific. The controlled-hunt application deadline has traditionally been mid-May, with results posted by mid-June. Internet applications are accepted. You must purchase a hunting license before being allowed to apply for controlled-hunt tags, or purchase bonus points. Unlimited general archery elk tags must be purchased by late August, before seasons open. In 2007 a non-resident tag cost $361.50.

While not a Boone & Crockett standout, Oregon has produced 175 archery record-book Yellowstone bulls during the past 10 years, three of these scoring better than 360 (no additional bulls showing until you reach into the lower 300s) but about 33-percent scoring better than 300 during the same period. Only three Booner bulls have appeared in Oregon in the past decade, typical bulls all, out of a total of 23 historically, proving that Oregon genetics have never been top notch. These three bulls are at the low end of B&C minimums (from 375 ⅜ to 360 ⅛ inches).

Oregon's saving grace comes via its Roosevelt elk, where it wins hands down as the species hotspot. Of the 153 B&C Roosevelt (275 awards, 290 all time) Oregon has produced, 44 of these have appeared in the period from 1997 to present, as well as holding most of the top spots to date. These observations mirror what archery hunters have accomplished while pursuing the state's Roosevelt during the past 10 years. From a total of 73 archery record-book bulls appearing during the past 10 years, 29 scoring better than 275 have appeared from 12 counties. Seventy-three archery record-book bulls scoring from 225 to 275 have come from Oregon during the past 10 years. See "Oregon" charts for both Rocky Mountain and Roosevelt harvest information.

UTAH

Conservative management in premier elk units has the Beehive State overall trophy elk quality on a quick upswing, while in the past archery record-book bulls have been relatively rare compared to other prime Southwest states. Interestingly, while archery trophies have proven relatively rare in Utah, Boone & Crockett bulls show more frequently than in many other western states. This is easily explained by the fact that in past years archers were allowed to hunt only in August, well before the rut, and were all but excluded from some of the state's very best trophy areas. Rifle hunters, on the other hand, were given prime hunting dates during the best rut periods in the very best trophy areas. This situation has improved in more recent years, with more of the state's premier units opened to bowhunting, and seasons moved forward and into mid-September rut dates. This is a state to keep an eye on in the years to come; with an estimated herd size of 63,000 head Utah could soon rival Arizona and New Mexico as a top trophy producer, though presently archers are only seeing a 13-percent success rate.

Utah elk tags are offered via unlimited general archery elk permits, limited-entry, or Cooperative Wildlife Management Units (CWMU) systems. Utah's over-the-counter general archery-elk license options are scattered about the state, with the best options including the units along the Utah/Wyoming border northeast of Salt Lake City, Morgan-South Rich, Chalk Creek, North Slope, Summit-West Daggett and East Canyon hunt areas. The best bets for monster bulls in limited-entry units include San Juan, Plateau Boulder, Mt. Dutton, Fillmore and Oak Creek South Hunt areas. About 85-percent of the bulls entered in the archery records from these limited areas score better than 300 P&Y inches.

Cooperative Wildlife Management Units offer the rich man a trophy-elk opportunity; sans fighting crowds in unlimited areas or bucking slim draw odds in limited areas. CWMU provides economic incentives to landowners for habitat protection by providing permits they can sell at their discretion. Such permits typically sell for $4,000 to $6,000, with prices escalating annually.

Utah awards bonus-points. Applicants can purchase points each year without applying, or earn them after failing to draw a limited tag, which directly increases your odds of drawing a tag. Fifty-percent of permits are reserved for those with bonus points. Ten or more years might be required to draw one of Utah's better

UTAH – 10 Year Time Frame from 1997-2007

County	P&Y total	P&Y 350+	P&Y>300	P&Y>260	P&Y N/T	B&C total	B&C N/T*
Garfield	19	3	9	3	4	17	
Millard	9	2	4	2	1	12	
Sevier	9	1	5	3		6	
San Juan	5		4		1	10	
Beaver	3	2	1			6	
Piute	1		1			6	
Juab	2	1		1		5	
Toocle	1				1	4	
Utah	7	1	3	3		4	
Wasatch	7	1	3	2	1	3	
Carbon	3		1	2		3	
Rich	9		4	4	1	3	
Sampete						3	
Iron						2	
Emery						2	
Cache	1			1		2	
Duchesne	7		4	2	1	2	
Uintah	3		1	2		1	
Morgan	2			2		1	
Statewide Totals	**96**					**92**	

*N/T entries are included in B & C totals.

Pope & Young records (59-percent over 300 inches) don't reveal the potential in Utah. B & C records, though, show the potential for some huge bulls.

elk hunts, though first-time applicants certainly have some chance of winning a tag. Applications are unit and weapon specific.

Utah's traditional application deadline is mid-February, with results provided by late April. Internet applications are accepted. You don't have to purchase a hunting license to apply or earn bonus points. In 2007 a general non-resident elk permit cost $388, a limited-entry permit $795, Premium Limited Entry bull tags $1,500.

Ninety-six archery record-book bulls have come from the Beehive State during the past 10 years, 12 of these bulls scoring better than 350 inches, but more than 59-percent scoring better than 300 inches. To get the real picture of Utah elk hunting potential you must scour Boone & Crockett records. This is where the state's potential really shines. One hundred and nine bulls scoring better than 360 have been taken in Utah, 79 of these in only the past 10 years, showing a herd quickly coming up in quality. Refer to "Utah" chart for county harvest details.

WASHINGTON

Washington elk genetics leave much to be desired, with only 23 Boone & Crockett Rocky Mountain bulls taken across time, though 10 of these were taken in the past 10 years. These have come from King, Columbia, Spokane, Walla Walla, and Kittitas counties, with Kittitas the only one accounting for two. Though the state includes much prime habitat, poor management and unlimited Native American hunting rights allow few bulls to grow to full potential. As a consequence record-book Washington Rocky Mountain elk are rare.

All archery hunters may purchase a general archery elk tag over the counter. There are a few units that include special permit hunts, with a $54.75 (in 2007) special permit application fee and odds of 1:7 to 1:130. Too, applicants must first buy an elk tag for inclusion in these drawings. Bonus points are awarded, which can be either purchased or accumulated following unsuccessful applications. The best limited trophy areas might require up to five or more years to draw, though each applicant has a chance to draw from the very first attempt. Limited hunts require specifying an East or West tag and weapon choice. The deadline for applications has traditionally been mid-June, with results available late July. Internet applications are accepted. General tags can be purchased any time throughout the season. A non-resident tag cost $394.20 in 2007.

Rocky Mountain elk hunting in Washington is best in the Cascade Mountain Range surrounding Mt. Rainier. The best bet for Roosevelt elk success lays in the Olympic Mountains west of Seattle and in the southwestern portion of the state across the Columbia River from Oregon.

Washington State shows no real trophy trend in any given area, a scattering of only 44 archery record-book bulls showing between 1997 and 2007, only three of these scoring better than 350, but 45-percent of the total scoring better than 300 inches. Only seven Boone & Crockett Yellowstone elk have been taken in Washington during the past decade.

Washington's Roosevelt elk situation is certainly better, but pales in comparison to Oregon. Seventy-eight total Washington Roosevelt bulls show up in Boone & Crockett records, only 16 of these taken in the past 10 years. Archery hunters have done better in the record-book race, taking 37 Roosevelt record beaters in the past 10 years. Interestingly, 24 of these score better than 275. The chart below provides more detail.

WASHINGTON - ROCKY MOUNTAIN ELK - 10 Year Time Frame from 1997-2007						
County	P&Y total	P&Y 350+	P&Y> 300	P&Y> 260	P&Y N/T	B&C total	B&C N/T
Yakima	9		4	5			
Lewis	8		3	5		1	
Kittitas	5		3	1	1	2	
King						1	
Columbia	4		2	2		1	
Spokane						1	
Walla Walla						1	
Statewide Totals	44					10	

Despite plenty of prime habitat, Washington is perhaps the poorest state in the West for record-book bulls.

WASHINGTON - ROOSEVELT ELK - 10 Year Time Frame from 1997-2007

County	P&Y total	P&Y 275+	P&Y 220 to 275	B&C total
Grays Harbor	11	8	3	3
Jefferson	13	9	4	2
Wahkiakum				1
Clallam	3	2	1	8
Lewis	3	2	1	1
Pacific	5	2	3	
Cowlitz	1		1	
Totals	**37**			**16**

Though not producing the total Rosey numbers of Oregon, Washington's top end makes it worth investigating.

WYOMING

With one of the earliest application deadlines in the West, it's easy to forget Wyoming. But the state hosts an estimated 94,000 elk and diligent archers enjoy some of the best elk hunting in the West in regards to ease of obtaining a license

While showing lackluster Rocky Mountain potential, Washington's Roosevelt elk are its saving grace with plenty of big bulls coming from coastal areas.

County	P&Y total	P&Y 350+	P&Y> 300	P&Y> 260	P&Y N/T	B&C total	B&C N/T
Park	35	5	21	9		15	
Albany	33	4	22	6	1		
Johnson	25	7	7	10	1	4	
Sheridan	16	2	7	7		1	
Lincoln	19	6	5	8			
Crook	3	2		1			
Natrona	5	1	4				
Fremont	10	1	2	7		0	
Teton	2	1	1			6	
Carbon	15	1	9	5			1
Converse	10		6	4		2	
Goshen	*	*	*	*	*	1	
Campbell	*	*	*	*	*	1	
Sublette	*	*	*	*	*	1	
Natrona	*	*	*	*	*	1	
Hot Springs	*	*	*	*	*	1	
Washakie	*	*	*	*	*	1	
Statewide Totals	203					39	

*These counties are not included in the P&Y data

About 65-percent of the archery record-book bulls taken in Wyoming during the past 10 years score better than 300 inches.

in relation to trophy quality. Once your application is submitted odds are quite good you'll be hunting this fall. Several areas in the Cowboy State offer top-notch bowhunting success and trophy potential.

Non-resident options include general or limited-quota elk license. General licenses are good for any area not under limited-quota rules. There are some archery-only areas in the northwest corner of the state that often have licenses left over after the drawing, but wilderness areas are common there, requiring non-residents to hire a guide.

Units 38 through 41, the Bighorn Mountains, have plentiful elk and occasionally account for bulls scoring in the 400-inch class. Access is good in these areas and non-residents have an even chance of winning tags. The Laramie Range is another top archery elk area. Access can prove more limited, but extra effort can be rewarded by trophy bulls.

In 2006 Wyoming began offering optional elk preference points to non-residents for an additional $50. You can purchase a point each year or apply and earn them the old-fashioned way, increasing odds of drawing later. Seventy-five percent of licenses are reserved for those with the most preference points, a random drawing conducted for the remaining 25-percent. If you choose not to participate in the preference-point system, you're still included in the 25-percent random drawing.

Wyoming's application deadline is normally around the end of January, but

Archery insiders Paul Viacunas and Garret Armstrong tagged this 360-plus bull in central Wyoming after drawing a hard-earned tag.

you will know if you'll be hunting by late February. Internet applications are not accepted. A leftover-license application period allows latecomers a second chance for a tag in mid-July. A regular elk license cost $493 in 2007, a "special" elk license $893; the latter giving the rich man a leg up in drawing a license (both including $12 application fee).

Between 1997 and 2007, 203 archery record-book bulls have appeared in Wyoming, 27 of these bettering the 350 mark and 65-percent of them scoring better than 300 inches; placing it just behind Arizona (and in sixth place) as an archery record-book producer. Boone & Crockett records reveal that trophy production remains even keel in the Cowboy State. Of 110 total B&C bulls taken since 1983, 39 of these (typical and non-typical) have appeared in this decade. See the "Arizona" chart for more details on trophy production.

Chapter 4

Going Guided

I t's one of the most enduring precepts of elk hunting; client and guide working together in the quest for a trophy bull. The guided hunt can evoke a great many images, dependant on location and terrain. Many will involuntarily think of horses, creaking saddles and leather-faced guides wearing cowboy hats and ragged beards. The more modern version might conjure images of a well-groomed young-ster in high-tech mountaineering togs, earning money between college semesters, confidently piloting an ATV instead of a trusty steed. Today the guided hunt could just as easily include a four-wheel drive truck with hard rock pounding from a stereo and a peach-fuzzed young-ster at the wheel; a financially-set professional temporarily on vacation, getting away from the office a couple weeks; or a retired game warden

Finding productive elk ground and then getting there can be hard work. An outfitter allows you to hit the ground running for higher success rates.

who has experienced enough killing himself but enjoys sharing in the success of others. All of these describe guides I've worked with. All are out there because of a love for the outdoors and especially anything to do with elk. A common western bumper sticker pretty much says it all; "Elkoholic."

Opposite page: Pack-stringing into wild places is not only part of the adventure during a guided hunt for elk, but gets you into country that is normally lightly hunted.

ELK HUNTING PERSONALITIES

And with various guides comes a wide assortment of personalities and hunting approaches. The youngsters are most often gung-ho and ambitious, liable to run a client into the ground right out of the starting gate through innocent exuberance. Older guides may prove more contemplative, hunting by their wits and not outright brawn.

Most experienced guides simply adjust the pace and their hunting style to meet the abilities of the individual client. One way or the other your guide makes sure you see, get close to, shoot at, and hopefully, tag elk. It's up to the outfitter to read each client and pair them with a guide who will work best with them.

If a couple decades of guiding elk hunters have taught me anything, it's that bowhunting clients also come in all shapes, sizes—and especially capabilities. The occasional client really doesn't need a guide, but these are rare. Some intuitive hands only need someone to show them an elk then they can confidently take the wheel from there. Such clients make a guide's job easy; clients best served by a guide willing to back off when the need arises.

The greater majority of hunters honestly couldn't kill an elk in unfamiliar country on their own in a month of concerted effort. They need a savvy, hands-on guide able to work around these obvious handicaps. This is not to suggest these clients are bowhunting morons. They are mostly whitetail hunters, many of them extremely successful, but elk hunting has its own set of rules, a completely different pace, and settings that could not be more remote and foreign.

The guided hunt can mean more quality time relaxing and enjoying your elk hunt rather than conducting camp chores.

MAKING THE CASE FOR GUIDED

While plenty of elk are killed on public lands every year by do-it-yourselfers, the odds are normally stacked against you. Fact is, on average only 20-percent (sometimes much fewer) of public-lands hunters take home an elk. The professional elk guide shatters these odds by investing untold hours becoming intimate with his particular elk ground, learning the ploys necessary for bowhunting success in that particular location. A couple elk hunts in the northern Rockies, for instance, does not make an expert in the drier Southwest or vice-versa.

With the high costs of today's elk hunts it might be easy to

Pack animals owned by an outfitter makes getting bagged meat out faster, a highly-important consideration during warm archery elk seasons.

assume the average outfitter is rolling in greenbacks, but this simply isn't true. Reimbursed at bare-minimum wages, the professional elk hunter might have hundreds of thousands of dollars invested in scouting alone over many year's time, not to mention gasoline consumption, public land-use fees, insurance and upkeep of vehicles. Quality elk guides spend hours and days in the field that would simply prove impossible for someone more distantly removed to invest. They do it because it's the rare guide who doesn't take great pride in leading clients to success, bringing in the biggest antlers. Friendly competition between other guides keep them striving to find ever-better hunting ground, or more successful approaches to ground they know best.

REALITY CHECK

Of course, booking a guided elk hunt does not guarantee an elk; nor would most of us have it that way. What you are purchasing is your guide's knowledge of terrain and hotspots, hunting skills and perhaps special equipment needed to streamline your hunt considerably. Booking an elk hunt with a quality outfitter means you hit the ground running, looking at elk instead of looking for elk, chasing elk rather than chasing leads, stalking elk instead of scouting elk. The guided elk hunt also provides much-needed elk hunting experience, allowing you to see lots of elk, learn more about the animals' behavior and how to hunt them effectively. This is invaluable experience for those who wish to hunt on their own later.

Booking a guided elk hunt comes with responsibilities. First you must find an outfitter offering services that are right for you. Finally, you must arrive as highly prepared for that hunt as possible.

Elk hunts are as varied as the country they inhabit, and come with just as varied a range of price tags. Private-land or Indian-reservation hunts have emerged as some of the best (and most expensive) elk hunting in the business. High suc-

The guided hunt simply increases your odds of success. Guides live in elk country and spend time scouting—impossible for anyone living far away.

cess on big bulls comes with a price, Arizona Apache reservation elk hunts, for instance, now command from $20,000 to $25,000. Heavily-managed private-ranch hunts can also fall into that category. But then again, many private-land hunts simply don't come with the possibility of 400-inch bulls, or even 300-inch bulls, and can prove relatively affordable. Lower-priced public-land hunts might mean sharing a tent camp or lodge with a crowd of hunters; a real experience in itself, sharing your adventure with a group of like-minded individuals. Interestingly, remote wilderness camps often entail lower price tags, because fewer hunters care to rough it and the going price is set by what the market will bear. In short, if big bulls are common, and hunting convenient, expect to pay more. If trophy quality is average, and more work involved, a highly-affordable option can be the result.

MAKING THE LEAP

Booking a hunt you have saved many years for can be a daunting experience. Unfortunately, there are crooks and chiselers in every business, and outfitting is certainly no exception. Horror stories abound. This makes word-of-mouth the safest bet in elk hunting, and what legitimate outfitters count on most of all. A friend or acquaintance who has risked an archery hunt with a new outfitter and hit the jackpot is a Godsend. Baring such a break, a proven booking agent (such as Safari Bowhunting Consultants) is the next logical approach. Booking agents in the habit of dispensing bum advice don't remain in business long. And, these services typically cost the client nothing, because commission is collected directly from the outfitter.

Doping out a quality outfitter yourself is certainly possible, but should be approached with caution. Outlets for such information are limitless; from magazine advertisements and articles, to outdoor television endorsements, sportsman's shows and Internet web sites.

After you have discovered a promising outfitter, take the time to talk to him via telephone, taking careful notes as you proceed. This serves to provide a basic gut feeling about the man. Again, your foremost concern is determining if a particular hunt, and outfit, is right for you. Determine if an outfitter and his guides truly understand bowhunting and all that it entails. Determine what kind of country you might be hunting in to assure it fits your physical abilities. As I have hinted, wilderness hunts are not for everyone. A 12-mile horseback ride and sleeping in cold, drafty tents might not be your idea of fun. Establish whether you will be hunting public or private ground, and in regards to the latter, how guides work around other hunters. I've witnessed many misunderstandings wherein clients who'd purchased a unit-wide "private landowner tag" believed they would be bowhunting behind locked gates when, in fact, public land was involved.

The camaraderie of camp life can be a huge bonus to the fully outfitted elk hunt; meeting and sharing your hunt with archery hunters from around the globe.

Remember, guides make a living with their trucks. Treat a guide/outfitter's vehicle as you would your own.

MORE DETECTIVE WORK

During your chat ask for a list of references; the more recent the better. Ask for lists of clients who were both successful and unsuccessful. It goes without saying that a fellow who has tagged the biggest bull of his life will have nothing but praise for an outfitter. What reveals more about an outfitting business are past clients who went home empty handed and still have nothing but accolades for their experiences. The worst combination might be the hunter who got his elk, but also says he would never return.

It must be remembered, too, that you just can't satisfy all of the people all of the time. Talking to references entails a bit of detective work in itself. I've guided clients who, even after tagging a super trophy, remained bent out of shape because of a seemingly unimportant event such as a forgotten coffee pot. Too, if a reference appears overly flattering, find out what the reference's relationship to the outfitter is. Some unscrupulous outfitters will use family and close friends as references. Also ask the outfitter for references spread over various hunt dates so you might determine if an unhappy client simply experienced an off week, or if an entire season passed that way. Sometimes weather, rut timing, or some other unforeseen circumstance conspires to create a bad week (plain bad luck, for instance), while the following week proved exceptional. One red flag I have begun to witness regularly, even in camps I've worked in, are huge camps with a large volume of hunters killing a few huge animals. Sure, the outfitter has pictures of three monster bulls to show, but what of the greater majority who went home without seeing a bull at all? Another common scenario is an outfit who has a great past record, but something has changed to make hunting less than what it once was in their area. Outfitters should be able to show you evidence of recent success, not a stack of pictures from the late 1980s.

REVISITING PRIORITIES

Priorities are also important when choosing an outfitter. I've visited camps where trophy animals abounded, where everyone got shooting, but food was horrendous, tents leaked and guides were little help or downright surly. I have visited camps where I ate like royalty, had my bed made each day with fresh linens, but there was little in the way of quality game available. Quality game but mediocre accommodations are fine with me. I don't care how good the food is if I'm seeing no animals. You may feel differently.

On a recent guided hunt for Roosevelt elk I found the accommodations and food more than adequate, even got my trophy bull. Problem was my young guide seemed to harbor Grande Prix fantasies, motoring his truck over treacherous, corkscrew mountain roads with squealing tires, ignoring repeated requests to slow down. I chose not to let it ruin a good hunt but have guided many hunters who would have been too petrified to continue; who would have packed up and demanded a ride to the airport.

There is also the matter of physical abilities. Elk can often be found in country offering a virtual cakewalk, while in still other places you need to be in marathon-type shape to get through a single day. If you are physically limited in some way this is information you want to quiz an outfitter and references about carefully. Even in rough country special accommodations can often be made. I've successfully guided senior citizens by finding the perfect water-hole or stand site in otherwise nasty terrain. Brutal honesty with yourself and your outfitter is absolutely necessary to avoid misunderstandings.

Booking a hunt with a well-prepared outfitter allows archery hunters the opportunity to worry only about the hunting and not about things like setting up a camp.

The night life after the hunt is finished can add to your enjoyment of the hunt, but don't allow bad manners or "partying" to spoil a good time for others.

Only after doing your homework, discovering the perfect outfitter and hunt for your needs, personality, and realistic abilities, should you commit to a deposit. Depending on procedures for drawing tags, waiting lists and outfitter preferences, as much as 50-percent may be required. This deposit might also prove nonrefundable. Many outfitters will not offer a refund should something prevent you from making your hunt, but happily apply a deposit to a hunt at a later date. Make sure you understand an outfitter's policies to avoid misunderstandings should unforeseen events interfere with your hunt dates.

LET'S GET READY!

After you have booked your dream hunt it's entirely up to you to arrive as well prepared as possible. Ask the average elk guide his two most common challenges and he will invariably complain of clients who are so out of shape they are unable to hunt effectively, and bad shooting once a hard-earned opportunity is presented. Believe me, your guide fully understands that you'll not arrive in the kind of physical conditioning he's privy to. If he is a good guide he won't hold this against you. Be that as it may, he simply can't carry you up that mountain or across that deep canyon when the bull of your dreams bugles or appears in the binoculars. And while a good guide also does his best to calm you down before an important shot, he certainly can't shoot your bow for you.

Elk hunting is a highly physical dodge. The fast-paced lives we all live today leave little time for regular workouts. Sitting behind a desk long hours does nothing to prepare you for the physical rigors of high-altitude elk country and the heart-breaking pace that must sometimes be mustered to set up an archery shot. Living close to sea level is another very real handicap, the air suddenly appearing to have no substance once in elk country. A few days' acclimation to the West's thinner air is typically required before the flatlander hits his stride, though it has been definitively proven that top physical conditioning actually shortens the required adjustment period following sudden altitude change. You have invested hard-earned money for your elk hunt. Make the best of your investment by devoting the time to endurance training, or the money asked of a personal trainer. If time permits, arrive in the area a couple days early—a prime opportunity to spend vacation time with a loved one.

WORK OUT FOR SUCCESS

Concentrate primarily on strengthening your legs and cardiovascular system; the heart and lungs. Bicycling or mountain biking is low-impact exercise and a good way to begin getting into fighting shape. If you don't have a safe area to ride,

Getting bagged meat out fast is priority one during early elk hunts. Having an entire camp of guides to get the job done makes for a more enjoyable experience.

Elk country is rough on an archery hunter. The better shape you arrive in, the more your guide has to work with, the better your chances of success.

a stationary bicycle is a good second choice. Other low-impact exercises made to order for a mountain hunt include Nordic Track and especially stair-climber machines (which effectively mimics long, uphill climbs). Note that while it certainly doesn't hurt to whip the rest of your body into shape, strengthen your back and stomach muscles, tone your upper body, overdoing it to the point of soreness can affect your shooting. Sore muscles that make it painful to draw your bow can lead to frustrating target panic.

A gym is certainly a boon but not absolutely necessary (though some seem to gain greater resolve when the price of membership is at stake). Old-fashioned jogging is as good an exercise for elk hunting as possible. Start out at a reasonable pace, jogging a half or full mile to begin and working to lengthen your runs. It will hurt at first but becomes easier with each passing day. As you hit your stride increase the pace, or lengthen your runs. Personally, I've discovered I receive as much of a workout sprinting two miles (on forgiving grass or dirt) as I do methodically jogging eight. This requires less time from my busy schedule and also seems to be easier on my aging knees.

To develop climbing muscles (calves), and make small work of those innumerable ridges and mountainsides, run office building stairwells, stadium bleachers or steep hillsides when available. As you gain stamina a couple weeks into

Opposite page: You'll win few friends on a guided hunt with bad shooting. Practice to extend your range to assure success when that trophy bull pauses in bow range.

your regiment don a daypack full of sandbags during these workouts. If it doesn't hurt, you're not getting into the kind of shape you'll need to operate at top performance in rough and tumble elk woods. Start months ahead of your hunt, not at the last possible moment. I've witnessed plenty of hunters who've shown up in elk country gimping from such last-minute workouts. It's no way to begin a week-long elk hunt. (See Chapter 14 – Building Physical & Mental Endurance for more detail on smart endurance workouts).

WORK FOR BETTER SHOOTING

Shooting well is just as important to a successful elk hunt. Shooting well in eastern whitetail woodlots is quite different from the same term applied to elk country. I say this because Eastern bowhunters seem to have the greatest difficulties. While 35 yards might be considered a long stab in the heavily-vegetated East, it's considered a slam-dunk, in-your-lap shot while bowhunting elk; especially on public lands where elk are innately more wary. The archer able to stack arrows tightly at 45 yards has a much better chance at elk-hunting success. The average elk guide will expect at least this level of competency. Extend that effective range to 50 or 60 yards and you're nearly assured success with a competent guide in prime country.

Effective maximum range on elk means keeping all of your arrows inside a 14-inch circle; instead of the tighter eight-inch vital offered by a deer. Of course you must be able to pull this off with broadhead-tipped arrows, not field points. Shoot from odd positions to assure you can make the best of a fleeting opportunity; sitting on your rear, from your knees, leaning awkwardly from behind cover. Remember too, it's all about placing a sharp broadhead in the sweet spot, not brute power. You don't need an 80-pound bow. And for God's sake, buy a laser range finder and use it before every shot. The West can be deceiving, wide-open spaces, unfamiliar vegetation and falling terrain tricking even the most accomplished 3-D champion.

Today's archery equipment is all-around better and more efficient—especially faster. This all spells increased accuracy at longer ranges. The gear is certainly capable; you must simply bring yourself up to speed. Super bow tuning is pivotal. Small shooting flaws at 20 yards magnify tenfold at 40 or 50 yards. Tune and retune that bow until it's shooting perfect arrows every shot. If such detail is beyond your capabilities, pay a pro-shop professional to help you.

While your current whitetail bow is likely up to the elk-hunting task, an equipment overhaul or assembling an elk-specific rig can automatically take inches off your long-range groups. Ditch the total-containment arrow rest so handy while installed on stand and replace it with a modern drop-away. Add a stabilizer if you don't use one, or a longer model if you do, to help hold pins on distant targets more steadily. Purchase a sight with a longer extension bar and five (or more), fine-diameter fiber-optic pins. Use a wrist sling to assure an open-hand grip that eliminates bow torque and left and right misses. Finally, buy the best arrows available; the straightest, most precisely-matched brands and models made. This is your long-awaited elk hunt; don't cut corners now by purchasing discount-priced arrow shafts.

If riding a horse will be part of your elk hunt, a visit to a local riding stable might prove a wise investment to better prepare you for your adventure.

Extending your effective range means shooting with an eye toward constant improvement, hiring a shooting coach if needed. Hone your shooting form and strive for complete follow-through with every shot. And push yourself. Strive to shoot farther. Practice at 70 or 80 yards. No doubt you'll not be shooting at an elk at such ranges (unless a finishing shot on a wounded animal is called for), but after a summer of 80-yard practice, a broadside elk at 50 appears child's play. Only by pushing to shoot farther will you discover small flaws in shooting form that can turn into the difference between a heart and paunch shot when ranges stretch. This is a worthwhile investment toward success. The better you shoot, the more your guide has to work with, the better your ability to deal with a rare opportunity at that bull of a lifetime. (See Chapter 12 – Big Bull Minimums for more detail).

ATTITUDE IS EVERYTHING

Part of the unwritten guide/client contract is also that you arrive with a good attitude. I've stated it before and I'll say it again, booking a hunt does not mean you have bought an animal, or even a shot at an animal. You have contracted a guide's superior knowledge of the game and the country in which they are found, his best effort during the period of your hunt, as well as services and transportation while in the field. Hunting is hunting–bowhunting is something else altogether. Your guide has no control over game, weather, or the unforeseen activities of others who might be using the same forest (though part of what you pay for is to work around such contingencies). Occasionally tires blow out and cause you to miss the first half hour of a morning hunt. A lunch hour might be spent in an auto mechanic shop because your guide has been going full bore a month straight and has received no opportunity to have a repair done. Your guide might even be the one to blow a stalk on a trophy bull. He will hate himself and apologize endlessly, but these things happen.

Whining, complaining and turning sullen will not help matters when things have turned sour. Defining your hunt by how much it costs per hour (as I remember one client doing) is asinine and simply ridiculous. A guide faced with such a personality is more apt to give you less than 100-percent.

More importantly, perhaps, don't attempt to guide the guide. This is more common than you might believe; the plutocratic executive used to plying his will, control freaks that have a difficult time handing the reins over to anyone. If you are unwilling to take advice or direction, why pay for a guide? If he's doing something that you're unhappy about or uncomfortable doing, talk to him about it openly but politely. Stated diplomatically, there's no reason your guide should take such input personally. Most importantly, your guide doesn't care how you hunted elk somewhere else, or how you hunt deer at home. This is not there, and elk are not deer. Your guide normally has good reason to conduct a hunt in a certain manner. There may simply be circumstances you are unaware of. You might even learn something new.

And there just may be that guide who iniquitously gives you what you ask for. I recall a certain client who after attending three private-land Colorado elk hunts was a self-proclaimed expert, two mule-deer-sized raghorn bulls proof of that elk-hunting prowess. Each time we arrived anywhere near elk an argument ensued regarding calling, or more pointedly, my patent refusal to call at all. Calling works, even on heavily-pressured bulls, we just hadn't encountered that labyrinthine situation yet. I listened to diatribes on how his Colorado guide skillfully called in bulls on a daily basis. In time he insisted I obviously didn't know what I was doing.

We found the vast herd strewn across a wind-swept ridge of juniper and pinon. There were at least 100 elk in evidence, six behemoth bulls in a fervor to command the masses of cows frolicking to and fro, chirping and mewing frantically. It was an orgasmic sight, the setting ripe for a "run-n-gun" stalk, all that confusion creating subterfuge that would tip the odds in our favor. I'd seen the situation before and recognized it as the kind of break any confident elk hunter dreams of, when a careful stalk allows you to pluck an otherwise untouchable herd bull from the confusion. My expert demanded that we set up and call.

I knew better but felt he needed the hard lesson, so gave in. "Okay, if you insist," I said, adding silently; "You'll be sorry." We circled to accommodate the wind, slipped in close and set up to the music of screaming, grunting bulls and the constant female and baby elk chatter. I produced a series of beautifully-plaintive cow mews, just to show the expert that I knew something about operating a call after all. The ridge grew conspicuously silent, as if I'd just kicked the jukebox 45 off track in a crowded barroom, feeling all attention suddenly directed to our position. A few cows chirped, a bull grunted softly. The expert looked excited, believing all those elk had fallen silent to charge over to investigate this comely cow suddenly arrived to join the party. I produced a careful cow chirp in return. Then the ridge truly grew silent. I called away to an empty auditorium for another half hour before we decided to investigate.

Those elk were gone. Vanished without a peep. We never did see them again, or figure out exactly where they had gotten off to.

MAKING FRIENDS & INFLUENCING PEOPLE

Now let me speak as a client and not a guide, because I've certainly been in those shoes as well. Become friends with your guide, become interested in his world and life. He's not hired help, but a hunting partner, and may actually be able to teach you something you would never have known otherwise. Be as polite as it is possible to be to everyone involved in your hunt. Don't be afraid to jump in and help when something needs to be done; like setting up a tent, watering horses, gathering fire wood, butchering or packing someone else's elk. Share your booze and cigars. You want your guide to like you. If he decides you're a decent fellow he just might work that much harder for you. And remember, too, anything is possible when it comes to equipment breakdowns, personal problems, labor disputes or a glitch in communications or logistics. Relax. Everything will work out just fine. You're on vacation after all. This is supposed to be fun, remember?

This isn't tired Pollyanna blather. I learned these lessons the hard way. When I was young in the outdoor-writing business and had just begun to muster enough notoriety to rate sponsored hunts and television film crews I remember suffering through several stress-filled hunts. Everything gone wrong was seen as a personal affront, a waste of my personal time and hunting opportunity. I felt I had to produce a dead animal at the end of every hunt or my career was finished. I wasn't having much fun, and bowhunting is what I love more than anything on earth. In time I learned to take things as they came, mostly to relax and just let the hunt unfold. Interestingly, not only did hunting become fun once more, but success became more frequent.

TIPS ON TIPS

Tipping is a personal matter, but remember that most guides depend on tips to cover gas or vehicle-repair costs–to simply make ends meet. Some have suggested 15-percent as a standard rate, but don't be afraid to tip more if you believe your guide deserves it. And tipping doesn't only cover a dead animal. The guide who has worked hard, gone beyond the call of duty, even on an "unsuccessful" hunt also deserves a tip. I've been tempted to leave a camp without offering a tip only once, but in the end could not bring myself to do it. Perhaps the man had something going on in his life I had no way of guessing and I was only seeing him at his worst. I guess I prefer to think the best of people…

Find An Elk Outfitter

Alberta Professional Outfitters
Association
#103 6030 88th St.
Edmonton, Alberta T6E-6G4
(780) 414-0249
www.apos.ab.ca/

Arizona Elk Society
P.O. Box 190
Peoria, AZ 85380
www.arizonaelksociety.org/

British Columbia Guide & Outfitter
Association
P.O. Box 94675
Richmond, BC V6Y-4A4
(604) 278-2688
www.goabc.org/

Colorado Outfitters Association
P.O. Box 849
Craig, CO 81626
(970) 824-2468
www.coloradooutfitters.org

Idaho Outfitters & Guides
Association (IOGA)
P.O. Box 95
Boise, ID 83701
(800) 49-IDAHO
(208) 342-1919
www.ioga.org/

Montana Outfitter & Guide
Association (MOGA)
2033 11th Ave., #8
Helena, MT 59601
(406) 449-3578
www.montanaoutfitters.org/

New Mexico Guides & Outfitters
(registered)
New Mexico Dept. of Game & Fish
www.wildlife.state.nm.us

New Mexico Council of Guides &
Outfitters
P.O. Box 93186
Albuquerque, NM 87199-3186
(505) 822-9845
www.nmoutfitters.com

Nevada Outfitters & Guide
Association (NOGA)
HC 60, Box 76506
Round Mountain, NV 89045
(775) 964-2145
www.nevadaoutfitters.org/

Oregon Guides & Packers Assn.
531 SW 13th St.
Bend, OR 97702
(800) 747-9552
www.ogpa.org/

Utah Guides & Outfitters
(state tourism board)
www.utah.com/hunt/guides

Washington Outfitter & Guides
Association (WOGA)
P.O. Box 1125
Twisp, WA 98856
(509) 997-1080
www.woga.org/

Wyoming Outfitters & Guides
Association
P.O. Box 2650
Casper, WY 82602
(307) 265-2376
www.wyoga.org/

And don't forget all the others who have made your visit an enjoyable experience; the cook who created the best peach cobbler you've ever tasted, the wrangler who caught up and saddled your horse each morning, the camp hand who thoughtfully had a warming fire lit in your tent or cabin stove when you returned cold and wet after that evening thunderstorm, who woke you up each morning with a cup of steaming coffee. These folks work hard too, and also depend on tips to keep their children clothed and the mortgage current.

Every hunter deserves at least one good guided elk hunt in their lifetime. Hell, I am a guide (or was, until recently), but I still welcome the camaraderie, education and knowledge of a new piece of elk habitat that comes by way of a quality guide. I'm not being pretentious when I say I know one hell of a lot about bowhunting elk in a great many places in the Southwest; but am also more than willing to admit that when I hunted Roosevelt elk in Oregon, a species and area I had never glimpsed, I needed all the help I could garner. I've killed more than 12 archery elk to date, have guided clients to three times that many, but when I draw a highly-coveted tag in a strange area I won't hesitate to seek assistance once again. Learning a piece of new elk country can take years. This is an enjoyable process, granted, but hunting time is precious and sometimes you simply want to make the best of a limited hunting opportunity, to assure you see more animals, to increase your odds of success. This is what going guided is all about.

Hiring a guide or an outfitter can be well worth it by providing access to remote places that are not only beautiful, but are often full of elk.

Chapter 5

Do-It-Yourself Planner

Each year an ever-greater number of adventurous bowmen make the pilgrimage to the West, lured by her lofty mountains, sage-covered mesas and river-break prairies. Most arrive entertaining long-held dreams of arrowing what is arguably the West's most majestic big game animal, the Rocky Mountain or Roosevelt elk. This is remarkable only in that this raging fad did not begin decades earlier, considering the amount of readily-available public lands and wide-open accessibility to such a popular and coveted big game animal. Small wonder, while whitetail deer are undisputedly this nation's most popular big game animal, due mostly to widespread availability and backyard convenience, they lack a certain amount of variety and unquestionably leave much to be desired in way of the vast vistas and wide-open wilderness that the West's best elk haunts offer in plentiful supply. Bowhunting elk can require a daily dose of mental and physical toughness whitetail seldom demand. And unlike the very best whitetail ground, a major portion of the West's most productive elk country is made of public lands open to all of us.

As we have already established, the prospective elk hunter, but especially those on their own, must weigh desires and expectations and balance them with the realities of modern bowhunting. If world-class trophies aren't a priority, choose unlimited areas or states with shoe-in draw odds to assure an elk hunt every year (which makes gaining important knowledge easier). High-odds bowhunts don't necessarily mean a trophy's not in the cards, either. Some areas offer plentiful Pope & Young quality animals but not the slightest possibility of world-record potential. There are middle-ground options where trophy animals roam public lands yet drawing a tag isn't difficult, but working extremely hard for success is portion. If you are to succeed on your own you must be willing to invest in plenty of research, as well as putting forth much more effort once you hit the ground. An extra measure of luck never hurt anything either…

Opposite page: Bowhunting elk on your own brings a higher sense of self-accomplishment and pride in success. This requires a more intense planning and conditioning.

New arrivals to the West, elk ground in particular, can easily become daunted. Proper preparation leaves you feeling more confident.

There's certainly a strong case to be made for a quality guided hunt, namely, high-odds success and a quick education in hands-on elk hunting difficult to substitute through reading or simply watching hunting videos. There is certainly no shame in this and every archer who can afford it deserves to experience at least one quality guided elk hunt in their lifetime. But there's the catch. Guided hunts in good elk country cost serious money. Some of us will simply never be able to justify such an extravagance when the house needs a new roof, the kids outgrow their clothes on a monthly basis, and the flood of bills just keep rolling in. Hunting on your own becomes the only real alternative for a good many hunters.

WHY UNGUIDED?

There's also much to be said for earning the extra satisfaction that comes with self accomplishment. This is something no amount of money can substitute for. But there are other hard realities to consider. Arriving in any new area, bowhunting unfamiliar game, means the odds are stacked firmly against you. It is natural that the optimistic hunter should observe a posted success rate of 20-percent and automatically see themselves as part of those lucky few. It's easy to overlook the glaring truth that 80-percent of archers in that area, during a particular hunt period, return home without an elk.

But this mere number does not paint a complete and detailed picture. It's simply impossible to determine how many of those hunters missed an easy shot because they did not invest the time necessary to become proficient with their equipment; how many of those archers hunted the wrong areas or habitat types out of pure naivety and never saw an elk at all because they did not invest the time necessary to research their hunting area thoroughly; how many of those hunters started their hunt in poor physical conditioning and could not trek into the most productive areas or spent more time in camp nursing blistered feet more than doggedly pursuing the elk all around them. Some simply do not possess the skills necessary to succeed in elk woods.

I recall once setting up a group of Texas hunters in prime elk country—one of the best units in New Mexico's Gila region during that period—in exchange for whitetail hunting on leased private ground. I was nearly destitute while attending that Texas university and could no more swing the expense of a deer lease spot than pay cash for a brand-new, fully-loaded pick-up truck. It seemed a fair trade. I provided advice acquired after years of bowhunting and guiding in the area, made a three-day scouting trip with them between semesters, loaned them some important camping equipment, even divulged specific canyons and ridges where I had never failed to encounter trophy bulls.

The intrepid archers returned from their elk hunt empty handed and completely disgruntled. They were even inclined toward bowing out of their end of the deal. None of them had released an arrow. Upon closer quizzing I found they had heard bulls bugling nightly (from camp!), had seen elk daily, had even witnessed a couple behemoth bulls. These guys were 3-D target champions and highly successful whitetail hunters, one of them with twenty-something Pope & Young bucks to his credit, but the conditions they encountered in those foreign elk woods simply proved well beyond their bowhunting abilities.

A DIFFERENT KIND OF INVESTMENT

Self accomplishment aside, doing it on your own, unfortunately, is the only financially-viable option for most of us. This is especially true when groups of close friends or family members wish to share the hunting and/or camping experience together. There's no need to show up handicapped by predetermined success rates, though. Like the professional guide who regularly bucks established odds to get visiting clients their elk, the ambitious and determined non-resident archery hunter with a healthy dose of free time, better-than-average bowhunting skills and an adventurous attitude can enjoy a rewarding and successful elk hunt just like the guided fellow. Remember, too, going it on your own also means doing all the hard work that comes with elk hunting; showing up to set up and maintain your own efficient base camp, climbing daily into rough and tumble high country without benefit of horses or mules, or packing a bagged elk out of the pits of a bottomless canyon.

Desk-jockey research is where this operation begins; pouring over record books in search of an established track record or new trends (see Chapter 3 – Trophy Ground), visiting state conservation web sites to discover success rates in a state's

As enjoyable as bowhunting elk can be, it also comes with plenty of hard work. Are you physically ready for that challenge?

various hunt areas, calling game biologists and Forest Service personal for possible leads, and always keeping your ears perked for any information that might take you one step closer to a prospective hotspot. Don't expect the information you gather, or the questions you will ask later, to reveal a specific hillside or canyon. General information such as a particular unit number, an entire National Forest area, or a single county is good enough for starters. And like doping out a respectable outfitting business, this research involves finding an area that is right for you in respects to desired trophy quality, animal numbers, type of physical conditioning demanded and logistical realities. For instance, there's simply no use delving any deeper into a perspective area if you quickly discover that pack animals are required to access the best areas and you own or have access to none.

MAP WORK

This is a long and ongoing process. Once you have settled on a particular hunting area the next logical step is to purchase appropriate maps. Forest Service (www.fs.fed.us/) or Bureau of Land Management/BLM (www.blm.gov/nhp/index.htm) maps of the areas you have in mind help provide a better idea of what you are up against. If the area involves scattered private holdings that must be worked around or avoided altogether, you should also find detailed land-status maps of the area to steer clear of trespass trouble. Forest Service land is normally represented in green, BLM in yellow, state-owned lands in sky blue. Private lands appear as white blanks. General maps of this kind give you an overview of the area; roadways, trailheads and trails, major rivers and creek beds, stock tanks and ponds, and perhaps a vague idea of the lay of mountain ranges.

For a more detailed overview of an area, US Geological Survey topographical plats, found and purchased online at (www.usgs.gov/), provide a bird's-eye view of an area via contour lines. With a little experience you learn to gain a virtual three-dimensional view of a land mass. Contour lines that are closely spaced indicate steeper terrain, those spaced more widely reveal more gentle topography, while few or no lines show flat mesas or flats.

Maps make it easier to locate places where you'd expect animals to live; without expending a single drop of sweat, exerting one bit of energy, and in the comfort of your own home. Obvious points of interest garnered from general maps include permanent sources of water or large swatches of land with few or no roads. Correlated to topographical maps it is possible to determine if these areas also include attractive elk habitat. Look for long ridges that elk love to travel, hanging benches that provide bedding areas, meadows where elk come to feed at night, and so on. Once you have narrowed down the prospects, some additional calls to the state game biologist you have spoken to before might automatically eliminate, or earmark, some of the places that have jumped out at you. Of course, a biologist is only useful if he or she has actually spent time in the field or in the air—something which is becoming rarer today, computer models quickly taking the place of aerial surveys and on-the-ground field work.

Preseason scouting means locating sign made today or yesterday, because elk travel widely and you must hunt where they are now.

FURTHER SLEUTHING

Another potentially useful source of elk-hunting information is the Natural Resources Conservation Service/NRCS (formally Soil Conservation). They are easily located on the Internet by typing www.nrcs.usda.gov/. This federal agency compiles comprehensive data on flora and fauna around the country, sometimes down to the very food elk need to flourish–another way talking to game biologists helps you narrow down productive elk habitat. This information is often so accurate that it enables you to pin-point feed-rich areas down to a specific hillside or canyon. NRCS field officers also catalog water sources, sometimes even specific animal populations. It must be kept in mind, though, that some of these reports are decades old and recent activity, especially logging (or lack thereof), intensive cattle grazing or land development can have quick and detrimental affects on elk habitat.

Another fun and sometimes profitable mode of scouting online are aerial photograph sites providing a satellite's view of a potential hunting area. These can prove especially useful in Roosevelt elk country where clear-cuts and other logging activity can actually attract elk to emerging second growth, for example. These sites might also reveal prime meadows not revealed in detail by standard maps; places where elk like to feed and gather during the rut. Look to TerraServer USA, (http://terraserver.microsoft.com/), GlobeXplorer, (www.globexplorer.com/), or US Geological Survey aerials, (http://geography.usgs.gov/partners/viewonline.htm/) for such information.

GROUND WORK

As important as homework proves, no amount of desk research can truly prepare you for what you might find once in an area. One way or the other, to beat established success rates, you must get on the ground and invest in some amount of old-fashioned scouting. Greedily saving vacation time becomes important, because time is your best ally when bowhunting elk—the more the better. The more time spent scouting before season opener the more likely you are to get your elk, simple as that. This means showing up—if even just the occasional weekend —to discover areas elk are actually using this year or even this week. This is something guiding has taught me again and again. Conditions change from year to year, determined by factors such as weather, moisture and ranching activities such as where cattle have been pastured most recently. Elk will tolerate cattle, sometimes living side by side with them, but this does not mean they prefer it that way. I have a long list of hotspots that can provide wide-open hunting one year, and reveal not a single elk track the next. Even in areas I am highly intimate with, I must check them out before venturing into these places with clients during a particular year, even month or week.

While Rocky Mountain elk are nomads, less likely to burrow into a particular

Opposite page: An abundance of rubs tells you an area holds plenty of rutting bulls. If sign is lacking, keep moving until it is discovered.

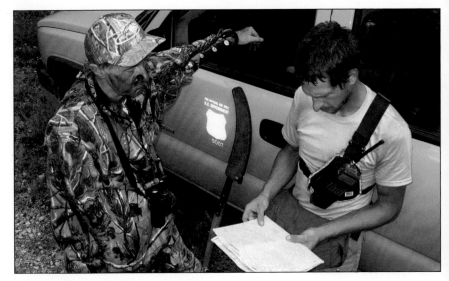

Locals who work in the woods, like Forest Service employees, can prove invaluable in unfamiliar elk country.

area indefinitely, scouting does reveal basic patterns, areas where elk obviously aren't, feed and water conditions particular to a given unit corner or end, cattle grazing activities and so forth. It also gives you a better idea of where concentrations of more inaccessible cow elk are located (not those every hunter with a tag will notice)—which will attract bulls with the coming of the rut. Most importantly, you gain an understanding of the general flow of the terrain and gain a better "feel" for the attractiveness of an area. You might even discover rut sign from the previous season (old rubs or wallow pits), activity that could be repeated again this fall.

It has long been my contention that pre-scouting is important enough that even should you be forced to subtract those days from actual hunting days due to vacation limitations, it's better than arriving to begin a hunt haphazardly and disoriented. Two or three days of pre-scouting immediately preceding your hunt also gives you the important opportunity to become better acclimated to altitude, allowing you to hunt more efficiently once opening day arrives. Others will be quick to point out that preseason scouting is often wasted effort, because the sudden hunting pressure that comes with the first few days of season opener can instantly push elk into new locations and patterns. The first couple days of season can catch some elk unaware, but this much time can also be required to allow elk to settle into a new set of movement patterns. In areas with intense hunting pressure, this may very well be the case. It is also easy to contend that conditions often change for the best as a season progresses, many hunters surrendering after an initial flurry of effort, or as the season pushes deeper into prime rut dates when bulls begin to bugle more openly or the biggest bulls begin to participate and become more visible.

Your approach depends on where you hunt and the resulting hunting pressure. In areas where I most often bowhunt elk I see only the rare hunter. For the most part I tend to ignore obvious and easily-observed concentrations of elk, such as those in summer mode and still feeding in a meadow easily observed from a major highway or Forest Service artery. These areas seem to be literally attacked on opening morning.

Getting started early gives you an opportunity to talk to cowboys, ranchers or Forest Service personnel you meet in your hunt area, querying them about recent elk sightings. These are folks who actually spend a good deal of time in the field and can sometimes prove an invaluable resource for timely information. The average range cowboy can prove a proverbial curmudgeon who has little patience for outsiders, but many more welcome friendly conversation in their lonely existence. In fact, I've encountered a few cowhands in my time that proved downright difficult to tear away from, willing to talk the day away. Sharing a cold beer or soda, even promising a chunk of elk meat should your hunt prove successful, can be a further help in loosening the tongues of taciturn types. Dropping in on area ranch houses is always time well spent, even taking time to casually help with chores if the opportunity presents itself; handing the fellow under the hood of a pickup needed tools, holding a corral panel in place while he fastens it with wire, helping unload a load of baled hay.

Focus midday scouting efforts in areas sure to concentrate elk sign, investigating remote stock ponds or secreted meadows with obvious feed. Follow wandering fence lines seeking broken-down crossings or open gates lazy elk employ while traveling. Finding a good vantage is the best way to make the best of prime morning and evening hours, putting quality glass to work looking for game in the open during the coolest portions of the day.

THE DROP-CAMP ALTERNATIVE

If you are unwilling or unable to invest the time needed to research and scout a productive elk area, a drop-camp is an excellent option for elk hunters who want to do it on their own. This involves hiring a packer to take you into productive elk ground, perhaps even providing camping gear, but then leaving you to your own devices. These arrangements can cost a quarter to a half of what is charged for a fully-guided elk hunt and typically include periodic visits from your packer to assure meat is packed out promptly. This is an especially useful approach in designated wilderness areas or remote regions lacking easy access, areas where backpacking is certainly possible, but where trucking a downed elk out after a kill becomes a logistical nightmare. Booking a packer involves the same careful research required of locating a reliable outfitter (see Chapter 4 – Going Guided).

I know of several outfitters in the Gila Wilderness area of New Mexico, for example, who offer drop-camp options with various degrees of service. Some hunters supply all their own food and gear, the outfitter simply ferrying them into productive elk country for a reasonable daily or per-trip fee. Others allow the outfitter to supply camp and food, simply showing up with personal gear and loading up to make the ride. For slightly more money, a camp "manager" can often be

Off-season scouting is time well spent. Make a vacation of it with family to better learn a piece of elk ground.

hired, a wrangler who shares camp to keep stock on hand in case meat needs to be hauled out or hunters choose to ride deeper into their hunting area. The camp manager also serves as chief camp cook and bottle washer. The latter options can prove to be a wise move, because professional experience assures all necessary gear arrives where it's needed, and eliminates the possibility of items being jettisoned during loading to make weight allowances. Pack animals can carry only so much, their numbers dictated by stock-trailer space, so conservative packing is always in order.

At the very least, consider lining up a packer to haul elk meat from the field for a fee after the kill. If you down an elk in a remote area, or are simply physically unable to pack an elk from the bottom of a deep canyon, local cowboys or even the owner of a trail-ride stable can often be contacted well before the hunt and an arrangement made. Ask at local general stores or gas stations located in elk country and the odds are good you will locate someone with horses who is willing to make a few extra bucks packing out your elk.

THE ALL-IMPORTANT HUNTING PARTNER

Having an even-tempered, highly reliable buddy, or buddies, to share the experience with is absolutely necessary to a successful do-it-yourself or drop-camp experience. This is not something you can do by yourself, because an injury could quickly turn life threatening without someone to go for help, and wilderness camping and hunting is hard work. Daily chores are a large part of the experience, hard work compounded by the fact that you are hunting long hours in rough terrain. It can prove physically taxing. A hunting partner unwilling to pull his weight, to pitch in when back-breaking work such as packing an elk back to camp needs to be accomplished, can make for a frustrating week. It has been said often that you really never know a man until you spend a week or more in the woods with him, and this is especially true when remote and rugged wilderness elk country is involved. Nasty mountain weather can conspire to turn the most patient man moody and downright pathological when staying in the tight quarters of a dank tent. Many hunters have returned to civilization after such an experience bitter enemies. Choose your elk-hunting partners with care.

It's a wonderful thing when one partner happily compensates for the shortcomings of another. For example, one person handling the cooking while another volunteers to wash the dishes and keep the water jugs filled with filtered drinking water—one partner tidying up camp early in the morning while

Keeping your way means more time hunting, and added confidence to trek off the beaten path. Maps and a GPS are key.

the other tosses together a quick lunch for both. It's also nice to know beyond a doubt you can trust the other person to calmly handle a tough situation should something go terribly wrong, a person who won't panic if you don't show up on time or should you injure yourself.

My hunting partner Steven Tisdale and I have been on countless wilderness hunts together. He's the kind of guy I would trust to hunt with anywhere, any time. If I should return to camp late and bone tired he has something hot ready to eat and all the dishes washed. I'm happy to do the same on those nights when he's running late. No one has to ask the other to do a thing; we just jump in and do what needs to be done so we can hunt as much as possible. There's seldom a discussion about how to divide necessary tasks. If an elk needs packing, we both drop what we're doing and get it done, no questions asked, no recriminations about lost hunting time, no jealousy whatsoever. He might kill a bigger elk than mine this year, but I know my time will come around next time. Such hunting partners are precious because they can be so tough to find…

A CLEAN, WELL LIGHTED PLACE

Even without a drop-camp scenario, proper camping equipment is highly important to a successful hunt. Bringing in hunting partners help spread the burden when special equipment such as weather-proof tents, sleeping and outdoor cooking gear and other necessary camping paraphernalia must be assembled for

A do-it-yourself hunt means you are better able to share the exciting experience with friends and family.

an efficient elk camp. One buddy might own the perfect tent or camp trailer, another needed cooking gear and so on. The West and its sometimes rugged weather is no place for discount-store tents that topple during high winds or leak during a downpour or crumple under a burden of early high-country snow. Purchasing top-quality camping gear is an investment against future elk hunts and pays for itself with time.

GENTLEMEN, START YOUR ENGINES!

With a proper camp erected and the scouting done, elk hunters await opening day with reverence. This is when all your research and preparation are proven valid, or obvious holes are found in the chinking. Now is the time to pull out all the stops. Perhaps you have packed into a remote area in order to beat crowds, or simply located a hotspot that takes a little bit of extra effort to access. Locating remote or overlooked areas where other hunters won't interfere with your efforts is always smart bowhunting. A day of elk hunting begins early, in the cold dark of morning, arriving in your chosen area and positioning yourself well before good light arrives. You might not see camp again until late into the night. To stay in the game catnaps in the shade of a tree during the heat of the day become part of the routine, awaiting cooler evening temperatures when elk go on the prod once more. Carry a lunch and water in your daypack so the necessity of back-tracking out of a remote hotspot is eliminated. Early bowhunting seasons often provide short windows of opportunity at the seams of each day, sometimes only the first couple hours after sunrise and last hours before sunset proving productive.

Successful hunters make the best of midday downtime by engaging in additional scouting, checking out a place on the map you have not yet had time to investigate, pushing over one more ridge to see what's on the other side. Hunting time is precious. Make the most of it. You can lounge, play cards and socialize when you get home. This is no time for laziness if you're serious about killing an elk. It's common while I'm guiding to drop my client off at the lodge during midday to watch television, nap and chat with others in camp while I'm out hiking, looking over a water-hole, investigating an untried meadow or an area on the opposite end of the hunt unit. When going it on your own, these are things you will have to accomplish yourself.

ELK-HUNT MINDSET

The biggest mistake most archers visiting the West make while stalking elk is being too contemplative. Elk hunting is a completely different game than deer. Elk demand an aggressive approach, covering as much ground as possible, as quickly as possible. Only when you discover smoking-hot sign or hear nearby bugling should you slow down, yet this pace still won't resemble the snail's pace of still-hunting deer. Elk aren't hard to see, relatively, so gobbling more ground is generally not a handicap. There's a lot of country out there, and it's easy for a bull to vanish into swallowing cover with the coming heat of day and never be seen again should you dally while making your stalk. Get on them quickly, slowing only to make the final approach. The finer points are to be covered in greater detail in the chapters to follow, but developing that aggressive mindset is paramount to elk-hunting success.

Regular success in elk woods translates into hunting aggressively; a mode many newcomers to elk hunting, who were raised on deer, fail to understand.

A drop-camp is a great way to hunt on your own without breaking your back; getting you and gear in, getting meat out more efficiently.

You'll also need to carry a daypack and a few survival items. Western elk country can easily kill you. Carrying the right gear can keep you out of trouble. A compass, topographical maps and GPS unit should be at the top of your list, to assure you don't become lost and find yourself in a survival situation. Make sure you carry extra batteries for your GPS unit, and keep the instructions in the same Zip-Lok bag as your unit. Other important and standard daypack gear includes an emergency space blanket at bare minimum, both a handheld and head-lamp flashlight, a compact backpack stove and titanium cup stuffed with tea bags and instant soup, surveying tape to mark a trail back to downed game, plenty of water and lunch.

Of course, you'll need a sharp folding saw, two knives, stout parachute cord, fly-proof game bags and sharpening steel in case you get lucky. Skinning, quartering and hanging an elk for later packing is no small task. Keep a pack frame in your truck or camp and be prepared to schlep your animal from a nasty place in a hurry to avoid meat spoilage in warm early-season weather. Hang meat in the shade, but also remember that hanging it over a cooling stream or spring can give you precious hours or days before packing is absolutely necessary. If you're worried about packing meat you'll not venture as far out as may be asked of the hunt. I've always concentrated on getting an elk on the ground first of all, only worrying about packing them out later. Packing meat is hard work, but part of the hunting experience. It won't kill you, though it may seem like it at the time.

Mapping It Out

Topographical Maps:
U.S. Geological Survey; (888) 275-8747; http://topomaps.usgs.gov/

U.S. Forest Service Maps:
U.S.D.A. Forest Service; (202) 205-1470; www.fs.fed.us

Land Status Maps By State:
Arizona: (602) 417-9200; www.az.blm.gov
Colorado: (303) 239-3600; www.co.blm.gov
Idaho: (208) 384-3300; www.id.blm.gov
Montana: (406) 896-5000; www.mt.blm.gov
Nevada: (775) 861-6400; www.nv.blm.gov
New Mexico: (505) 438-7400; www.nm.blm.gov
Oregon/Washington: (202) 452-5125; www.or.blm.gov
Utah: (801) 539-4133; www.ut.blm.gov
Wyoming: (307) 775-6256; www.wy.blm.gov

Optics make the Western hunter. Even when covering ground, you should stop often to scan the country around you for game. To make the most of the vast vistas afforded by the West you'll want something in the 8x40 to 10x40 class. The West is big, glassing distances typically well beyond those your compact, shirt-pocket whitetail models are suited to. Learn to use binoculars effectively and you'll see more game in the West. Let glass cover the long distances for you, carrying you effortlessly across deep canyons, off sharp mesa edges. When all else fails, when water-holes prove unproductive, when calling's out of the question, glassing up elk and stalking (spot-and-stalk) is your avenue to success. (See Chapter 13 – Gearing Up for more details).

As you can see, bowhunting elk on your own is no easy task. Planning such an endeavor takes on the dimensions of a military campaign. The best way to assure everything comes off without a hitch is to begin planning months ahead of your hunt. There are important decisions to be made regarding where and how you will hunt, applications to fill out and mail in before deadlines, diligent homework to accomplish, and the effort of getting into the best shape of your life. (See Chapter 14 – Building Physical & Mental Endurance). The cooling days of August and September, with frost on the meadow grasses, the river-bank trees afire with the colors of autumn, long plumes of steam rising from the nostrils of feeding elk, and the eerie whistles of rutting bulls may seem only a distant hope, but it will be here soon enough. You can kill an elk on your own, but only if you are better prepared and willing to work harder than the average guy. Being prepared not only increases your odds of success, but assures a greater level of enjoyment. And having fun, after all, is what elk hunting should be all about.

Chapter 6

Calling All Elk

It was still black dark outside but I pushed the truck door until it clicked, ambling up the fence line by mostly feel. I'd planned to catch a quick catnap while awaiting shooting hours, but the harsh-edged bugles had begun to fade and I wanted to keep the obvious behemoth within earshot. It was one of those silver-twinkley starry mornings when the Milky Way shows as a solid belt across a furry sky of purest black, frost swishing in the grass as I advanced, the magnesium handle of my compound biting through thin wool gloves. Meteors skipped off the earth's bell jar intermittingly, creating momentary streaks of light then fading to nothing just as suddenly while the barest hint of silver seeped into the ragged ridgeline well above. The bull was simply wandering, not going places and despite the loose stones under foot and inky remnants of a determined night I was able to shadow him at a safe distance for a couple miles, keep him within easy earshot so there was no fear of losing contact. His deep bugles reverberated down the hollow, seemingly bouncing away, punctuated shortly by incessant, chuckling grunts that tickled my spine and made me breathe with an open mouth despite the leisurely pace.

The sun climbed the back side of the 2,300-foot ridge standing between us as if laboring under a burden, making me feel as if I occupied a deep place instead of a gently-wrinkled series of meadows and coulees creating an expansive bench beneath its sudden flanks. I peered up that ridge and its brightening crown of multihued radiance knowing all too well I'd be climbing it soon enough, puffing and wheezing to keep this bull in earshot as his herd clattered up its steep ramparts, hurried by rising heat up the trails paralleling the fence that didn't have an end for all I knew. I suddenly realized I could see better with each ticking second and hurried my pace, reaching the edge of a familiar swale of blue gamma and bunchgrass, sunflower and Indian paintbrush. Crows released jarring barks, jays squabbling in piñons overlooking the open glade. Coyotes chattered from behind a screen of nearby trees and the big bull bugled once again. He couldn't have been more than 500 yards away.

I broke into open meadow and he was there, across the barbed-wire fence not 250 yards away, sauntering straight away across an ocean of featureless grass,

Opposite page: The bugle is to elk hunting what the crack of a bat and pop of glove leather is to baseball and what keeps avid archers coming back for more, season after season.

clicking along patiently, splotches of tan cow-elk rears flashing through boughs at the far bank of piñon and juniper ("white rump" creating the label "wapiti" in the Shawnee dialect). He was as big as his bugle had hinted, or more accurately, his antlers were beyond belief. I dropped into a point of trees, snaked my bugling tube around on its lanyard cord and popped a turkey diaphragm into my mouth. The whistling bugle came out better than I could have hoped considering my suddenly dry mouth. It was three-note perfect and spike-bull trilling with just the hint of half-formed grunts at the end. The bull swapped ends as if hit with a powerful cattle prod. He glared in my direction. Like Robert Ruark's Cape buffalo, he looked at me as if I owed him money. He glared and he waited, daring the upstart to utter one more note. I tucked the grunt tube under an arm, directing it behind me, and produced another high-pitched squeal.

The bull lunged into a lope and came after me without pause of consideration, screaming in defiance. I had just enough time to snatch an arrow from my Catquiver and get it on the string with uncooperative hands as the bull reached the fence 60 yards away. He hung his head over the top wire between two steel T-posts and simply hopped over in a single smooth bound. It was an amazing show of strength. He walked quartering-to as I came to full draw, following him with what I guessed to be the appropriate pin, letting him come, fighting to concentrate on vitals and not those orgasmic antlers. He turned and slowed slightly, broadside at 45 yards (I guessed), the mere hint of a bugle emanating from deep in his chest. The arrow was away.

Then abruptly in his side.

He reversed directions in a blur and ran through the fence like so much Popsicle sticks and twine, white fletching bobbed from his side then spun away as the aluminum shaft popped. He'd broken two T-posts cleanly at ground level and severed two strands of stout barbed wire, but when he came to rest on his side only 70 yards away the only mark on him was a neat, red-bubbling slice of a two-blade broadhead through his ribs. Laying there on his side his skyward main beam hit me in the middle of the chest. He was something alright; something like 364 inches wrapped around an even seven-by-seven point rack. He was the biggest bull I'd ever killed; a bull that would take me a decade to better.

That was 1988. Long ago in an era long gone.

I've killed a couple higher-scoring bulls since—both undeniably harder won —but none so exciting nor spectacularly gripping. None of those bulls to come resulted so directly from calling or more pointedly, bugling.

CALLING ADDICTION

What is it about calling in a bull elk that is so tantalizing, so downright addicting to so many archers? Stalking amongst a milling herd of mixed cows to tag the herd bull certainly requires more raw skill and steely nerves. Having a monster bull trot into a water-hole or wallow and present a broadside shot at slam-dunk range is nothing to get snooty about, certainly an event able to quicken the pulse. Still, when archery hunters present their most exciting elk-hunting scenarios they almost always involve calling. Gary Sefton, game calling champion puts it sim-

ply, "It's all about com-
municating with
another species, manip-
ulating him to your
needs. There's magic
and romance in that."

From bringing a
whitetail buck running
while feigning a fight
by rattling two sal-
vaged antlers together,
to employing a clev-
erly-designed cedar
box or cut slate and
simple stick to imitate
the hen a spring gob-
bler wantonly seeks, to
creating a faux bugle
or cow call with a
stretched scrap of latex
and hollow tube, it's
the stuff of bowhunt-
ing legend. Nothing
excites hunters like
bringing game to a call.
It's evidence of our
superior intellect, our
adaptability, our sta-
tion as the world's top
predator. I've seen a
hunter coolly pinwheel
a trophy bull freshly

Bugling must be approached carefully, because when bowhunting modern elk it can oftentimes literally blow your chances of success.

arrived at water beneath a tree stand. The same hunter ineptly blundered shots only days before, much easier, much closer shots, at bulls running into a bugle bulge-eyed, screaming and snot-flinging, intent on physical violence. Is that it, this threat of violence that so stirs the emotions? I cannot really say for certain.

LITERALLY "BLOWING IT"

"Addicted" to calling is the only way to put it into accurate words with so many of today's elk hunters—addicted even to the detriment of success. Too many archers are blowing on too many elk calls in today's elk woods. To blow on an elk bugle, especially, in heavily-hunted, public-lands elk areas today can mean liter-ally blowing your chances of success. Many hunters seem to forget that elk calls are but a single tool in what should be a many-pronged approach to successful bowhunting. The fault is multifaceted. Hunters arrive with brand-new elk calls

A mature bull elk in the average hunting area today has been subjected to a barrage of calling techniques, making them understandably wary of man-made calls.

in hand without a complete understanding of the complicated details of timing, animal disposition and what they are actually relating with their calls. They employ calls during desperate moments, calling to wildly-spooked animals, hoping against hope for a miracle or perhaps a mentally-challenged or suicidal specimen. They lazily call from open truck windows, from atop ATVs only recently switched off. They arrive before season opener to "practice" their calling on live subjects. All of this quickly educates elk, making them understandably wary of foreign calls.

Just as importantly, elk come to calls and are missed, or spooked through the myriad pitfalls all hunters are subject to. More archers are trekking our forests every year in search of elk-hunting dreams. Elk are subjected to an increasing amount of hunting pressure, calling the most obvious correlation they have between man and danger.

Aside from ATVs, nearly every single one of my frustrations with bowhunting modern elk comes directly from hunters charging around the forest incessantly blowing on bugles. They blow at elk from upwind, they bugle endlessly when real bulls have yet to begin festivities, they call to bulls obviously not interested, and the cycle continues. And even after repeated failure they just don't seem to put two and two together. They rush to the next bull and try again, and again, ruining it for everyone around them as well as themselves.

ELK-CALL EDUCATION

Wishful thinking might be blamed, but I believe lack of understanding is the underlying issue. The newest calls make producing a realistic bugle or cow call nearly automatic, or at least easier than ever with a minimum amount of practice.

Knowing how to call is one thing; understanding exactly when and where to call and under what particular circumstances, and more importantly, absolutely when not to call, requires hard-earned experience. Having failed to evolve with the changing face of elk hunting makes gaining experience in today's hard-hunted woods particularly problematic. Even hard-hunted elk can be called in when the timing is right. Sometimes I couldn't even tell you for certain what makes a situation right; you simply feel it. Smaller (younger) bulls are normally the regular victims of calling success, but even older bulls make occasional mistakes. The key is being in the right place at the right time, then recognizing when systems are go and taking advantage of a rare opportunity. More discipline is necessary to simply put the call away and try something else. I invariably keep a bugle and several cow calls on hand while bowhunting elk. I might go days between touching them even when on elk daily.

Call manufacturers' heavily-edited videos and television shows make it look so easy, assuring continued sales, making every archery hunter believe. With all due respect to call manufacturers, it must be clearly pointed out that the leading moguls of the multimillion-dollar call business and the resulting video do not hunt elk in the same places that most of us do. When you are in the business of securing footage of big critters responding drone-like to the latest call sensation you can ill afford to hunt workingman public lands. You instead must hunt prime Indian reservations or sprawling private ranches or only the very best limited-quota units available. You also happen to have the available funds to make this happen. That is not to say calling doesn't work, because it obviously can. Lacking the funds to hunt exclusive or high-dollar real estate, when limited to affordable public-lands, you simply have to work harder, hunt longer, to find those situations where calling will do the trick. Therein lays the meat of bowhunting modern elk.

A NEW AGE OF ELK CALLING

If finding a productive area to ply your best calling efforts is easy enough, getting there may not be. In the most basic terms possible, in order for calls to work with regularity, especially when dealing with mature bulls, you must hunt where bulls have not received an education to the evil ways of man, where they are hunted most lightly.

We regularly bring even trophy gobblers to our calls because they are cursed by a short life span and a peanut-sized brain. While a four-year-old gobbler would be considered an old timer, a bull elk of the same age is just reaching prime breeding age. In better habitat elk easily reach the ripe old age of 10 or 12 years old. That gives them plenty of time to gather useful survival knowledge, most pointedly for the purposes of our discussion here, learn to avoid man-made calls. It goes without saying that to find naïve bulls you must hunt where others have not, or can not or will not.

The obvious answer when public land is involved is designated wilderness areas, though plenty of rugged elk habitats pass as de facto wilderness due to lack of roads and ready access. As much as I hate to say it, a good portion of today's

archery hunters are simply lazy. True wilderness requires backpacking, and then the horror of removing lots of meat in a timely fashion, or the extra work or expense of employing pack horses or mules. De facto wilderness can be created by a single hellish canyon or ridge that's intimidating enough to dissuade the masses.

My buddy Billy Lee of Mimbres Guide Service specializes in wilderness pack- trips deep into the Gila Wilderness. His camps are normally located no less than 10 miles from the nearest maintained road. Consequently, calling is a regular part of his hunting repertoire. He regularly calls in even trophy-sized bulls for his clients with a savvy combination of

Elk calling can be productive in the right place and time. That normally means lightly-hunted areas.

bugling and cow calls. I've bowhunted and guided in that very country off and on for a couple decades and even there you must know your ground well to get away from hunting pressure, which Billy certainly does. The edges are pecked at constantly during any given elk season. Billy will also be quick to caution that just as often he finds it more prudent to put his calls away.

Tavis Rogers is another bowhunting friend who regularly makes calling part of his successful bowhunting routine, bringing bulls in close to be dispatched with his primitive longbows. He hunts central Colorado high country so vicious you have to be an absolute animal to get through a single morning's hunt. Starting at 10,500 feet above sea level and climbing vertically from there, is not for the weak. Cross a single heart-break ridge or gut-busting canyon and you have elk all to yourself. The way he tells it the five-point and small six-point bulls he calls in arrive on the run, sometimes making him fear for being stepped on. Even in that country, though, he admits that when you find the rare behemoth—translating

---

into a 330 to 340 bull in that part of Colorado—he puts the calls away and initiates a careful stalk. When they get that big they have retreated into such places for a reason and are normally call-wise.

CALLING COUNTRY

So, if essentially any type of elk-calling success, bugling in a bull especially, is something you can't live without, you'll obviously need to direct your efforts into discovering areas that receive light hunting pressure. Wilderness isn't your only option. This can also translate into prime limited-entry areas. Private lands are another solution, if a reasonable trespass fee can be arranged or if you simply have the available funds to make that happen. The other solution is to hunt the edges of such places. I've guided in at least one area of northern New Mexico where National Forest lands abutted huge private holdings that were hunted only lightly. Of course I wasn't the only one with this bright idea, so traveling to a far corner of this boundary, accessed only after several hours of concerted hiking, produced the best results. The edges of big Indian reservations, national parks or off-limits national wildlife refuges can also produce bulls that have experienced less hunting pressure. Hunting the edges of the notoriously-productive (and expensive) White Mountain Apache Indian Reservation in Arizona's Unit 1, 27 or 3C is *de rigueur* for hunters lucky enough to draw one of those hunts. I have friends in Idaho who have a prime honeyhole just outside the fences of Yellowstone National Park where they seldom fail to take nice bulls every season.

Like I have said, sometimes it only takes a single ridge or deep canyon to shake the masses. When necessary, I don't hesitate to load a decent-sized daypack and simply go hunting without regard for calendar or clock. Where night finds me I pitch a basic camp and spend the night, saving the wear and tear of returning to a truck or main camp every night. I carry a lightweight one-man bivy tent against possible rain (or a sheet of folded plastic), compact "cycling" sleeping bag to get me through a cold night, a fleece vest for a pillow and morning cold, a mini backpack stove, a couple foil packages of dehydrated food, and water where needed. With the normal gear such as knives and flashlights that the average elk hunter carries, the entire pack might tip the scales at only 25 pounds.

Talking to hunters around the country has shown me that dogmatism is always a dangerous trap. Friends in certain areas of Montana, or Colorado, for instance, find regular success through bugling due to lower hunter numbers in their general hunting area. If you seem to be on your own in a particular hunting area, calling will likely prove more productive. When other hunters are obviously prevalent, more caution is in order.

LOWERING STANDARDS

Calling success can also hinge on a willingness to tag younger bulls. Young bulls of two to three years old, like teenage boys, can prove horny little cusses and also like teenage boys, prone to rash behavior. Even on public lands that receive a good deal of hunting pressure, these naïve youngsters can often prove downright foolhardy.

If smaller bulls make you happy, regular calling success comes much easier. Small normally means younger, less educated elk.

Only a couple years past, I arrived at a road end well before daylight, leaning into my ATV against the morning chill, drinking hot tea from a thermos and listening to three bugling bulls. Due to intense hunting pressure (limited public lands funnel all hunting pressure through a single road) big bulls were getting into the swing of the rut but had also been harassed for nearly 12 days. They were bugling mostly under the cover of darkness, retreating to off-limits private ground with daylight. I wanted to get a jump on them. With the first hint of light I set out after the bull sounding most mature (never a sure science, because small-antlered bulls often produce deep bugles), feeling my way across treacherous ground, producing the occasional cow call to keep them talking. When it was just light enough to see 50 yards I caught up with my bull, a dandy 350ish six-by-seven with black antlers. He was traveling down a ridge spine with no cows in evidence and I hurried to cut him off. I wasn't quite quick enough, marooned in an open gully watching him march down that point.

He was well within range but in a hurry to get somewhere, flashes of tan hide showing through gaps in ponderosa pines as he passed. I sidestepped to take advantage of a discovered shooting lane ahead of him and waited. When he approached the gap I hit him with a cow call. He didn't miss a beat, continuing down the ridge. I called more emphatically, but to no avail. I was about to regroup and scramble around for another attempted interception when clattering rocks behind me snapped me to. A 250-inch five-point (young in the Gila region) pranced enthusiastically toward my position. I froze, hoping he would pass without alerting the big boy I'd almost received my shot at. Nothing doing. The youngster had those cow calls pegged, coming to me as if on a string. At five yards his eyes widened, his head came up and he backed a few steps like a horse that has just discovered a snake. The small bull didn't blow my cover, but he held me up just long enough that I wasn't able to take advantage of the big bull crossing the sudden cut 100 yards below. I saw the original bull again but he had clammed up and quickly slipped into the safety of private land.

The point is, that area had been pounded for nearly 12 days, every road churned to dust by ATV tires. And that bull still trotted foolishly into my desperate cow calls. Had I wanted him he would have been all mine.

These are so-called satellite bulls. Yet not all satellite bulls are youngsters. It's all relative to who's in charge. And timing is everything. Sometimes you simply get into a fracas, large herds of mixed bulls and cows that seem to have boiled over in emotional fervor. This is difficult to read accurately, because sometimes it seems that two large herds have simply crossed paths to create momentary confusion while matters are sorted out. The herd is on edge, but far from receptive to calling. On still other occasions my best guess is that a cow, perhaps several cows, in the herd have slipped into estrus. There's no other way to explain the mass chaos amongst the wound-up bulls, the fact that they have lost some of their innate wariness and typical caution. When encountering this kind of situation there seems to be an electric buzz in the air. You will not call in the herd bull due to simple biological principals, but the satellite bulls around the herd become highly vulnerable. You could easily hunt several seasons without witnessing such an event, but it's something to behold.

HERD-BULL HERESY

Before I elaborate, this herd-bull business might deserve a bit more explanation. Calling to herd bulls is a waste of time, not because he's so savvy and knowledgeable (though even as a lone animal that is very likely the case in today's woods), but because he's bound by duties that prevent him from responding at all. Think of this logically. He has all the girls. He has nothing to fight about. He has nothing to gain. Leaving all those cows to respond to a call leaves all he has worked so hard for open to cutting by sneaky satellite bulls. His typical response, no matter if it is a bugle produced by you or by any real bull around him, is to prod his cows in the opposite direction, to distance himself from the competition; oftentimes to even become completely silent. You want a herd bull to become tight lipped, blow a bugle at him. Guaranteed results…

Satellite bulls, on the other hand, have nothing to lose by investigating a call. They want in on the action but are either too young or too weak to actually do anything about it. They become frustrated and frustration spawns desperation and recklessness; especially when you have discovered the kind of melee described earlier.

My biggest bull resulted from calling, if not directly. It involved just such a melee, a magic evening fallen into after eight days of bowhunting. I had dogged the herd for miles. They finally stalled in a wide, lush meadow. I was stranded at its edge, wantonly leering at the monster herd bull over all that wide-open, featureless grass. It was hopeless and darkness would soon reclaim the land. Then, almost literally, lady luck arrived, or I should say a laggard cow, or perhaps a com-

pletely new arrival. I had nothing to lose, the bull as far removed as if he was situated on the moon. I began cow calling to this late-coming cow.

At first she didn't respond, but I became more insistent, more pleading, like a lost calf demanding attention. She slowly began to swing my way. The bull had taken notice and was bugling lustily. I continued calling to this cow. It was something to do to pass the time before I slipped away under the cover of darkness. It was practice against future calling opportunities. The cow had decided I needed closer inspection and began to saunter in my direction, pausing occasionally to stare at my position. I had begun to notice a change in the bull's demeanor. Judging from his tone he was obviously ordering this cow to join him. But he was being ignored. Suddenly I saw hope. I put more heart into my high-pitched cow calls, pulling the curious cow ever closer. The bull began plodding out of the middle of his safe haven, moving closer with every step. I used my laser rangefinder to stay abreast of progress until he was beginning to hold promise. At 60 yards it was apparent he was coming no closer, stopping to produce a demanding bugle. My arrow punched through both of his lungs in mid bugle. He didn't make it out of sight. That seven-by-eight-point non-typical scored 386 inches.

HYPER COWS

So-called "hyper" cow calls can also come in handy during these situations. These are loud, aggressive cow calls that imitate the calls of a cow in estrus, demanding to be bred. Even in the heavily-hunted Gila region, when they first hit the scene they produced wondrous results; a solid 360 bull I called in to 27 yards for a client who promptly missed him with his recurve bow the most spectacular of my recollection. The bull certainly didn't charge in headlong, but did deviate from his course to swing by our position. Since then I have lured many bulls within range with such calls, though nothing that I deemed big enough to punch my tag on. Interestingly, most of the bulls that responded arrived silently, which is something to keep in mind during any calling sequence.

EXCEPTIONAL RESULTS FROM EXCEPTIONAL CIRCUMSTANCES

Another recent notable event resulting from calling would be difficult to reproduce with regularity, but does show how accurately reading a situation can create a happy ending. A client and I had dogged a very nice bull and his dozen cows several miles but failed to so much as glimpse them. By 10:30 morning sun was bearing down and the elk fell suddenly quiet. We continued stalking up the tight canyon blindly, but promptly jumped the cows and sent them flowing over the ridge to our right. But luck was on our side, because the bull had bedded apart from his cows and the wind was in our favor. From our left, hearing his departing cows, our bull suddenly let loose an inquiring bugle. I read the situation instantly and produced my bugling tube. Now this was an established herd bull with plenty of hunting sea-

Opposite page: When the rut kicks in, satellite bulls that hover at the edges of large herds become most susceptible to calling.

In general, cow calls are a safer bet than bugling, because these are social calls that bulls hear regularly.

sons behind him, in an area that certainly received hunting pressure. In fact, we could easily hear vehicle traffic from a state highway nearby.

I bugled and the bull immediately screamed in retort. So I bugled again. The same angry bugle followed. It had become obvious the bull believed an upstart had designs on his cows. I turned and told my client that whatever he did to stay on my tail. The bull was attempting to flank us to reclaim his cows. We nearly sprinted up that canyon bottom, matching his pace as he side-hilled above us, throwing bugles back and forth between us, doing my best to imitate his every call in way of mocking him. After three quarters of a mile our bull had enough. He was coming! I saw those incredible antlers tilting through the piñons and dropped to my knees, hissing behind me for my guy to draw his bow. The bull emerged at 15 yards, scrambling out of the deep cut to our left, coming straight on. I held still and tried to make myself look little, hoping my charge had followed orders. The bull continued, coming dangerously close. I was going to have to do something.

When it appeared the bull would certainly step on me—his front hooves were a couple feet from my head—the bull paused. My client later said the bull dipped his head, sniffing between my shoulder blades. His eyes widened and when he spun to turn my guy thrust his bow fist at the bull's armpit and triggered the release. It was a perfect heart shot and the bull didn't make it out of sight. It just doesn't get any more exciting than that!

MAKING CALLING WORK

In areas where calling is a high-odds proposition, where hunting pressure is light, or there are plenty of younger age-class bulls to ply, certain strategies can make success more likely. One of these involves hunting with a friend or guide. The shooter sits 50 to 100 yards forward of the caller, depending on terrain and vegetation, more open terrain inviting more distance between hunting partners. The shooter should have selected a spot that provides plenty of open shooting lanes to cover developing contingencies, but also cover in the form of shade, tree trunks or brush. In more open country a triangle of large-boled pines can do the trick. The shooter stays put and does not move other than to make the shot. The caller sits back and attempts to read the situation as it unfolds. This is important because his job is to not only call, but to shift his position to keep the shooter directly between him and the bull as he angles in; do his darnest to keep the bull moving toward the shooter and not around him. For example, should the bull swing left of the shooter, the caller moves right. This also creates realism, because few actual elk stay put long while calling to one another. This also helps the shooter catch elk off guard. A lone caller is directing attention to himself, any arriving bull owning a fair idea of exactly where the sound is coming from and focused on that spot of ground. An elk responding to a caller set well back from the shooter isn't yet anticipating danger when he passes within range of the shooter, making him more vulnerable to a clean shot.

Another worthwhile ploy might be labeled "multiple calling." This employs the use of several cow calls of various makes and models in an attempt to imitate a small herd of cows and calves. This is made easier with hand-held "bulb" calls (one in each hand twisted to create different pitches) in combination with standard mouth calls. It can also work especially well when hunting with a partner, or by spreading several hunters along a ridgeline. Even bulls, or herds, that aren't particularly interested in calls might swing by for a closer look if you can arrive in their travel path. If more than one caller is involved, call to each other like a herd of wandering elk—though it's important that each caller have honed calling skills —placing the shooter well ahead of those working their calls.

Set up in relation to prevailing wind presents some tricky considerations. The common assumption is that any animal responding to a call swings downwind out of sage caution. This may very well be the case, but also remember that elk live by their noses. It's a simple biological principal for animals to approach from downwind because it quickly helps them hone in on the object of their desires. Even when you have a solid bead on your calling subject and have care-

Multi-calling is one productive way to make elk calling work, convincing a bull a herd of cows has wandered into his world.

fully considered the wind during set-up, don't assume another, undetected animal, or the animal you are directing your effort to, will not maneuver to bring the wind into their face. Seek situations that make this more difficult; backing against a sudden drop-off that carries scent over their heads, or extra-thick or rough terrain that discourages using that ground at all.

OFF-BEAT PLOYS

Another trick for more productive calling, and a relatively new development, is the elk decoy. A bull responds to a call and naturally expects to find an elk when he gets there. Even the spring gobbler arriving to a call only to find a conspicuously empty meadow grows suspicious. So it is with elk, though the elks' size compounds this suspicion. It's more understandable that a hen turkey should remain hidden. When a bull arrives in the same vicinity of a calling cow elk, there should be some visual clue to her presence. The two models I'm most familiar with, from Renzos and Montana Decoy, are photo-realistic models printed on collapsible cloth with spring-wire frame. A quick twist allows you to easily fold them down to daypack size and they weigh nearly nothing. When ready to deploy, just release them and they automatically pop into shape. All animals key into particular glaring aspects when seeking another of their species. For elk this is the lighter posterior patch, so accuracy isn't highly important, simply something to represent that patch of light tan. My buddy Keith Jabben, owner of Precision Designed Products, even fashioned a functional decoy out of a painted piece of cloth, quickly tied between handy trees when needed.

Rattling can also create realistic sounds elk respond to, attracting the same attention as a schoolyard brawl. I've always been surprised this has not caught on. It's common to see elk callers using a stick to bash nearby trees and vegetation while calling, but toting a set of heavy mule deer or smallish elk antlers is an effort that can be well rewarded. Incorporating rattling with bull grunts and even cow calls can add realism to any sequence.

The first time I tried this, maybe 25 years ago, I didn't really believe. It was somewhat of an experiment. I coaxed a husky-sounding bull into bugling and set up to rattle. A massive eight-by-eight bull soon emerged onto a defunct logging road a couple hundred yards away and I almost choked. He was a world record and likely would still be today. As I watched, the bull seemed to lose interest and fade into the trees. I was young and impatient. I dropped my antlers and began a desperate stalk. Picking up his tracks in rain-softened ground I tracked the bull (you guessed it) back to the very place I had only recently abandoned. The bull stood over my antlers, obviously growing nervous over the offensive human odors still lingering on the damp ground. He faded away and I never saw him again. If only I had waited…

Opposite page: Before going into a full-blown calling sequence, take a bull's temperature. If he seems to shrink from a certain type of call, back off a tad or try something different.

Calling with a partner is a good idea, producing a wider variety of calls to feign a traveling herd or more than one elk.

TAKING THEIR TEMPERATURE

Any type of calling, whether bugling or cow calls, should be initiated carefully. Get a feel for a particular animal's disposition before you begin a full-blown calling sequence. You might call it "taking his temperature." If he's fired up and responding to aggressive stuff, proceed with vigor. If he seems to shrink from aggressive calls, back off and take it a bit easier. For the most part, non-aggressive social calls will do you more good than aggressive, or challenging calls, when dealing with even lightly-hunted elk, but especially so with those who are hunter savvy. Aggressive calls depend heavily on rut timing and discovering an animal with an aggressive demeanor. Social calls are those elk hear on a regular basis, even if the rut is not in full swing.

A challenging bugle may find a bull simply not in the mood for a fight, even a solitary, wandering bull without cows. A spike squeal or simple, none-edgy "here-I-am" bugle without challenging grunts is more likely to coax a bull to respond and reveal his position, or even swing past out of sheer curiosity. Subtle cow chirps can get a bull talking when loud, "naggy" calls may turn him off. Also, too much calling can raise an instant red flag. When in doubt produce high-pitched calf chirps, calls that even amongst actual elk herds are more common in areas where hunting pressure is common. These younger animals simply don't know better, are more emotionally immature and likely to break silence when adults are maintaining silence.

Take your cues from what actual elk are telling you. If bulls are bugling only sporadically, tromping through the woods bugling continually obviously isn't going to go over well. The same applies to cows. Elk have incredible hearing. The occasional soft chirp is certainly heard when elk are in the area. Just because they don't respond doesn't mean they can not hear you. Any more can send them packing. Too, when employing subtle calls in areas where elk are hunted hard, take your time. Don't expect elk to sound off enthusiastically just because you have called to them. Take a seat and give it 15 or 20 minutes when you know you are in close company with elk, when fresh sign or earlier calling tells you that you have arrived in the right place. Not every elk will charge in wild eyed and slobbering. You just might be surprised to find an older sage bull slips in on you as quiet as an alley cat. Any time you blow on an elk call this is a possibility, so keep your eyes peeled, stay on your toes and keep an arrow nocked.

This is especially true, and effective, when you have established a regular travel schedule through a fairly predictable travel corridor, via careful scouting or simple observation during the course of a hunt. Any time a set pattern is observed, arriving well ahead of even silent elk and engaging in subtle social calls can result in a bull responding silently out of pure curiosity. Spend 30 to 45 minutes on such a set up, at a site that makes it difficult for bulls to circle downwind to catch your scent, watching and listening carefully.

No doubt communicating with another species through calls you have produced yourself is one of bowhunting's most thrilling experiences. But caution is in order. Too many hunters have overdone this calling business. If you are in the market for only the biggest trophy bulls, your calling will have to remain extremely prudent indeed, used only when a situation is deemed perfect, or patiently anticipating a silent approach. A trophy, a 10-year-old or better bull, has seen a few things. He didn't get that big by making rash decisions, by running headlong into a potentially dangerous situation. Odds are he did so one time. He may have a scar to prove it, a healed over broadhead against a shoulder blade or neck vertebrae to remind him of that time he allowed hormones and lust to get the best of him. If you are willing to trek into areas where others will not, will be happy with younger, smaller-antlered animals ("trophy" is in the eye of the beholder), calling can certainly bring regular success. Still, you must operate by a different set of rules, live by the code of bowhunting modern elk. This means that you should use your head first, read each situation carefully, and understand when it's time to put the calls away.

Calling can often be enhanced by using it in combination with a decoy, giving arriving bulls a visual cue.

Chapter 7

Dogging Bugling Bulls

"**D**ogging" elk, relentlessly shadowing a bugling bull, waiting for your opportunity to slip in on him or into his herd undetected and receive a shot is one of bowhunting's most enduring endeavors. Archery hunters have been successfully tagging bulls in this manner since the very beginning. Before calling took such a firm grip on the elk-hunting consciousness, before hunters made regular use of an elk's vulnerability at water-holes or wallows to earn close shots, they followed bugles and stalked the bulls producing them. This is elk hunting at its most classic, and fundamental. It offers unique challenges not presented by any other North American game. I could venture that this is elk hunting in its purest form. In heavily-hunted areas where calling proves a low-odds proposition, where water is overabundant, it offers your best avenue to regular success. When the very biggest bulls are at issue it just may present your only prospect for triumph.

Dogging bugling bulls pulls together a wide variety of hunting skills. This is nothing like the tedious, slow-paced business of stalking trophy whitetail or mule deer, even crawling up on an open-country pronghorn. Success while dogging elk means running like the wind; or moving like the hands of a clock. The trick is in understanding and choosing which is required at a particular moment. It can indicate making big, risky moves, or sitting patiently motionless for minutes on end. It can prove one of the most physically-demanding pursuits in all of bowhunting; following a bull or herd for miles over gut-busting terrain while gulping thin air, or completing a mad-dash circling to accommodate changing wind or to set up an ambush. It at once demands an aggressive attitude and meticulous stalking skills. It's this incongruous combination of elements that throws so many seasoned archery hunters off track.

Opposite page: "Dogging" bugling bulls can mean running like the wind, or stalking like the hands of a clock. The trick is in knowing when to apply one or the other as necessary.

Locating a bugling bull, and then keeping track of his movements, can mean the "dogging" hunt begins well before daylight.

MIXED BAG OF TRICKS

The biggest stumbling block appears to be maintaining an aggressive mindset. The average archer perceives all bowhunting as innately contemplative and slow-paced. "Stalking at a snail's pace" is a hackneyed term indelibly yoked to bowhunting as a whole. But this doesn't accurately represent all elk hunting. Elk are long-legged creatures evolved to cover vast amounts of country in a hurry. Their very size dictates that in order to survive, to remain abreast of needs for ample nutrition, they must cover plenty of ground. The average elk saunters faster than you jog, but when a bull gets it in his mind that he wants to be somewhere else, you can be hard-pressed to simply keep him in earshot. There's also that obvious factor of rough terrain and thin air that makes it impossible to keep a dogged pace over many miles; the same pace an elk goes about leisurely. Physical conditioning is as big a part of dogging elk as honed stealth skills and an ability to convert on difficult shots.

But then the tables suddenly turn; you catch your bull, arrive on the edges of a milling herd, and must suddenly employ the patient stalking skills required to bag the most neurotic cougar-haunted deer. This is a hefty bag of tricks for a single archer to shoulder, but required for regular success.

THE EARLY BIRD

In the world of dogging elk, the day begins early and most often ends late. Three a.m. wake-ups are commonplace, dragging in at awful hours to inhale fuel and catch a few hours sleep. The midday power nap is a must for long-term survival, to remain hunting at peak performance after a week, or two, of full-out mountain bowhunting.

Prime feeding and bedding areas may be separated by many miles of ridges and canyons. It seems to me savvy trophy bulls understand where hunting pressure originates; the roads, trails and parking areas we use to access their world. Access roads and highways in rough elk country typically follow bottoms and flat places where lush meadows and grass more readily takes root. Elk take advantage of these prime feeding areas under the cover of darkness, understanding that with the first hinting of daylight hunters will arrive to molest them. Too, being nomadic by nature, where they bedded yesterday typically can't be counted on today as a place to anticipate an arrival. Consequently, morning hunts typically commence in darkness, simply being on hand to keep tabs on the movements of the biggest bulls.

I usually like to arrive at my chosen hunting area two hours ahead of shooting hours. This may mean simply parking my truck, rolling down the windows to catch a catnap while listening for bugling. I might move to another likely spot and listen again if I hear nothing within a half hour. Only after discovering bugling bulls do I settle in and await daylight. So long as those bulls remain within earshot, I'm allowed to catch up on sleep. Should they begin to recede, it's time to grab my gear and follow. In more remote areas I might climb a ridge or point under darkness to arrive above a feeding area or along a proven travel route, whatever it takes to keep deep-throated bulls readily available the very minute shooting hours arrive. It's commonplace to stay on a bugling bull from 3:30 a.m. until late-morning heat arrives to shut down the festivities, covering six or eight rough and tumble miles in the interim. It can assume all the qualities of work, but is oftentimes required to stay abreast of the biggest, most wary bulls in heavily-pressured public areas.

I also keep my options open. Returning to the truck or camp and a cooler of iced-down sports drinks and hearty lunch is a wonderful thing after an exhausting morning of hiking, but can also prove inconvenient in many areas. All that running back and forth in rough country can dull your edge. If I've blown a stalk, not covered an enormous amount of country, or caught my bull only to find him somehow lacking, that option always awaits. If a monster bull has simply outdistanced me, or wind or terrain has simply prevented me from closing, I carry food and especially fluids in a roomy daypack allowing me to stay on hand to await prime evening hours. I've enjoyed some of my soundest sleep beneath a shading juniper, wiling away the unproductive and hot hours of midday. A compact paperback book is always welcome during these long waits.

NAPPY TIME

Unproductive is certainly what midday proves during warm early seasons. Cooling thunderstorms or a persistent cold front bringing wooly, overcast skies can certainly prompt midday elk movement, but whether you believe in global warming or simple climatic cycles, today's September elk hunts seem warmer than ever. Bowhunting bedded elk is a low-odds proposition no matter how good you are. A single bull in just the right spot might invite a successful stalk (one of my better bulls came this way at 1:15 p.m., bugling from his bed) but this is the exception rather than the rule. Elk choose their bedding areas with care, in my

experience places fraught with swirling breezes, making them especially difficult to slip up on in even the best conditions. Blundering into a bedded herd and scattering them to the winds is a good way to lose contact with a trophy bull you've set your sights on. This is difficult to explain to a tightly-wound client wanting his money's worth via all-day hunts, but playing it safe is always best.

Still, to every rule there's an exception. A friend and I were once jarred from a sound midday nap by a pair of bugling bulls, seemingly in our laps. We'd dogged a large herd miles into remote country, finally losing them when temperatures soared and the herd bull clammed up. Awoken from hard sleep we went on auto-pilot, grabbing gear without a word and slipping down to cut the closest bull

Dogging bugling bulls involves long hours of hard work, making the midday nap highly important to survival.

off. We'd stalked only 300 yards through heavy cover when we detected snapping limbs nearby, falling to our knees and nocking arrows. Within minutes the 330-inch six-point emerged in a shooting lane at 40 yards and my buddy sent a broadhead through his lungs. I can't positively pinpoint what sparked that midday action, especially under so hot a sun, but I'd guess that bull simply scented the herd we'd been dogging after a midday wind shift and wandered in to stir up trouble. That was certainly an example of how packing a lunch and being on hand during midday "downtime" worked to our advantage. It certainly wasn't the first time that has happened.

THE SIREN'S SONG

Obviously, bugling is important to success while dogging. Bugling is what maintains that thread of contact as you desperately attempt to close the distance. A distant bugle tells you to pick up the pace, push harder. A nearby bugle tells you to slow down. Any bugle at all provides the starting point to every hunt. Trouble is, in areas that receive persistent hunting pressure, bulls can prove disinclined to bugle at all. Sometimes you must provide a spark of encouragement. Provok-

Opposite page: Bugling is the music that motivates. It makes it so much easier to keep tabs on a traveling bull, giving us clues as to when to hustle, when to slow down.

ing calling through calling of your own can prove a large part of dogging success, but there's a razor-thin line between encouraging bugling and shutting it down completely. A single whistling spike bugle or short series of subtle cow calls can get a bull started or set you back on track. It often seems a bull answers simply to humor the hunter, well aware of the potential consequences. If pressured, such a bull is certain to be sent packing or clam up. Like calling elk in general, this requires reading each individual situation, taking a bull's temperature. As a general rule, less is best.

When bulls are reluctant to talk it's highly important to make the best of each rare bugle, get an accurate fix on a bull's position. Have a buddy call while you stand well aside, or direct your calls behind you where it will impact your hearing less. Immediately after you call, cup your hands over your ears to create larger receiving dishes (this is far more than pantomime, it really works). Once you've detected a bugle don't waste any time, move into the area without hesitation, using binoculars often in an attempt to locate your elk instead of resorting to more calling. Only when you've nothing to lose, when you have lost contact altogether, should you risk additional calling. Remember, by refraining from calling you take a bull by surprise. He has no idea you are in the area. Persistent calling can put a bull on edge, keep him on high alert and make him more difficult to approach.

Since dogging is about hearing bugling more than seeing actual bulls, covering a lot of ground quickly is more effective to getting started.

FICKLE FOOTWORK

Returning to the aggressive aspects of dogging elk; moving quickly yet silently is a skill that can be difficult to master. A herd may be only a couple hundred yards ahead of you, even closer in denser areas. This is when most hunters get left in the dust. They slow down, become overly cautious, and the herd quickly outdistances them. Miles can

After you have followed a bull miles and begin to close the gap, "stalking slippers" make your footfalls quieter.

be covered closing the gap on a traveling herd. As mid morning arrives, bugling in particular can become more sporadic, even cease completely, making it easy to lose your bull. The odds are tipped in your favor if you have made visual contact by the time calling tapers off, following elk by catching an occasional flash of tan or observing legs churning through undergrowth, or audible clues such as clicking rocks, cracking branches or the soft chirping of young calves. You might even have to do some amount of careful tracking when that contact is temporarily severed. You must move fast, but remain ever cautious.

Keep in mind, a traveling elk herd doesn't move through the woods without creating a certain amount of racket. They're big animals, and a large herd adds an element of confusion. Members of the herd simply can't keep track of every individual around them. In other words, a certain amount of stalking noise is acceptable. While it's best to reserve noise to unintentional mistakes (elk are becoming spookier in heavily-hunted areas), the occasional twig snap or gravel crunch isn't as likely to send animals into retreat like it might a deer.

CAT-FEET PRECAUTIONS

Smart elk hunters take measures to assure their ground-gobbling footfalls are as quiet as those of a cat. Standard procedure for decades was to simply remove your boots and proceed in stocking feet. I can't begin to tell you how many miles I've run in my socks, trying to close on traveling elk. In New Mexico's dry Gila region this included regular encounters with cactus, and pin-like piñon pine needles. I made a habit of packing an extra pair of extra-thick wool socks for just these occasions, added padding against sharp rock. It's a common tale, the hunter who's removed his boots to make an approach only to have the bull move off once again with the archer in hot pursuit, leaving his footwear behind, never to be seen again. Word to the wise: If you choose to remove your boots while stalking elk, lash or stash them on or in your pack.

Even when you have your target bull in sight, remaining aggressive, yet careful will result in more shots.

Many hunters tote leather moccasins designed specifically for stalking game; steer- or buffalo-hide soles certainly serving better than wool socks against stone-bruising rock and stabbing cactus. The only drawback is they are not suited to persistently wet weather. More recently savvy archers have come to depend on commercially-available "stalking slippers" specifically designed with stalking big game in mind. These include heavily-padded felt/faux-fur soles and silent-fleece sides to slide over hiking boots and muffle the noise of treading dry pine needles, gravel or small sticks. Synthetic materials make them compatible with wet conditions and machine washable after becoming caked with mud or pine pitch. Combined with a waterproof pair of soft-soled lightweight hikers or "cross-trainers" they allow you to move across crunchy terrain with minimum clamor. They're also indispensable during those defining moments when close to elk and ultimate stealth is in order. The only drawback is standard "furry" soles can prove slippery on pine needles, so care must be taken to avoid a spill or undue movement when elk are close.

FINISHING TOUCHES

The last 100 yards is where your efforts are suddenly dashed or rewarded. Closing the deal, whittling that last 100 yards down to your effective maximum range means an ability to think on your feet, make quick decisions. While this is likely the most critical stage of your hunt it doesn't mean aggressive moves are not called for. Thinking on your feet means making hard decisions, weighing the consequences of gambling a couple more steps and the possibility of spooking your elk against waiting and perhaps allowing elk to walk out of your life. It's common to slip across an open gap with elk in plain sight, take a couple quick steps to find a shooting lane, dash just a bit closer to get your shot. A wide-open cow playing interference for the herd bull may stand at 20 yards, but has her head buried in grass, busily munching. An inattentive calf might allow a plain-sight maneuver to make a shot happen. When that same cow lifts her head, that calf turns his attention your way, stand stock still. Don't so much as blink or even think too loudly. Ignore the itches that invariably develop, the mosquito on the tip of your nose, the scratchiness in your throat that threatens to choke you, no matter how long it takes. Wait for them to calm and begin feeding again. It's absolutely amazing what you can get away with sometimes if you just hold still long enough.

The last truly monstrous bull I witnessed, a bull scoring something like 400 to 410 Boone & Crockett inches, surrounded by no fewer than 50 frantic cows/calves and perhaps seven satellite bulls (who could keep track?), presented a classic example of what slipping into a large mixed herd of elk is all about. This bull also showed that satellite bull size is relative to the herd bull, because several appeared to be solid shooters, which by Gila definitions means 350 inches.

The elk appeared as if they had gone mad, dashing in circles, screaming and chirping non-stop. The poor calves were beside themselves, frantic and panicked by all the unprecedented confusion. I might have killed that herd bull in all that pandemonium, but for the fact they occupied a piece of relatively open ground with only the occasional juniper and scrub cedar cover. And I certainly could have killed one of the better satellite bulls had greed not gotten the better of me.

I would duck and dodge from tree to tree, pinned for long periods, taking chances to keep abreast of developments, so close to receiving shots at the behemoth but the possibility never quite came together. Several times frenzied calves rounded ground-hugging cedars to meet me face to face, running into the herd to sound the general alarm only to be ignored, adults too caught up in their own problems. For more than an hour I was surrounded by elk, never more than 30 yards from cows or satellite bulls at any given moment, never more than 90 yards from that herd bull. Several times I would be pinned by animals threatening to step on me, but I stood stock still and let them pass. So many times it seemed I would finally get my shot at the big boy only to have him dash away to horn a pesky satellite bull pinching a cow. Three of the satellite bulls presented shot opportunities, one of them threatening to step on me as I hunkered in a patch of waste-high sunflowers. When darkness crept over the land, the party still in full swing, I allowed them to slip away unaware. I never saw that bull again. I did kill one of those satellites, wearing easily-recognizable antlers, a week later. He grossed

367 inches. Kind of makes me wonder how big that herd bull really was…

Like anything hard-won, experience is paramount. You must be willing to take chances or you will learn nothing. I've sat motionless as a cow or calf or small bull munched grass at mere feet, waiting for the herd bull to clear brush; stood hugging a cedar while an entire herd passed at 10 yards, waiting a boss bull bringing up the rear. I've been busted plenty of times, no doubt, but I've also won these cat-and-mouse games under seemingly impossible conditions. You have to play to win. You have to believe.

THE CONCEALMENT EDGE

Today leafy three-dimensional or "Shaggie" camouflage outfits help you in this game of stealth by making you invisible. These suits include three dimensional leafy-cut surfaces, or sewn hanks of cut material, jute rope and burlap, that break up your human outline like no flat camouflage can. It creates its own shadows, scatters light reflections, and creates more irregular edges that blend with any background. This is not to say flat camouflage is obsolete, because it just gets more effective every year, but 3-D camo gives you an edge when forced to make those risky moves with elk in plain sight. The point-blank elk that has caught peripheral movement or heard a misstep is hard pressed to discern a recognizable shape or to simply identify you as a threat.

Too, I wouldn't think of stalking elk without gloves and face mask, or camouflaging makeup.

Use every concealment advantage possible when stalking into shifting herds of elk, including 3-D camouflage suits and face coverage.

Dogging bugling bulls is extremely challenging but can be highly rewarding. It might be the only chance you have on a wise herd bull.

PLAYING THE WIND

Still, while 3-D camouflage keeps you covered visually, offending human scent carried on the wind, is your biggest enemy. In fact, unpredictable and changing wind currents have undoubtedly accounted for more foiled stalks on elk than all other factors combined. The broken, highly-varied terrain typical of elk habitat, combined with wildly fluctuating temperatures, creates this major imposition, but to be consistently successful it is something you must work with and around. The key lies in making a study of predicting, even anticipating, how terrain, weather and temperature changes affect prevailing breezes. This is important to any type of bowhunting, but especially so while dogging traveling elk. Every canyon or ridge crossed, every hour passed, has the potential to drastically change how wind influences your approach. There will always be instances when the unexpected occurs, when the most momentary of swirls blows your cover, but there are certainly rules to live by to keep such occurrences to a minimum.

In basic terms, cool air flows downhill, warm air upward. During cooler night-time, early morning and post-sunset hours, under calm weather conditions, air currents invariably flow down canyon bottoms, mountain slopes or ridges. Any elk standing directly below your position can potentially catch your scent. As morning sun arrives to warm the atmosphere it causes a turnaround, warm air pushing up canyon bottoms; or uphill in general. When this occurs, any elk standing directly above you might catch your scent. "Flow" is the most accurate term, as air, our atmosphere, takes on all the qualities of liquid in relation to how it interfaces with obstacles such as cliff edges, ridge points and canyon heads or bowls, especially confined bottoms. Hold that thought...

The problem arises when traversing terrain that presents several conditions simultaneously. Elk cross a heavily-wooded, shaded canyon head late in the morning, for example, and wind currents are dropping downhill solidly. One hundred yards farther along the same elk cross an open, sunny face and breezes are suddenly flowing uphill. Somewhere at the seams of these two distinct flow patterns these currents must meet, creating an area dominated by confusing swirls. There's also an all-important transition period to consider, the sometimes sudden transi-

Keeping tabs on the wind is everything when dogging bugling bulls. Light powders contained in a small plastic bottle make this easy.

tion between predominately cool air flowing downhill, and rapidly warming air moving up. Of course this has many variations according to terrain and climatic conditions, but where I've hunted most in New Mexico's Gila and Arizona's White Mountain regions, this can occur anytime between 9:30 and 10:30 a.m. on a clear, calm day. Closing the gap on elk during these dangerous periods is always dicey, yet the two scenarios described above also correspond to the timeframe when elk most often slow down, selecting bedding areas, wrapping up bugling for the morning. This sudden ease in pace also means this is generally when you have caught up with your herd. Evening hours, of course, reverse this process, prime hours at the edge of day and night muddling air currents once again.

FORECASTING WIND SHIFTS

Catch a bull very early in the morning, or late in the evening—typically after sunset and perhaps the most predicable of all timeframes—and your job is relatively easy. Air currents are usually completely honest during these periods. Any time between the hours when the morning sun has firmly established itself and evening sunset things can prove more complicated and unpredictable. The diligent hunter, while moving across broken terrain dogging elk, strives to anticipate wind changes before committing to a potentially-disastrous situation where scent might be carried to his quarry. Sometimes this means simply going on a hunch of what might happen and circumventing that gamble. Some common sense is also in order.

Scenarios are as varied as the terrain itself, but here are some examples: Elk move off a sunny mesa top, dropping off its edge to access a cool north slope bedding area dominated by thick vegetation. The wind has been steadily in your face across that wide mesa top, but as you descend that shaded slope cooler air is suddenly dropping like a stone. If you have continued to follow those elk straight off that side you've likely been caught in the sudden trap, elk below you suddenly receiving your scent. Or: You have dogged elk up a wide but deep meadowed river bottom spilling out of high alpine peaks; the breezes in that bottom curling back your eyelashes steadily despite the late hour. As the morning progresses these elk begin climbing out to cross a ridge en route to a far-removed bedding area. As they climb they reach sun-drenched slopes and the wind does an about face. If you have followed in their spoor you are busted.

Wind changes can also prove more subtle, even highly isolated in the form of swirls. You may have finally caught up with a bugling bull, shadowing him closely, waiting for a shot opportunity. He rounds a point and you follow. A front is pushing wind ahead of itself and down the face, but as you round that same point that steady breeze curls around the point, like water running around a midstream boulder and creating an eddy in a trout stream, and for just a moment the bull gets a nose full. It's not much, but it's enough. Game over. Bottoms and canyon heads often create these swirl traps, honest wind suddenly turning back on itself in an isolated vortex, perhaps only briefly, but just long enough to finish its evil work.

As I hinted earlier, I try to see air currents in terms of an invisible, (if multidirectional) trout river. If you have fished for trout with dry flies in small mountain streams you will have a clearer picture. The eddies and swirls and back-flows are where we toss our floating Royal Wulffs and Stimulators and hopper patterns because these are places that trout prefer to lay. Observe what a mid-stream rock does to the steady downward flow of water, creating easily-discerned backwash. Look what a protruding stump at the bank of a smooth run does to create a whirlpool. See how a sudden (underwater) drop-off causes water to curl back under itself. Now picture these scenes in terms of topographical features; a saddle in a ridge, a rock point, a bowl or sharp canyon head, the edge of a steeply-falling mesa edge.

You can see how certain terrain features can present obvious traps. Part of dogging elk is not only closing the distance, but closing the distance when the wind situation is to your best advantage, hanging back and avoiding potential traps, waiting for more opportune opportunities to allow wind to work for you. Remember, too, the wind-in-your-face approach is certainly ideal, but not absolutely necessary. Side-winds are just as viable, and in certain situations, even preferred. They can actually give you a bit more leeway to unexpected swirls. Sometimes you simply have to work with what you have in relation to how terrain allows you to proceed. Any wind that does not reach the noses of elk is perfectly acceptable. I've stalked plenty of elk with the wind flowing past them only a few degrees. It's risky, but sometimes necessary.

Keeping tabs of wind is obviously a huge part of elk hunting. Archers are more aware of this than ever, if the proliferation of commercially available "wind-checkers" is any indication. When I began bowhunting elk there was no such thing as convenient powder sold in compact squeeze bottles. Of course, like we did long ago, you can fashion your own. I've used the same bottle for years, something that dog medicine came in, wrapped in camo tape, with a flip-up dispenser that opens with the flick of the thumb, closes again as easily. Years ago I bought a large bottle of quilt-making "pounce powder" from a sewing supply store, no more than light, powdered chalk, allowing me to fill my wind detector when needed. I also fill that same bottle with dried puff-ball mushroom spores when available. This is my favorite, agilely riding the slightest breezes. A pocketful of milkweed or cattail fluff is also useful, or as I discovered, super-light synthetic materials (incorporated in egg patterns for instance) used for fly tying. Such options are also commercially available, with names such as "wind drifters." These can actually give you a more accurate assessment of tricky wind currents, visibly riding air currents to reveal swirls or sudden shifts 50 or more yards from where you stand. The successful elk hunter checks the wind obsessively, even when wind direction appears obvious.

Another quick note: Late August and September can bring unpredictable and sudden monsoon thunderstorms; especially in the Southwest. Those building thunderheads are a clear and visible indication of rising air mass. What this translates into are clouds sucking air toward themselves, creating sometimes strong breezes. As those thunderheads gain momentum and turn to rain they begin moving in the atmosphere, pushing air before them to create the opposite effect. So predicting wind direction can also mean keeping an eye on prevailing weather conditions.

Avoiding traps can certainly entail added effort. Circling to avoid a wind trap can mean backing off and jogging around an entire ridge point; running down a canyon bottom only to trudge uphill again from a safe distance to arrive above or in front of animals; side-hilling or ridge running to arrive below a herd walking a canyon bottom. This can come at the risk of losing contact with your herd, but you are still in the game. Let them get your scent and you've likely lost them completely, with slim odds of catching them again.

ELK THINK YOU STINK

Scent-control clothing, activated-charcoal outfits in particular, once had little use in the elk hunting seasons I'm most familiar with. Sure, they worked fine in whitetail woods, but simply proved too hot while running and gunning in warm early-season weather. This is no longer true. These companies have developed thinner, more airy versions of this highly-effective technology, without sacrificing scent-filtering qualities. I'm sure we will see further developments in years to come.

Lighter, T-shirt-weight anti-microbial base layers are also the rage today, impregnated with skin-safe chemicals or silver, killing odor-causing bacteria bred from the sweat of exertion at the source. Even activated charcoal powerhouses have conceded the effectiveness of these products, incorporating them into their own products.

There is also an entire world of "scent-killer" sprays available to hunters today, sprays that neutralize, actively absorb, or oxidize odors at a molecular level and weigh nothing, and certainly don't heat you up. Charcoal scent-elimination powders are also helpful, especially useful for taming the stink of hard-working boots; the latter even effective directly on the skin and doubling as camouflage, covering the shine of exposed skin.

I was once inclined to ignore these readily-available scent control options. I believed this was whitetail nonsense. I simply thought that the unique conditions of elk hunting weren't compatible with the entire program. Elk hunting is sweaty business, often with days between real bathing. Playing the wind, I believed, was the only tenant worth adhering to. The year I killed my 386 bull I decided to give the complete program a fair shake. I religiously wore lightweight ScentLok duds, changing into street clothes after each hunt and stowing them in scent free plastic tubs. I doused myself with scent-eliminator sprays before every hunt. In general, I made a greater effort to keep myself clean, even taking dips in bone-chilling springs and cattle troughs during midday. It was a lot of extra work. But, I had to admit it was all very much worth it. In short, I was being busted less often. I can even recall specific instances, when a sudden shot of cold air on the back of my neck raised a few inquiring noses, even mildly alarmed nearby cows, but not to the extent these very scenarios once had. The elk moved away, but calmed down quickly instead of departing in brush-crashing fashion. My only explanation is these elk certainly sensed me, but simply believed I was far enough removed so to not prove an immediate threat. You can't "forget the wind," as some misdirected ad suggested, but it can give you an added advantage, give you a few more seconds to get off a shot.

If you stalk enough elk the wind will change; elk will receive your scent. Modern scent-control options simply give you an additional edge. In today's elk woods the smallest added advantage is points in your favor.

WAITING AN OPENING

As important as staying abreast of wind developments is, so is studiously observing terrain features and how they might be used to your advantage. This is one edge seasoned guides possess, owning an intimate familiarity with hunting grounds. Keeping an accurate topographical map handy can also provide this benefit. For example, your elk are traveling in an established direction and you observe, or know, a deep saddle lays ahead. You put two and two together and deduce your elk will move through that saddle. Take advantage of the situation by doing whatever it takes to arrive there ahead of them to set up an ambush. The knowledge of a watering hole has also given me a drop on traveling elk, assuming they will drop by for a quick drink before bedding, physically killing myself to get there first and set up. The dogging elk hunter is always scheming, always looking for a bushwhack option.

Also keep your eyes open to vulnerable spots elk are approaching. These can be places where wind promises to remain steady, or just as importantly, where a perfect blend of cover or terrain and high-odds shot opportunities make closing the distance suddenly possible, even relatively easy. Successful dogging often means hanging back and awaiting these situations, though only a narrow window of opportunity may be presented. Time your movements to assure you are there when that window is flung open. This can mean using the lip of a mesa or sudden ridge to literally run in for the shot while elk are still within range of that rim; a narrow bottom allowing you to arrive within range of the opposite face as the bull crosses before sauntering up that slope; even chancing a big move when you detect a bull aggressively rubbing a tree or fighting another bull, his senses temporary disabled by rattling brush (or antlers) and all those boughs (or tines) in his face. On open ground such an opportunity can be abruptly presented by a single ground-hugging cedar or large-boled tree that provides a shield against a bold move.

DRAW CYCLE

Making the best of fleeting shot opportunities posed while dogging elk seems to thwart even the most seasoned hunter. The eastern whitetail hunter bound to his stands, even the western archer schooled on the careful art of sneaking up on bedded mule deer, can miss shot opportunities by being too contemplative. The hunting they are most used to normally allows the shooter to gather his thoughts and carefully set up for the shot. The modern archer has been brainwashed into

Opposite page: While bowhunting elk, range finders are crucial. Develop a system that allows you to access and to get rid of your unit without undue commotion.

the notion of the "perfect shot," something they believe only arrives through patience. Certainly patience can be rewarded, but as often in elk hunting, while dogging traveling bulls in particular, the perfect shot can develop in a finger snap, and vanish just as quickly. I'm certainly not advocating sloppy, poke-and-hope shooting, pressing less-than-ideal shot angles (especially not on an animal the size of an elk). I'm only stressing that shots at big bulls, in particular, can be hard won. You must have trained to make the best of what is offered.

That broadside shot we have waited so long for, worked for days and endless miles, may develop in the blink of an eye, through a narrow gap in vegetation, at a range well beyond that of the average whitetail. There's little time to think, you must react. A seemingly hopeless situation can suddenly turn into a quick opportunity. You must stay on your toes.

Knowing the range is as important as any other factor, obviously, especially in the confusing terrain elk are found in. You are also dealing with an animal with confusing dimensions, something much bigger than anything we regularly hunt. A quality laser range finder is a must, even for the most accomplished 3-D champion. Any time you are near elk you should assume a shot is imminent, envisioning possible shot scenarios and constantly gathering range information. The Rancho Safari Catquiver 2000 series daypack/back quivers I religiously employ include sherpa-fleece-lined range finder pockets at the hip. I can quickly and silently slip my rangefinder out, and more importantly, instantly slip it back in, get rid of it for the shot, without fumbling or taking my eyes off the target. If you use a bow quiver, belt-mounted range finder pouches are also available; just make sure it is quiet and facilitates fast access and reinsertion of your unit.

TRICKY RANGING SCENARIOS

Ideally you'll receive a quick pop off the bull himself. But elk hunting seldom presents ideals. You must keep your wits about you to assure your laser range finder does not provide a confusing misreading. Grass, or the smallest limbs, between you and the target can bounce laser beams back prematurely, providing a short yardage reading. Those same twigs or grass stems might have absolutely no bearing on arrow flight, but make receiving an accurate laser reading impossible. Horse-sense is important, and why eyeball range-judging skills earned through long practice shoots are still highly important. A grossly inaccurate reading should automatically send up a red flag. Clear thinking allows you to automatically switch to a more reliable ranging surface; the tree trunk directly above the bull's back or a stump or rock well to the side but judged to be at a similar range. With today's fast bowhunting equipment a couple yards long or short means little. Anything more than five yards can put you off the mark.

You can also use your range finder and quick thinking to determine if overhead branches will negatively affect arrow flight. You pop the bull at 40 yards, but half way to him overhead limbs appear potentially problematic. Quickly take a second reading off those limbs. Say they prove to be 20 yards. Quickly hold your bow at arm's length, placing your 40-yard pin on the bull's vitals. If your 20-yard pin is buried in those limbs, or cutting it close, your arrow will likely be deflected.

Spread your legs to lower yourself, or carefully sink to your knees. How does everything line up now? This is another area where 3-D shooting, as well as regular small-game hunting, gives you an edge. These exercises quickly help you memorize arrow trajectory. With practice you should instinctively know when overhead obstacles pose a threat to arrow flight, saving you a few precious seconds in setting up a difficult shot.

All of this may sound time consuming and confusing, but in reality practicing with your range finder as diligently as you would your bow should turn a maneuver requiring three paragraphs of explanation into a streamlined seven-second (or less) operation.

SHOTS AT ELK

Keep in mind elk present much larger vital areas than average deer. Eight inches constitutes a deer's vitals, while elk present closer to a 14-inch vital. This gives you some leeway on those longer shots likely when hunting public-lands elk, as well as allowing for trickier drills such as a slowly-ambling bull at closer range. And while an elk hit in the vitals can prove remarkably "soft," that same bull hit marginally and wounded can turn into the toughest animal on earth pound for pound. All of this is to say that while getting a killing shot off at a stalked elk requires the same aggressive demeanor that has gotten you here, it's also your duty to assure that you are up for the challenge. This is in no way advocating pushing beyond your abilities, but encouraging you to work harder to become a better shot, to gain the confidence necessary to make the most of difficult or fleeting opportunities.

Strive to extend your maximum effective range, to mentally imprint your arrow's trajectory at every range, to speed up your shot execution when that is asked, all while maintaining all-important accuracy. There's no better way to become a better archery hunter than to hunt. Take advantage of small-game opportunities in your area to better hone woodsman skills such as stalking, shot timing and working around shooting obstacles. Take advantage of off-season game such as feral hogs and spring turkey when possible.

Dogging bugling bulls is perhaps bowhunting's most challenging pastime. Twenty years ago, while dogging bulls, I counted on shot opportunities every three to four encounters. In today's hard-hunted woods and the resulting education elk have received, those numbers have climbed to a shot opportunity every six to eight encounters. This can prove utterly and absolutely frustrating, ending in failure more often as not. But there is no better way to learn about elk habits and bowhunting than bowhunting them from the ground, face to face. In the case of the very biggest bulls, the record breakers and sage herd bulls we all covet, there simply may be no other way. When it all comes together, when you manage to beat the treacherous wind and wicked terrain and the highly-attuned senses of the quarry itself, there's no better feeling of accomplishment in all of bowhunting. Dogging bugling bulls has always been a huge portion of elk-hunting success and for the foreseeable future will continue to prove the most straightforward and productive means day in and day out.

Chapter 8

Water & Wallows

So admit it. You haven't spent a lot of time in the gym, jogging or bike riding, or even taking an evening stroll around the block for that matter. In fact, you've been doing a lot of nothing; most likely spending your days behind a desk, or worse, leaving that desk only to plant yourself before the television. Your midsection is showing it too, bulging evidence of the junk food and sodas you have been putting away. Maybe your daily intake of cigarettes exceeds the total number of miles you walk during an average month. A typical flight of stairs leaves you wheezing like a sprinter outclassed in a distance race. In short, you're in no kind of physical conditioning to hunt elk; not in the real sense in any case.

Okay, so maybe you're not out of shape. Maybe you're as fit as a bull, only you traverse average mountain real estate like that same animal in a china shop. You were born with two left feet; stalking quietly proves beyond your abilities. Perhaps you're simply tired. It's been a long week; you've tried your damnest, pushed yourself beyond reasonable limits and have simply had it. You have time, but no longer the gumption.

These are the very scenarios I was faced with while engaged in the full-time occupation of outfitting nearly 25 years ago; the desperate situations that eventually forced me to take a closer look at the possibility of parking clients at water to receive shots at elk.

THE DARK AGES OF WATER

It's an all-too-common scenario: A guy works his entire life, gets the kids through college, pays off his mortgage and banks a few extra dollars. The graying archer treats himself to a guided hunt, only he's too far gone physically to actually hunt rugged elk terrain with the gusto required. Unique to the guiding trade as well, there are simply those weeks when you have too many clients and not enough help to offer everyone one-on-one attention.

Opposite page: Clear skies and warming temperatures encountered during early elk seasons offer the perfect combination for bowhunting success at water.

You struggle with this constant dilemma until eventually it's difficult to dismiss all those bugling bulls you've dogged straight to water you didn't know existed, all those freshly-muddied bulls obviously made that way by a nearby wallow. And you really need to park this dude somewhere convincing so you can attend to the guy who's actually physically fit and ready to go. So you deduce that perhaps this water thing will kill two birds with one stone. Most of your clients are eastern whitetail hunters used to the tedious (to a westerner) dodge of perching in trees, hunkering in a blind, patiently awaiting the arrival of game. They don't mind a wit. In fact, they welcome it. They are seeking fun and relaxation, and this elk thing is transforming into excruciating torture.

Then the funniest thing happens. These guys you park to simply get them temporarily out of your hair begin killing elk. Regularly. Some of the best bulls of the season. And unlike all those cases when stalking bugling bulls or calling are involved, they don't miss the easy shot, they pin-wheel their bull and create a short trailing job. It's what they are used to, shooting when they are ready and not when game dictates. It's a wonderful thing for everyone involved.

Like anything that's been right in front of your face all along, you wonder why it's taken you so long to make the connection. Better yet, we have all these sites to ourselves. No self-respecting western hunter would consider sitting a stand when so many elk are there to be stalked and dogged, and better yet, called to.

WATER-HOLE AWAKENING

Of course western archers eventually and happily took to the waiting game, guarding water. The situation has changed considerably. Hunting water is standard operating procedure with a majority of hunters holding elk tags today. Some-

A tree stand or ground blind is the normal means of concealment at or around water. The modern pop-up blinds makes that easier.

Scouting out productive water often starts with map work, but investing in old-fashion scouting is also important to discovering the best sites.

times it seems archers have forgotten how to hunt elk any other way. Discovering a prime water-hole without an overlooking tree stand or hastily constructed ground blind in place can prove a rare occurrence indeed in modern elk woods. Hunting rights to these public-lands sites can become hotly contested. Harsh words and fist fights are not uncommon where water is limited, where this ploy works best.

Still, bowhunting over water is as viable as ever. Elk still have to drink and water-hole hunting continues to provide an edge not allowed otherwise. Many of today's biggest bulls are killed at water. Water allows you to fool the veterans not likely to respond foolishly to calls, those herd bulls surrounded by myriad cows and demanding the most tedious approaches and highly-whetted stalking skills. Water-hole hunting is certainly not a cure-all method, as some modern elk hunters seem to believe, but simply another ploy to add to your widely varied bag of tricks, to increase your ability to tag a trophy bull under changing hunt conditions.

AN OBVIOUS SOLUTION

Archery elk seasons traditionally occur in late August through September. It's a good bet you'll experience warm weather during those months, and a better bet elk will develop a thirst that only a watering site can slake. When summer has yet to offer fall a firm foothold, daytime temperatures may hover in the upper 80s. Imagine a 700- to 800-pound animal covered in heavy hair suffering in that heat. Now, knowing elk drink, and being in the right place at the right time are two entirely different matters. There is water, and there's water.

Rutting bulls are perhaps the best bet around water because weather doesn't affect the effectiveness of your watches. Wallowing becomes more important than

Determining if water is used regularly by elk is easy; seek sign at the water's edge; fresh tracks and rounded droppings are key.

a mere drink. Elk seasons can certainly arrive with rainy weather across the West, transforming every low spot into a potential watering hole, making elk difficult, even impossible, to pin down to a single drinking site. Luckily, bulls are in the habit of wallowing, even when hunted hard, and are particular about where they conduct this business.

In short, you may be unable to course alpine altitudes in search of scattered elk, hump straight up a vertical slant after a bugling bull or perform two-mile sprints to flank a traveling herd—but you can still tag an elk this season by guarding water or wallows. The infirm hunter may not be able to depend on legs and lungs, but he can hunt smart. Don't assume this is going to be easy, though. You'll still need to invest some time on the ground—hiking, investigating, chasing leads or hunches—but you can do so at your own pace, not that of rangy elk. If the physical aspect of elk hunting has held you back, this is your opportunity to tag a trophy bull on public lands, by disengaging your legs and putting your hunting savvy to work.

LOCATING PRODUCTIVE WET SPOTS

Scouting productive water or wallows is easier said than done. Most hold a common trait; namely remoteness, sometimes obscurity. The biggest bulls are shy, which means the best holes normally receive the least amount of disturbance. Watering sites need not be large. A prime example is a highly-dependable watering site I discovered one late evening while following a bugling bull. The place was no more than a single trash-can-lid-sized pool of water held by a dip in solid rock, fed by a stingy seep. It's a tiny pocket of water but remains during the driest periods. It's clear elk make regular use of that water as conspicuous trails cut from both flanks of the canyon, and better yet, a sudden drop-off 50 yards below keeps elk from slipping in downwind. Finding that particular spot was a stroke of good luck, as there is no hint whatsoever of its existence on any map.

Another example of often overlooked watering sites are "trick tanks" or drinkers installed by conservation departments for the direct benefit of wildlife, most often funded by hunters' purchase of "habitat" or "conservation" stamps or validations. These are often placed in high places, on ridges or mesa tops, using an old satellite dish or similar water catcher to direct natural moisture into a holding tank, connected to a small trough through a float system. Other examples are simply improvements on tiny springs, a cement spring box that collects water or a pipe tapped into a rock face and dripping into a holding tank. Ranchers making use of public-lands grazing allotments often construct such water-saving devices for cattle, but they benefit wildlife as well. Many of these will not be shown on maps.

Other watering sites are revealed by pouring over maps, remembering that the too obvious can attract other hunters with the same water-hole hunting plans you hold. Look for tanks far from roads, more commonly today, at the end of a legally-closed or blocked road, and put in the time required to look each one over carefully. You might discover a gold mine that will serve you for years to come. Most Forest Service maps show all man-made water, springs and natural ponds. U.S. Geological Survey topo maps can offer more detail yet, also making it easier to punch sites into sophisticated GPS units to allow a quicker bee-line to a remote, roadless watering place.

Once in the vicinity you should begin to pick up game trails. This not only tells you this is a permanent watering site, but it can quickly lead you straight to the source. Typically a fork or "Y" in the trail acts as an arrow, pointing toward water. This is something to keep an eye toward while dogging bugling bulls or simply hiking in search of sign. Obvious trails mean concentrated activity, and water is typically the attracting factor.

FACTORS FOR SUCCESS

How productive a water-hole may prove depends on a number of factors. Obviously, there must be animals in the area. Too, prevailing weather or a naturally-dry climate may force elk to use what little water is available to them. There are places in New Mexico's Gila region, or in Arizona trophy ground in particular, where watering sites are wide flung and scarce, though over-hunting can quickly turn big bulls nocturnal. How productive a site may prove is easily determined at the water itself. Abundant sign around water is normally easy to discern; deep-cut trails angling off hillsides or over tank dam corners. Tracks around the edge of the water may be obvious, or less so in rocky areas. Beware that the tracks observed around water may have been made during another season. Age is easily determined, as waters' edges recede during dry periods—when water is most productive. Look for tracks in still-wet, soft mud, placing less credence on the

Elk visit water regularly to drink and to wallow, but just as commonly, to simply cool off during warm weather.

higher edges and "cement" imprinted tracks possibly made months ago.

Another problem is presented in areas with abundant cattle. Cow tracks can look awful similar to those of elk. Luckily the droppings of these two animals vary greatly; cattle leaving loose "flop," elk rounded pellets. Elk are big animals and normally droppings and other sign are obviously blatant. Just as important, large numbers of animals are not absolutely necessarily. A single trophy bull is all you need to punch a tag. Don't give up on an isolated spot ignored by others just because sign is scant. Fresh bull sign, bigger tracks mixed with tell-tale marble-sized pellets, is more important than lots of sign.

What constitutes a "good spot" can be directly proportional to how much security a site provides, as well as how critical that water is to the wildlife of a particular area. While remote watering holes, those wholly overlooked by most hunters, are often the most productive, don't automatically discount water found right off a well-traveled road. It just might be the only water available for miles, or concentrations of elk may simply provide plenty of elk traffic at the site. My buddy Kelsey Denton enjoyed an awesome week of elk hunting at just such a site. Located only 200 yards off a smooth Forest Service road, it seemed an obvious pass; until we took a closer look and discovered an abundance of sign. We were still reluctant to hang a stand there, but it was difficult to ignore seven wallow pits and a plethora of still-moist droppings. By week's end he had observed no fewer than a dozen bulls, and got a few shots at them as well.

At such sites it's normally prudent to post a buddy, spouse or offspring on the access road well away from the water to deter other hunters from disturbing your hunt. In the case of a pond found at a dead-end road, or when hunting alone, simply parking your truck in a way that discourages further travel and leaving a polite note in plain site can do the trick; something like; "Archery hunter on water below, please respect my hunt and do not disturb." It might discourage the most polite amongst us…

I also recall a few highly-productive water tanks so far from roads one wonders how they came to exist at all; perhaps constructed so long ago the access road has eroded into oblivion. Just as productive as the singular pond, natural springs seem to attract less attention from hunters than tanks that make choosing a surefire stand site easier. Springs may well up and flow for hundreds of yards, making finding a stand location more difficult, though even in these circumstances there seems to be that one stretch elk choose over all others.

It seems my most regularly productive watering sites (gorgeous, man-made dammed ponds included) are absent from maps. Whether these were constructed after a map's latest printing edition or were simply overlooked by cartographers during its conception, I can't say. What matters is the average hunter doesn't realize this water exists, so elk receive little pressure in such places. It goes without saying that these secreted watering sites are more difficult to stumble across. *Stumbling* across such water is certainly how I've located most of these places, but I have also had good luck making friends with and querying range cowboys in way of securing such information. It's the cowboy's job to know what water is available to his stock. Sharing an evening cooler of beer with a lonely cowboy is a great way to loosen his tongue and learn of such sites. Finding a commanding vantage and watching elk move, or walking out low-lying areas looking for a small water pocket, sometimes does the trick. Again, all it takes sometimes is a puddle.

MAKING YOUR OWN LUCK

This also brings to mind another useful ploy in heavily-hunted areas. It's certainly not unethical or against any laws I'm aware of to create a watering site of your own in more crowded hunting areas, places where all available watering sites are typically occupied. This entails plenty of work and advanced planning, no doubt, but can really tip the odds in your favor. Use half of a 55-gallon drum and some pipe to collect water from a tiny, secreted seep, or transport needed water and cement via ATV to an isolated arroyo to construct a hollow were summer rains can collect to provide a September stand site. I have friends in Arizona who, while bowhunting the state's more arid elk habitat, create success by transporting precious water throughout the summer to established drinkers that have run dry during an especially dry period.

WONDERFUL WALLOWS

As productive as watering sites can prove, depending on them for success makes you susceptible to the whims of Mother Nature. In alpine areas where water proves overabundant, or when persistent rain puts a damper on water-hole activity, drinking elk can become wholly impossible to pin down to a particular site. This is when wallows can save the day.

I have yet to hear a conclusive explanation as to why bulls wallow; whether to simply cool off, or add a layer of insect-deterring mud, or the opportunity to add odorous urine to their hides to impress the ladies while rutting. I suspect a combination of all these factors is at play. One fact remains: Rutting bulls wallow, rain or shine. It took some years to convince me that this was a situation I might take advantage of in respects to bowhunting, especially when persistent rain haunted a hunt; even after observing obvious wallows and mud-caked bulls during these wet periods.

The interesting thing about wallowing bulls, and what makes bowhunting such sites highly productive even during the wettest periods, is rain might have filled every bar ditch and meadow dip, filled every road berm and stock tank to brimming, but bulls invariably choose a select few holes for wallowing. I have also bowhunted areas in Colorado where small creeks, springs and seeps interminably dot the landscape, yet wallows show up in the exact spots every year. I remember a couple seasons past when nearly every evening produced slashing thunderstorms and torrential rains. The area we hunted, while harboring an abundance of whopper bulls, also supported a dozen watering sites for every one of them. Yet, the wall-hangers chose just three sites. One pond in particular soon supported a healthy scattering of bomb-crater wallows, while ponds 300 yards up and down the same canyon held exactly zero.

Seeps, isolated springs, damp meadows or simple low spots are all prime locations to look for elk wallows.

My theory follows that when you weigh 650 pounds or more you simply don't enjoy rolling atop sharp rocks. Then, too, some ponds simply don't provide the sticky mud needed by a bull determined to plaster himself in an adobe shell. Rocky ponds and sandy bottoms are automatically out; from there my theories become more subjective.

Elk wallows also seem to present all the qualities of whitetail scrapes (in particular) and rubs. Some elk wallows, like many whitetail scrapes and rubs, are simply spur-of-the-moment whims, aggressive-displacement behavior that poses little opportunity for bowhunting success

Hanging a stand out over bomb-crater wallows can prove more productive than water alone.

because repeated visits are not likely once constructed. Perhaps such wallows are created by non-dominant bulls and hold no social significance within the herd as a whole. Other wallows, or sites constituting many wallows in a concentrated area, become like the whitetail scrapes that represent "sign-post" social centers used by a multitude of animals, translating directly into continued and repeated visits.

Several prime spots discovered in the past come to mind, most providing year to year dependability, places you know certainly without pre-scouting will hold a wallow when the rut kicks in. One such spot is created by a lush, spongy spring seep where elk come to rake ugly scars into the poison-green clover and sedge. Apparently they've been at this for years because there's a permanent stand nailed in the pines that's been in place for so many years the lumber can no longer be trusted.

Petersen's Bowhunting editor, Jay Strangis, installed himself in a portable stand overlooking that very site and observed two different behemoth bulls in a single evening. Luck wasn't on his side and those bulls did not present shot opportunities, but the very next year I placed a client in that same tree and she arrowed a nice six-point directly beneath her feet the very first morning.

BIG BULLS IN SMALL PLACES

During wet periods wallows can show up anywhere rain collects to create muddy pools. Such wallows can also appear in the most unlikely places. One friend killed a 365-inch bull from a small depression right in the middle of a two-rut Forest Service road. Another prime place to seek wallows is along defunct logging skids. After logging is completed, roads are rehabilitated and berms pushed

On many watering sites, solid tree stands are out of reach. Ground blinds, positioned for wind, save the day.

up on sloping sections to impede erosion; small "dams" that puddle water during rains. Lush bends or sloughs of larger rivers and creeks also invite wallowing bulls.

One of my better bulls came from an ancient logging road. I'd stumbled upon the place while following bugling bulls days before. In a deep saddle separating two lush valleys a pair of dished-out puddles had collected where a bulldozer had long ago dislodged massive stumps. They showed only a scattering of tracks but no wallowing activity. Returning days later, after rutting intensity had increased, those dishes of water were a sloppy soup with discernable elk imprints at their edges, muddy droplets leading off into surrounding forest. It was still early and quite warm so I reclined beneath a nearby pine to have a nap in the shade and await prime evening hours, still hours away, and listen for bugling. I was awoken a half hour later by splashing and bovine grunting, sitting up to find a monster bull rolling enthusiastically in the farthest pit. I grabbed my bow and when he turned to silently slip away, quartering heavily, I sent an arrow into his ribs.

CREATING VIABLE HIDES

If you've bowhunted whitetail deer from portable stands you're well ahead of the curve in this water-hole dodge. You own a stand and are acquainted with the sometimes boring occupation of waiting. The remote nature of the best watering and wallowing sites indicate a light-weight hang-on style that can be set up quickly and quietly. I've long believed in lightweight aluminum hang-on models with

Opposite page: Dean Martin (not the singer), one of the Jersey Killers, tagged this nice 6x6 bull sitting a crude blind overlooking water. He scored on the very first sit.

attached backpack straps. Most of these compact models aren't the most comfortable during a long visual, but are simply easier to pack into remote canyon bottoms or distant meadows. Ever-present Ponderosa pines ask for a handful of screw-in or strap-on tree steps to get you into the lowest disguising boughs, though the occasional juniper, spruce or fir sometimes provides plenty of readily-available climbing branches, using a folding saw to create an unobstructed climbing path. Elk certainly aren't as wary to activities such as cutting stand holes or shooting lanes, but it still pays to keep human odors to a minimum. Freshly-cut brush or the glaring scars of sawed branches don't seem to alarm them in the least bit.

Just as likely, especially in "desert," sage or scrub cedar areas, is a ground blind constructed of natural materials. Elk aren't as wary at water as, say, pronghorn, but a little extra effort assures you can draw your bow undetected and assures a clean shot. I have gone to the trouble of digging pit blinds, camouflaged after with cut brush, but this isn't usually necessary. One of my favorite and effective ploys is to select a ground-hugging cedar, piñon or juniper and use a folding saw to selectively cut branches and create a concealing "cave" of overhanging branches. The glaring fact is that ground blinds make you vulnerable to wind currents, so sites must be chosen with extreme care.

THE JERSEY KILLERS

I remember well an evening sitting with half of a twin-brother pair from New Jersey, burly men who were having a rough time in the thin air 8,000 feet above their sea-level homes. We'd glassed a scattering of bugling bulls from a high rim during a morning hunt and returned to the vehicle to drive around and investigate during the heat of day. Further scouting revealed two widely-separated waterholes, one situated on relatively open ground, another ringed tightly by ground-hugging cedars and piñons. On the open pond we built a sketchy blind, a cedar-limb frame tented over with cut boughs. It stuck out like a beach ball on a putting green but was as good as we could manage in the limited time available before prime hours. Leaving one brother in the makeshift "wickiup" we made haste to the other pond and quickly cut a cave into the side of a piñon pine and crawled in.

A couple hours passed before bugling commenced well up the canyon our pond occupied. We enjoyed an hour of spirited bugling, the anticipation of nearing elk. The first cows and calves arrived in a rush, diving right in and happily splashing and kicking up water at rock-throwing distance. They were obviously overjoyed by the cooling water. We waited anxiously, bugles thundering down the hollow. The cows had cleared out and we thought we were out of luck, but a handsome 270-inch bull suddenly and silently appeared, wading up to his belly, drinking deeply, broadside at 25 yards. With fluttering hands and raspy breath my guy drew his bow and neatly centered both of the bull's lungs. While we shook hands and slapped backs another bull suddenly appeared, taking the place of the first. Of course he was bigger by 25 inches but we could do nothing more than smile and shrug. That bull drank and played in that water for a full half hour before allowing us to exit our hide and inspect our bull.

But it only got better. The other brother appeared in the headlights as we approached, smiling widely, his quiver an arrow short of a full load. "He got one!" his brother said immediately. This one kept us in suspense, simply taking us to a blood trail, refusing to divulge any information. Eighty yards up the hill lay a 335-inch bull, shot through the heart. We were a very happy truckload of hunters for sure!

POP-UP OPTIONS

Today the pop-up blind has replaced the hastily-constructed ground blind for quick water-hole concealment. Interestingly, the average elk seems to pay very little attention to these seemingly conspicuous hides, waltzing right in only hours after set-up as if the material blob has been there all along. Still, I never trust the biggest bulls to act nonchalantly "average." For this reason I stab pop-ups beneath umbrella-like trees or into tight brush, trimming as necessary. I use trimmed branches to "brush" the blind over and help it blend. Pop-ups also offer a scent-containment advantage not possible with a brush blind, more effectively holding offending odors inside instead of allowing them to easily ride errant breezes.

Recently I hosted an outdoor television crew intent on securing elk-hunting footage. After dogging public-land bulls for a couple days it became grossly apparent stalking a bull with a three-man team (guide, hunter and cameraman) might just prove impossible. I set them up on a wallow created at the edge of a lush spring seep, placing the blind in a tight place between two pines and planting brush around the blind so it absolutely disappeared. I waited a mile down the canyon, reading a good book and enjoying the music of singing bulls that arrived with prime time, anticipating my guys hurrying down the canyon at any time, animated and grinning like idiots. It was apparent they were literally covered up with elk up there, and from the sounds of things several bruiser bulls were among them. Yet complete darkness showed without their arrival.

After bugling receded I returned to retrieve them. They had quite the tale to relate. Indeed they had been surrounded by elk, no fewer than 50 cows and calves, several small bulls, parading before the blind for a full hour. The punch line was that a true behemoth, a bull scoring an estimated 370 inches, had set up shop directly behind the blind; clearly visible through the narrow screened viewing slits, at one point horning a pine sapling not 10 feet from the blind! This was confirmed by freshly-dripping pine sap and twisted limbs. They had fought to open the rear shooting port as the bull created his racket, unfamiliar with the simple hook-fastened workings of the window system. He'd even considered shooting through the wall of the blind. The bull was that close! Finally it was decided the bull would come around to join the others, so they patiently waited. Of course the bull did not cooperate, wandering away without presenting a shot. When asked why they hadn't simply cut the window-retaining cord with a broadhead they looked at each other with a sudden dawning. Apparently, it hadn't occurred to them!

WIND, OF COURSE

Like stand-hunting whitetail, the wind is your biggest adversary. In mountainous areas this might become more predictable, especially during the cooling early and late hours when most activity occurs around water and air moves predictably downhill. Problem is many animals, especially in remote spots, may arrive at earlier (evening) or later (morning) hours when breezes haven't settled into a predicable persistence. With increased hunting pressure I've also began to witness elk visiting water during midday when hunters are typically napping or lounging in camp and far from water. It's usually easy to determine from what direction the majority of elk are approaching by noting conspicuous trails and at which corner the brunt of sign is located at water's edge, setting up accordingly. In worst-case scenarios you may have to trim two stand trees, install two sets of steps, and move a portable stand morning to evening, move a pop-up as the hour dictates, or simply install dual ground blinds.

Employing scent-killing aids such as sprays and powders, activated-charcoal or anti-microbial clothing is an especially wise move when bowhunting from any stationary position, and can certainly give you an advantage in bottoms where winds often swirl. Installing yourself in a stand doesn't entail the sweaty exertion of other classic modes of pursuit, so becoming overheated is not the issue it otherwise would be, making "whitetail-hunting" layers welcomed. It's also a smart move to lash a light jacket to your daypack before setting out. The best bulls most often arrive at the very edge of shooting hours, when temperature drops of up to 20 degrees can cause unexpected chills, especially while sitting stock-still. Shooting your best means keeping shooting muscles warmed and ready for action. Shivering is not conducive to this end.

WATER-HUNT TIMING

Guarding water has traditionally been an evening venture, elk bedded after a long day understandably thirsty. This still holds true. Even while guiding I use water as an evening-only ploy, allowing a tired hunter to regenerate, dogging bulls or employing calling strategies by morning to give my hunter a well-rounded elk-hunting experience. Evenings are undoubtedly best, but this is not to say elk will not visit water, or wallows, during other portions of the day.

As I have hinted, a midday visit to water has become more commonplace in harder-hunted areas. I figured this out after backpacking into a vast, roadless primitive area. The only available water was found in widely-scattered stock tanks filled with green, slimy water. Every couple days I would hike to one of these tanks during midday to filter-pump water to renew our camp supply. I was in the middle of one of these monotonous errands (the soupy water clogged the filter endlessly, requiring constant cleaning); pumping away and daydreaming of other things, when rolling rock snapped me out of my reverie. I looked up to find a 360ish bull ambling into the water, drinking at the opposite end of the large pond for 10 minutes before slipping away once more.

Of course I hadn't brought my bow, my hands full of water jugs and pump. A stand overlooked that very pond, but after several days of waiting during prime hours my friend had seen nothing. After my experience I encouraged him to invest in an all-day visual, just to see what happened. That same bull arrived on schedule the very next noon hour. Unfortunately, the gagger bull rattled my pal enough that he missed the 35-yard shot across the pond.

Hunting water offers many obvious advantages. Foremost, it allows you to get close to trophy bulls that might otherwise remain out of reach while calling or stalking, or to beginning hunters lacking honed bowhunting skills. This becomes especially pointed for hunters who are overweight, cigarette smokers, coming on in years or otherwise not in the best physical conditioning. Just as importantly, shots over water or wallows are normally as controlled as it gets in elk hunting. Even a bull in a hurry is likely to spend a full 30 seconds greedily tanking up before moving on. This gives you time to calm your nerves, await a high-odds shot, even bumble an arrow off the rest (hopefully quietly), without losing a fleeting opportunity. For the eastern whitetail hunter versed on the finer points of stand hunting, the tedious nature of sitting stock still for hours on end, this is old hat. Hunting over water can also provide shot opportunities at game such as black bear or mule deer when seasons run concurrent with elk; or at least the thrill of seeing these interesting game animals up close and personal. There are many glaring reasons to hunt elk over water, but remember, too, this is only a single facet in a multi-tiered approach to elk hunting overall, not the be-all, end-all. Use it to your advantage when necessary, but don't miss out on all the fun offered by the complete program that is elk hunting.

Persistent rain can quickly put a damper on water-hole activity, but wallows continue to produce, even become more attractive with wet conditions.

Chapter 9

Take A Stand

Calling, dogging bugling bulls and sitting water; these are the primary modes of operation while bowhunting modern elk, the ploys nearly all hunters turn to in some form or fashion while seeking elk-hunting success. Still, it pays to remain flexible. As we have firmly established, calling doesn't always work according to the script; hunting pressure, weather and rut timing are all fickle factors in the final equation. Dogging simply isn't for everyone, a highly physical endeavor that oftentimes culminates only through the highest degree of stealth possible. Dogging also requires bulls that are actively bugling. Water-hole hunting, of course, is highly dependant on weather, namely rain or lack thereof, and in today's often crowded elk woods finding a productive and unoccupied watering spot or wallow can prove difficult indeed. If readers come away with nothing more from these pages I hope that it will include approaching each elk hunt with an open mind, especially when the going gets tough or an overall situation appears grim. Portion to this flexibility includes, when required, occasionally abandoning standard operating procedures and trying something different, something less popular with the average elk hunter today.

One such ploy is climbing into a tree stand or blind while bowhunting elk.

WHITETAIL PLOYS FOR ELK?

Whitetail hunters seem to understand little else but stand hunting today, so elk hunters traveling from the "East" should be well versed in how to proceed in this business. Of course, water-hole and wallow hunting include installing yourself in a stand or blind, and the same principals of stand placement and playing the wind apply, but here we are talking the finer points of true ambush, guarding points that, in general, have no immediate attraction for elk, sites that simply provide a high odds chance of an interception between points A and B. Diligent scouting can reveal such places, even better, a long-time familiarity with an area. More often likely ambush sites simply reveal themselves during the course of an average elk hunt, sites recognized by an astute elk hunter while dogging or stalking as a situation or condition likely to put hunter and prey in the same place at the same time.

Opposite page: Taking a stand can mean letting crowds work for you, using their activities to push elk past your position. This requires hunting smart instead of hunting hard.

For the worn-out elk hunter looking for a place to sit, this obvious elk trail should send up a red flag.

Elk, Roosevelt in particular, can occasionally prove remarkably predictable. This is especially true during early seasons before hunting pressure has scattered elk to the winds, and especially before bulls have become distracted by rutting activities that send them wandering widely. This closely parallels the situation often presented by early season whitetail. Bachelor groups of bucks are easily observed at the edges of open farm fields feeding like clockwork mornings and evenings. Even the biggest bucks can prove amazingly predictable for the archer willing to invest the time to observe these patterns from afar. With elk seasons kicking off as early as late August in many western states, the early-season whitetail analogy is often quite apt when applied to pre-rut elk. Substitute Midwestern agricultural fields for lush mountain meadows or even foothill valleys with scattered hay fields and the situation begins to sound quite familiar. This is certainly not the rule, of course, but something to keep in mind with an early season opener.

And also like whitetail, high-odds ambush situations can simply arise due to a high population density in a given area; terrain features and funnels simply increasing your odds of an elk ambling past your stand or blind. Again, Roosevelt elk come to mind, because they are relative homebodies and their habitat incredibly thick; certainly not conducive to long-distance glassing for the most part. Finding the right trail and setting up to intercept anything that uses it can reap huge rewards in terrain and vegetation types that make stalking about quietly most difficult.

FOLLOW THE FOOD FOR SUCCESS

Like whitetail, movement patterns most often revolve around food directly, or indirectly as bulls seek concentrations of cows attracted to obvious food sources. If you are lucky enough to gain access to elk in a private land area including irrigated crop circles, river-bottom plots or seasonal crops such as oats or barley, winter wheat, alfalfa or simple hay grass or an inviting vega (in Southwestern argot), taking a stand can provide your most obvious plan of attack. On more extensive fields this can prove hit or miss because elk are not as routine-oriented as whitetail deer and less likely to travel the same path day to day. That said, patience is eventually rewarded, because choosing a beat-down trail entering such a site means that given enough time, elk will eventually wander within bow range. In such cases a single cottonwood is all that's needed to hold a portable tree stand, though never discount a sweat-earned pit blind or even a brushed-over pop-up.

In elk habitat farther removed from civilization, open meadows of lush grass are more likely to create the appeal. Elk are grazers, primarily cropping grass for a living, unlike browsing deer that most often nibble broadleaf plants and shrubs for sustenance. Grazing elk need reliable grass to remain healthy, their sheer size dictating they also need plenty of it. Whether discussing the piñon/juniper (PJ) oceans of the Southwest, black timber regions of northern Colorado, northern Idaho or western Montana, or rolling Ponderosa pine forests scattered across any elk habitat, reliable grass is found most readily in open areas where acidic pine

The beat-down trail cutting off a ridge point, used by elk to access a nearby meadow, offers an obvious site for a stand.

Places such as this isolated winter wheat field, adjacent to prime elk habitat, are typically made of private land, access made easier if damage to crops is incurred.

needles have not poisoned the soil and abundant sunlight prevails. While scouting, keeping an eye on the grass situation is always the best clue to potential hotspots. Without it elk will be somewhere else. This normally goes for concentrations of cattle as well. While elk will and do regularly mix with cattle herds, given a choice they prefer not to. Unless obvious sign shows otherwise—round, marble droppings most revealing, en leu of loose cow flop—look elsewhere for elk feeding areas.

An overabundance of food makes this sort of approach less productive, but during periods of drought, in fringe areas with less than ideal habitat (so-called "desert" elk are a perfect example) or extremely-heavily forested areas, food is key.

New Mexico's Gila region during a dry year is a perfect example of what is possible. The forest becomes parched and arid. What little grass exists turns wiry and unpalatable. But even during drought years there always seems to be a cienaga (technically a marsh, but also a spring-fed meadow) or vega (technically a fertile plain, but also an open, grassy place) where grass is a bit greener. These can also constitute a bench below a mesa rim, a canyon head or low playa bowl where moisture collects more readily. While glassing early and late you seldom fail to find elk feeding in such places. While dogging evening elk across endless miles your quarry will invariably lead you to a grass mother-load.

Opposite page: Elk are big animals and must eat well to maintain their health. In heavily wooded areas, open meadows of lush grass offer an obvious focal point.

Clear-cuts created through logging activity, most common in Roosevelt country, quickly become elk magnets as second growth returns.

During a recent western Washington foray for Roosevelt elk, bowhunting a national wildlife refuge island, we discovered that elk moved to the ocean's edge each evening, where impenetrable walls of fir, spruce and alder abruptly ceased and marsh grass began. The only problem in that case was treacherous mud and extreme tidal shifts made stalking beyond difficult. An extensive system of deep, sloppy tidal cuts and sinuous sloughs made it futile to circle in the narrow time frame before darkness took over; though I tried and came close to a couple gorgeous bulls. After observing a Boone & Crockett-class bull in the same remote meadow two mornings running I alighted from bed at 3 a.m. in an attempt to complete the five-mile circle required to flank those tidal flats. Circling meant fighting jungle-like brush to get there, an exhausting undertaking in itself. I arrived by daylight and slipped within 70 yards of that 300-inch-plus Rosey, but when I began sinking to my knees in black mud I had to give up; the bull melting into that nightmarish Pacific Northwest vegetation across a small lagoon. We plan to arrive better prepared next time, our scheming now involving kayaks, and especially tree stands. There's no doubt in my mind this will turn the odds in our favor.

OPENINGS FOR ELK

Roosevelt elk bring to mind clear-cuts, recently logged areas creating openings where second growth vegetation flourishes to attract feeding elk. And though bowhunting Roosevelt elk seems to revolve around logging activity (positive and negative alike), Pacific Northwest forests certainly don't own an exclusive to this activity. Clear-cut logging is the Catch-22 of forest management. Yes it's ugly, and has the direct potential to silt in prime trout streams, but it also creates elk feed no matter where you are hunting. Whether bowhunting Oregon Roosevelt elk or Idaho Rocky Mountains, clear-cuts are worth scouting carefully and can offer prime opportunities for ambush along their edges, seeking obvious trails coming and going from adjacent areas of thicker forest.

Forest fire is Mother Nature's natural process for creating clear-cuts. Fire not only clears an area of old growth that poisons the soil and starves elk feed of sunlight, but returns important nutrients back to the soil. Two- to three-year old burns are elk (and other big game) magnets. They create open areas of lush new grass, shrubs and berry patches, in general a literal elk dinner table. They vary in size from a football field to thousands of acres. The smaller stump-fire burns can offer the best opportunity for dependable ambush, but don't discount larger burns that require more thought and thorough scouting.

The U.S. Forest Service keeps close tabs on recent burns, normally even mapping them precisely. Visiting a local Forest Service office and making nice with the right person can prove a virtual treasure trove of such elk hotspots. You might not receive precise map coordinates, but you might find someone who worked a fire crew and can give you general directions to such a site. Smoke jumpers are likely the best source for smaller burns, the brave ones who respond to extinguish an acre-sized fire before it turns into something bigger and more costly.

FENCE-CROSSING HOTSPOTS

Fence lines are the next-best ambush alternative to concentrated and dependable food sources, more pointedly, breaks or crossings in such fences. Not just any fence line, mind you, but a fence representing a major barrier between two points elk want to be according to hour or hunting pressure.

Fence lines can create funnels that make elk movement more predictable, normally revealed through broken wires, obvious trails or tufts of elk hair.

Elk are basically lazy when not pressured. They seek the point of least resistance. An open gate above an established food source can become an elk funnel.

The situation I'm most familiar with is the fence marking the border between Arizona and New Mexico in some of the Gila's most productive elk habitat. While Arizona's later archery season dates make that side of the fence a temporary haven, in the particular area I have in mind and have bowhunted extensively, the best feed is located on New Mexico's side of five-strands of barbed wire. Daily commutes between the two states becomes a regular routine with the area's elk. Walk a couple miles of that fence and you're sure to find a broken-down section and established trails leading east and west.

In fact, one such spot accounted for an archery-industry friend's very first elk. At 100 pounds soaking wet that gal obviously can't pull he-man bow weight, which meant her range was limited considerably. In the interests of creating a likely close encounter we tossed together a quick blind of logs and limbs, sprayed down the site and ourselves with scent-elimination spray and settled in downwind to await prime late-evening hours. Just before dark an eating-fat cow ambled out of Arizona following the beat-down trail, stepped over what was left of the barbed-wire fence at that section and entered New Mexico. My pal let that elk get 25 or 30 yards into the right state and let her have it at something like 15 yards. That elk never knew we were there.

STRADDLING THE FENCE

I think, too, of several areas in New Mexico where public lands open to the masses (lucky enough to draw an elk tag) sit adjacent to highly-exclusive private holdings; places where the price of admission is quite high and success rates and trophy quality beats surrounding Forest Service holdings. Despite the fact that these elk are more relatively safe on their private side of the fence, the compulsively nomadic elk nevertheless hop or duck over and under those fences to take their chances on the public side like kids who drive too fast or climb high things to cheat death and experience a cheap thrill perhaps. Of course, too, such places make obvious destination points for elk fleeing hunting pressure and looking for safe haven, so this traffic goes both ways.

I have friends up north who find regular bowhunting success by haunting the boundaries of Yellowstone National Park. The way they tell it, the more remote the location the more likely these highly-protected bulls are to wander out of off-limits park and onto wide-open (over-the-counter) public lands for the taking. In any case, they take 300-inch-plus bulls nearly every year. Such opportunities can also be offered via state parks and wildlife refuges, and especially federal national wildlife refuges. If there is a clear boundary, with one side of a fence off limits and including zero harvest, there will nearly always be some amount of overflow from displaced animals, more reliable food sources found on outside areas with lower population-densities or a simple wanderlust elk are inclined to.

Burns quickly become elk feeding areas for the same reasons clear-cuts are productive; new growth that is more nutritious and palatable.

Regarding state boundaries or private holdings, doing everything possible to assure your elk dies on the right side of the fence is important.

POTENTIAL TROUBLE

The only real drawback in this business is that while a well-placed arrow is very deadly, it's seldom immediately so. Even 30 seconds gives an elk plenty of time to return to or make the wrong side of a fence. And while it's perfectly legal to shoot an animal on the right side of that fence, retrieving it where it comes to rest can pose a more ticklish situation. Even when that, too, is perfectly legal (so long as you have a blood trail commencing on the correct side of the fence) it can create hard feelings with landowners and no one—even those beyond reproach—is comfortable subjecting themselves to game warden scrutiny. This is a long-winded way of saying it's best to do whatever possible to make this scenario less likely.

When a situation permits, back off a bit instead of setting up right over the fence or boundary in question. If setting up right on the fence line is your only viable option, allow your animal to travel as far as is practical onto the correct side of the

There is no food or water at this site, but ridge-running elk obviously cross here often. Setting up nearby could result in a high-odds shot.

fence before taking a shot. In general, a mortally-wounded animal will run in the direction it was facing before the shot. When that rule holds, departing animals offer less concern than those entering off-limits land. That said, there's also the factor that an animal will often do an about face to flee a shot. That animal knows what lies behind because it has only recently passed over that ground; while the terrain before him offers uncertainty, especially in light of the sudden danger encountered.

Check your game laws carefully in this regard. You are likely to find that the law can prove quite fuzzy. You might need to ask landowner permission to retrieve an animal, or even be required to be escorted by a conservation officer in the case of a wildlife refuge. If you plan to hunt such an area, know the rules before you proceed.

WORKING THE LAND

Topography is another obvious factor working to funnel elk past a particular point, a point where sitting in ambush can really pay off. Elk are wanderers by nature, though hunting pressure also has the potential to shove elk here and there and in front of a waiting archery hunter.

Old-fashioned scouting reveals such places, but U.S. Geological Survey maps can give you a good jump on locating likely ambush sites. Deep saddles separat-

ing adjacent valleys or basins are always an obvious hotspot whether ambushing elk or trapping valuable bobcats' pelts. Unpressured elk in no particular hurry to get somewhere naturally choose the path of least resistance. No use climbing a mountain when you can skirt that mountain and pass through a saddle 1,000 feet lower in elevation. Long, narrow ridgelines can also provide obvious travel routes. Rutting bulls, in particular, seem inclined to maintain the high ground while cruising for receptive cows. Long, isolated ridges become bull highways when the rut kicks off, allowing a bull to cover a lot of ground while maintaining a visual and audio advantage over two large swatches of land.

In the Southwest my favorite ambush sites are found at the edges of abrupt mesa's rimmed in broken volcanic rock. While the relatively flat tops of such places offer obvious feeding ground in the form of rolling grass meadows and pastures, the edges can prove quite treacherous. Be it a gentler ridge creating an "off-ramp" from higher country, or a just-passable cut in a sharp rock rim, such places normally reveal well-used trails to thicker bedding cover below.

The best example of an ideal elk ambush site created by topography alone is found in an area I've bowhunted extensively. A high plateau of lush meadows and gentle cuts dotted at regular intervals by watering holes attracts nightly elk traffic. While all the food and water they need is found on top, the widely scattered Ponderosa pines create a cathedral-like under-story of wide-open habitat offering scarce bedding cover. To find their daytime beds they travel off this top, dropping off sudden rims to access tangled PJ and oak ridges, benches and points below. One such point includes an isolated peak higher than the adjacent plateau at its end, a deep saddle between the plateau and this small peak. A multitude of age-old trails begin in that saddle, side-hilling the small peak and dropping through small cuts in the sudden and rocky rim. A thousand feet below all those trails converge on an open saddle of Ponderosa before plunging into even thicker scrub oak. Maybe 15 trails converge in an area no larger than an average neighborhood convenience store parking lot. It's an obvious enough ambush point that a pair of makeshift ground blinds have become permanent fixtures in this place, tidied up each season, added to and well used. It's a rough place to clamor in and out of each morning and evening, but I'm sure plenty of elk have fallen to hunters there.

Sitting for elk certainly doesn't offer the immediate, heart-pounding excitement of other approaches. It's tough to ignore, though, that the sound of elk approaching your position has the potential to frazzle the nerves. Even more appealing in this day and age, when elk are abundant but hunter numbers are just as high, sitting a stand offers the opportunity to allow crowds to work for instead of against you. Too, having a reliable stand site simply gives you an option when dogging bulls has left you a bit ragged and foot sore, allowing you to stay in the game while regenerating. For those who have arrived out of shape (and you know who you are) you can still get your elk by playing it smart—by taking a stand.

Opposite page: Terrain features can determine how and where elk travel. This hanging bench in otherwise steep country shows a well-used trail any archery hunter would recognize.

Chapter 10

When Elk Won't Bugle

The bugle of a rutting bull elk is the single, spine-tingling, primal event that makes bowhunting elk so popular. The way most hunters see it bugling bulls are practically fundamental to the sport, but in the times we live in dependable bugling can often prove rare. This is to be expected during early seasons when hunt dates arrive well before the rut begins. Bugling, after all, is a biological function of breeding activities. But it's also difficult to dismiss climatic changes and even increased hunting pressure as obvious factors to diminished bugling. I can't say I actually buy into the concept of global warming in the context of man's alleged hand in it. An average volcanic eruption spews more toxic chemicals into the Earth's atmosphere than our automobiles can muster in two decades, or all the cow farts accumulated over five more of those decades. I'm ever suspicious of special interest groups creating emergencies in an effort to fund their questionable agendas. These are the same people, for the most part, who would also take away our hunting if it were in their power, and science has shown that this isn't the first time major climatic shifts have occurred on our planet.

But the fact remains; it used to be colder, on average, during archery elk seasons than it is today. I used to leave camp shivering, even while dressed in wool sweaters and wearing long-handles beneath my camos, equipped with gloves and stocking caps against biting chill, puddles from last night's rain skimmed with ice, frost swishing in the grass as I crossed a grassy meadow. Lately I depart camp in the dark morning wearing long-sleeve camouflage T-shirts and cotton pants and find I'm sweating during the first good uphill pull. Heavy-hided elk aren't particularly interested in the rigors of rutting when it's hot like that.

A DIFFERENT BREED OF ELK

Hard-hunted bulls, especially the very biggest, have also learned that to sound off with a far-reaching bugle is to call down trouble. I also have to think that in

Opposite page: Early season openers, too much hunting pressure or hot weather can mean elk hunts without bugling. Locate elk the old fashioned way—by glassing.

Gaining a vantage point makes more of your hunting time when seeking tight-lipped elk, allowing you to cover ground effortlessly.

the larger picture, we could be slowly eliminating the genes of those in the herd inclined to aggressive bugling. My synopsis follows that a warming climate pushes back the rut until it ultimately coincides with traditional rifle-hunting dates. Bugling bulls attract attention from hunters equipped to gun them down from afar with very little required hunting skill. The bulls that bugle the loudest and most often get it first. At least this is how it has begun to play out in my native New Mexico.

I've pointed out before that the biggest-antlered animals in a herd, be it whitetail deer or elk, aren't necessarily the most aggressive. In fact, a completely non-aggressive bull, one who doesn't participate in the rut with full-out gusto, is more likely to live to a ripe old age, to grow antlers of giant proportions, simply because he puts himself at less risk. Elk have personalities, and that personality may simply mean they aren't interested in breeding activities. Could we be creating a race of elk inclined to homosexuality? In all seriousness; the highest-scoring elk don't always fit the archetypal picture of boisterous herd bull; translating into a lack of bugling that can make them more challenging targets.

An elk hunt without bugling is like a turkey hunt without gobbling, a NASCAR race without crashes. It's easy to feel cheated. Still, what are you going to do when you finally draw a hard-earned tag only to arrive to just such conditions? Give up and go home? Not likely. You make the best of it. Mule deer, after all, don't make a peep and we still manage to take a few of them with our bows. When elk won't bugle you simply set aside your preconceived expectations and carry on. You resort to bowhunting at its most elementary. This is elk hunting without smoke and mirrors. This is hunting via straight-ahead, simpleminded spot-and-stalk and still-hunting ploys.

"DOGGING" WITHOUT BUGLING

Glassing and stalking, spot-and-stalk in common hunt-talk, indicates first spotting an animal from a distance then using terrain, favorable wind currents and stealth to sneak within range, or maneuvering to allow that animal to come to you. Spotting game is the first step, followed by creating a viable plan to bring you closer after considering all factors within your control. Still-hunting, at its most basic, means moving through habitat slowly and quietly in hopes of approaching unsuspecting game. Each has its advantages according to terrain and prevailing conditions. In general, spot-and-stalk ploys are best in areas where seeing game from a distance is feasible; in more open or broken terrain. Still-hunting is normally reserved for denser vegetation, where spotting game from a distance is more difficult.

BACK TO BASICS

Before the stalk begins you must first find game. This is the "spot" in spot-and-stalk. You might find game by simply covering a lot of ground, bumping into a bull. More likely, and more productive when time is a factor, this is accomplished with binoculars. Mounting a commanding vantage makes the most of these efforts, allowing quality binoculars to carry you effortlessly across deep canyons and up

High-quality binoculars are important to any elk hunt, but most especially when elk aren't bugling and are more difficult to locate.

high ridges, cover miles with your eyes in minutes that would require days afoot. Locating bugling bulls can mean walking intermittently with a sharp ear tuned to that tell-tale grunting whistle, pausing to glass only sporadically. That talkative bull could be just over the next ridge. Without the benefit of the siren's song of lovelorn bulls, efficient spot-and-stalk hunting requires parking yourself and using your eyes and binoculars instead of your legs. Spotting an animal even so large as elk from a distance requires a careful look.

Remember, too, that elk country offers vast vistas, often stretching into tomorrow. Discovering a bull two miles distant is pretty much par and well within striking distance in most country. While something like an 8x32 is standard-issue while dogging bugling bulls due to their compact and easy-toting nature, sitting down for the long look entails something along the lines of a 10x40. There are many variations to these numbers; but the first number indicates magnification or power, the second the "objective" lens measured in millimeters. The larger the objective-to-magnification ratio, the better the glass cuts deep shadow and penetrates the dim light most commonly found when big bulls move during warm early seasons. There's also the factor that bigger glass are steadier in the hand, providing long hours of probing without eye fatigue.

SYSTEMATIC GLASSING

Effective glassing means learning to look *with* your binoculars, not merely *through* them. This holds whether engaged in pure spot-and-stalk hunting, or dogging a bugling bull. Seeing with optics means holding binoculars rock steady while moving only your eyes within the available field of view, moving to the next

In rough terrain it makes more sense to let your optics do the walking for you, covering in hours what might require days afoot.

patch of ground only when satisfied there's nothing to be seen in that quadrant. This soon becomes second nature with experience. Avoid panning across terrain and expecting to spot game as it passes through your glasses. Glassing approached in this manner makes it's all too easy to miss a small and inconspicuous patch of rump or hide that might give a bull's position away. It also quickly invites eyestrain and headaches.

Another trick used to remove the randomness of glassing is to develop a regular system to assure you don't unintentionally miss a patch of ground that holds game. By a "system" I mean a way of "reading" terrain thoroughly. I normally "read" terrain (a ridge or hillside or valley) like I read a book; left to right, top to bottom. When I run into blue sky or exhaust my field of view I start on the next "line" overlapping slightly and beginning anew. According to terrain type you might prefer to move binos up and down, bottom to top. It doesn't matter. There's no hard rule other than to develop and stick to a system.

Using good horse-sense can also save you a lot of time, help you cover more ground efficiently. You can obviously skip sunny spots when it's hot and game has sought cooling shade. When it comes to early-season bowhunting for elk I normally direct my attention to heavily-shaded north slopes. Even when it's comfortable for you, remember that elk wear a heavy coat. If you're not layered up or chilly they're most likely overheated and looking for someplace cool. The sharp demarcation between sun-drenched areas and dark shade can also reveal elk movement. Changing light can flush elk from their beds to escape warming sun, and movement is always easier to detect than a stationary subject.

PLANNING AN APPROACH

After game is spotted creating a sensible plan of approach is a must before continuing. Factor wind direction, whether that animal is traveling, milling, or bedded, surrounding animals and disguising terrain features. Most important, take mental notes of the area the animal occupies before rushing headlong into a stalk. Earmark obvious landmarks for latter reference; a rock outcrop, a conspicuous dead tree. Things can look completely different once in the immediate area and it's easy to become disoriented during a stalk. Bedded animals allow more time for contemplation; traveling critters more decisive action, but invest in this all-important step before beginning.

In rare instances allowing your bull to bed before starting a stalk can provide the best approach. This is more often the case in high alpine habitat where elk bed at the edge of timberline, in short, where cover proves thinner rather than in areas where vegetation is thicker or terrain flatter. In thicker terrain actually observing an elk bed can enter the realm of pure luck. This is especially true when elk are traveling; and it's the rare elk that is not going somewhere. In the case of traveling bulls, it can closely resemble dogging bugling bulls, but without the obvious advantage of pin-pointing bugles. This alone makes it a trickier undertaking.

Remember, too, that while keeping the wind in your face is basic bowhunting lore, it may be easier to relate on paper than in practice. Especially in broken terrain, wind currents can prove tricky. Chapter 7 includes a lot of detail on playing

Glassing for silent bulls on distant hillsides and ridges efficiently means employing a system to assure you see more animals.

and predicting wind movement so I'll not belabor the point here. It bears repeating, though; learn to anticipate obvious stumbling blocks and potential wind traps. Just like when dogging bugling bulls, wind is everything. In most respects pure spot-and-stalk provides parallel challenges to dogging, though without bugling and raging hormones the pace by necessity slows considerably. Remember, too, a direct in-your-face breeze is not absolutely mandatory. Side-winds are viable, even quartering winds, so long as your scent does not reach the nose of your quarry.

STALKING STIPULATIONS

Stepping softly is obviously important but also comes with qualifiers. A bedded animal demands the utmost in patience and stealth. A moving animal may ask for an aggressive approach to maintain contact, or in the case of an elk fleeing approaching heat, to avoid being left behind completely. Elk herds often allow a certain amount of noise even without rutting distractions, creating so much clamor themselves even when simply ambling peacefully. A bedded or lone elk will not. Sometimes moving quickly and silently simultaneously is in order. Other times moving as quietly and slowly as a stalking cat fills the bill. Each situation must be read individually, something that becomes easier with experience, so learn from your mistakes and invest in small-game hunting to become better acquainted with the finer points of stalking.

DETAILS MAKE THE DIFFERENCE

In very general terms, the best stalking situation is one that allows you to approach elk from above, from over a ridge crest or cliff lip in particular. Terrain and wind currents ultimately dictate these matters, and just as likely you might find yourself using an erosion cut for cover from elk situated higher than you, or coming around a point on the same level with a bull or small elk herd. Using a subtle roll of land or even something as simple as knee-high grass or shrubs is not out of the question, requiring you to slither on your belly or crawl on hands and knees.

Heavy, hard-bottomed boots have foiled many otherwise well-executed stalks. Boots with soft foam soles are a boon, but may not provide the support necessary in treacherous footing. I'm repeating myself (Chapter 7 – Dogging Bugling Bulls), but "stalking slippers" offer a good solution, offered by a multitude of manufacturers and mandatory should bulls fire up later in the season and dogging bugling bulls become your new approach. They simply muffle the crunch of gravel or the

snap of twigs, silencing your steps like cat's paws, making moves on even bedded bulls feasible with honed stalking skills. In extreme cases, don't be afraid to shed your boots and proceed in sensitive stocking feet. It pays to keep an extra pair of dry socks in your daypack if you plan on employing this approach.

CLOSING THE DEAL

The last 100 yards is where all your efforts pay off or are suddenly dashed. You might have to take chances. An extra measure of caution might be asked for. You may actually be able to see your bull clearly, enabling you to read body language, freeze if he's obviously sensed something (swiveling ears, turning antlers), moving when his attention is clearly

As with dogging bugling bulls, stalking success hinges directly on playing the wind. Light powder does the best job.

Stalking elk without the benefit of bugling is certainly more challenging, but persistence pays off in the end.

directed elsewhere or his eyesight blocked by obstacles, grass or terrain. Use binoculars often, even when you're very close, reading body language to better gauge your every move.

Sometimes the best action is no action at all. If you discover noisy ground clutter, lack of cover or a blocking cow makes moving closer impossible, sit tight and wait. If you're lucky that animal, with time, might just come to you. You'll never know if you force the situation and blow it now. Your bull is just as likely to wander away, but this might also carry him to a place that better allows you to close the distance. Patience is highly important, because spooking a non-bugling bull can mean he's lost forever.

THE VANISHING ART FORM

Still-hunting, while once a much-used bowhunting mode of operation, is quickly becoming a forsaken bowhunting technique. This is a shame, because still-hunting can prove important when bulls aren't bugling, another useful tool in the well-rounded elk hunter's bag of tricks. When cover is thick or terrain flat, translating directly into limited visibility, you really have few other options when bulls fail to bugle. It can prove deadly during a day with light drizzle to quiet your steps and a wind stirring vegetation to create visual confusion. In short, during early seasons when many depend on water-hole hunting for success, heavy rains that put a damper on such well-laid plans increase your odds of success while still-hunting.

Simply walking through the woods slowly and silently isn't what makes for still-hunting success. I can't stress this enough. Effective still-hunting is a bit more involved than that. The best description I've heard is something close to a Zen-like state where the archer moves through the woods wraith-like, seeing and hearing all. Pardon the hackneyed expression, but approached effectively it's truly as close to "becoming one with the forest" as is possible. Moving silently and playing the wind are all important; no doubt about it, but just as importantly is sensing elk before they sense you.

Still-hunting by nature is a stop-and-go affair. The hunter takes a couple quiet and deliberate steps (watching all the time for game) then pauses to probe ahead thoroughly, scanning for any hint of game, then using binoculars to check and double check any suspicious features before moving forward once more. Each new advance changes the perspective and a new search for elk begins.

A reoccurring beginner's mistake is expecting to discover an entire elk broadside in the open, or at least an obvious patch of tan glaring from forest clutter. More likely you'll discern only a flickering that could just as well be a bird as an elk ear; a flash of antler; the curve of an elk rear against a vertical tree trunk; chocolate legs poking from beneath brush; a light patch of hide that could just as well be a sun highlight on rock. Investigate the smallest clues with binoculars, carrying on only after 100-percent certain that it is truly something else. Elk are big and

Still-hunting thick cover during warm elk hunts isn't the most fun way to hunt elk, but may be periodically required for success.

seemingly brightly-hued, but a confusion of harsh light and deep shadow can help them blend amazingly well.

It also behooves you to soak in the small sounds of the forest that can alert you to the presence of game. A chattering squirrel might just be scolding a passing bull, a squawking blue jay amusing itself by trailing an elk herd. You might detect the click of hard hoof on rock, antlers pushing through tight saplings, even an involuntary grunt, like an old man who talks to himself without knowing so. Engage your nose as well; a bull in particular can reveal his presence through a distinctive sweetly-musky/uric odor. Just as often you've stumbled upon a fresh puddle of urine which provides confidence game is near, but it could also be a bull upwind and just out of sight. I've located more than one bull by first smelling him.

Tune in all your senses; soak in your surroundings like a sponge. This requires intense and concerted concentration. I can't still-hunt effectively for more than a few hours before I begin to lose focus and become sloppy, tripping over obstacles and visually missing obvious game.

Once game is spotted, your spot-and-stalk skills should kick in, using all your powers of stealth to move closer or get a clean shot.

GROUND-LEVEL SHOT TIMING

Slipping up on a bull, whether spot-and-stalk hunting or still-hunting, without the benefit of distracting rut activities can prove more challenging than those approached at the end of a long dogging. These added challenges are also part of getting off a clean shot. The aggressive movements of drawing your bow are much more difficult to pull off when not surrounded by chirping calves, milling cows and screaming satellite bulls. Shot timing becomes even more critical, making or breaking your considerable efforts thus far. Obviously, you can't simply draw your bow when it's convenient for you.

A bull with his eyesight temporarily obscured by brush or a tree trunk offers the best possible situation not only while gaining the last few precious yards that earns you that shot, but in drawing your bow undetected. Something as simple as keeping a tree trunk or rock between yourself and a bull's head provides both on these advantages, leaning out to take your shot only after coming to full draw and anchoring solidly. A moving animal allows you to jerk your bow to full draw as an animal's head passes behind such a vision-blocking screen, awaiting the next opening before releasing. An elk that has you pinned in the open might dictate holding stock still, allowing him to pass, drawing your bow when his attention is focused forward before *cautiously* taking a quartering shot.

I say cautiously, because elk aren't deer, and though outdoor writers are fond of recommending it, most have little understanding of the amount of animal and the sturdy ribs that must be penetrated for a successful quartering shot on elk. I've seen seemingly beautiful quartering shots on big bulls turn into heart-breaking disasters when a well-placed arrow failed to find vitals or glanced from a rib.

Part of your responsibility as well is to find a clean shooting lane or hole. Off-season practice helps immensely, solidly imprinting your bow's trajectory on your mind's eye to better gauge what constitutes a useable shooting hole. A single small branch can interfere with a seemingly wide-open shot, while a basketball-sized hole in the right place lets you "thread the needle" easily to reach vitals. An elk standing behind brush with only his back showing can invite you to drop an arrow into his vitals. Stump shooting or bowhunting small game in forested terrain is the best practice here and the reason I always

Fleeting shot opportunities, common while stalking, ask that you be intimately familiar with your equipment.

carry a Judo-tipped arrow while bowhunting elk, shooting my way back to the truck during midday down time.

Of course the best shot is a standing shot. Moving elk, though they are big, present a ticklish situation, making a misplaced and wounding shot more likely. A slowly-ambling bull under 30 yards presents little problem, offering a decent margin of error. An animal in a hurry or farther than 30 should be stopped before taking any shot. Wait until the animal's sight is obscured, get your bow to full draw and pan with him until an opening is found. As the animal's shoulder enters your shooting lane produce a quiet cow chirp or mouth grunt. Be on him and ready to dump the string as soon as he stops, because he will certainly turn to see what has produced the attention-grabbing sound. The longer you take to aim the better chance he has of pegging you. And yes, elk can and will jump the string.

Bowhunting elk without benefit of bugling is the sport at its most basic, but is a situation that sooner or later you'll certainly be faced with in modern times. Pre-rut, early-season bulls might leave you no other options, while heavily-hunted public land elk can become tight lipped even during prime rut dates, bugling only under the cover of darkness. Bowhunting elk without bugling is better than not hunting elk at all. It certainly proves more challenging, sometimes much harder work, but honing your stalking skills opens more opportunity for bowhunting success in a wider variety of elk-hunting situations; especially, as they say, when the chips are down.

Chapter 11

Roosevelt Are Different

While Rocky Mountain or American elk have achieved cult status among much of the nation's bowhunting fraternity, the lesser-known Roosevelt (Olympic or *Cervus canadansis roosevelti*) elk remains somewhat of a mystery in even serious sagittary circles. I liken them to Coues whitetail that I've spent so much time, sweat and blood pursuing in my native Southwest haunts. While extremely popular regionally, eliciting near religious fervor in their own right, few far-removed hunters consider them worthy of their efforts. Aside from an obviously limited range that makes them less accessible to the average archer, there are real physical and climatic aspects that create less of a burning desire. Firstly, in our goal-driven society, there's the obvious factor (like Coues whitetail) of smaller average antler size than their Rocky Mountain cousins. Sure, the biggest Roosevelt antlers might score in the 350s to 360s, a big bull anywhere, but this is like saying the very best Rocky Mountain elk score in the 400s. Roosevelt bulls of such dimensions are as rare as diamonds and just as precious.

ONE FOR THE BOOKS

While a 260-inch Rocky Mountain will land you a permanent place in Pope & Young records, 375 a coveted spot in Boone & Crockett all-time records, Roosevelt's magic numbers are much lower: 225 inches for archery-killed bulls and 295 to make the minimum for a "Booner." In short, what might be looked upon as a "raghorn" in Rocky Mountain country could very well constitute an archery trophy, or more accurately a "book" bull, when in the Pacific Northwest's coastal ranges. To put this in more familiar terms, a 225-inch bull could look like a typical five-by-five with only average tine length and mass.

It's also interesting to note that Roosevelt elk include a unique set of measuring criteria, with aspects differing from American elk. Most specifically, this includes allowances for "crown points" like those found on European red stags. Officially

Opposite page: Roosevelt elk provide archery hunters with the opportunity to pursue them through dense habitat in a unique setting.

Any bull Roosevelt can be considered a "trophy," but the P&Y minimum is much lower, at 225 inches versus 260 for Rocky Mountain.

this includes any points projecting from the main beam or from another point on or above the G-4 (the well-defined "Royal Point"), that are not typical in location. This also includes points occurring on the royal, on other normal points, originating from other crown points and on the bottom and sides of the main beam above the royal. Such points are added to the total to boost score, no matter symmetry. This special concession was advocated and lobbied for aggressively by the Pope & Young Club's first president, Glen St. Charles, a longtime Washington resident and early archery pioneer who bowhunted Roosevelt elk extensively on the Olympic Peninsula when modern bowhunting was in its infancy.

UNIQUE FEATURES

What the Roosevelt lacks in outwardly-impressive headgear, he makes up for in sheer body mass. More lush and dependable feed, combined with mild winter climate (compared to typical prevailing Rocky Mountain conditions) create bulls that can easily tip the scales at more than 1,000 pounds. Roosevelt bulls are simply huge bodied, sheer size that can come as quite the shock to those who have handled a good number of American elk.

Opposite page: Pacific Northwest coastal Roosevelt means stalking dimly-lit understory of old-growth forest, making binoculars highly important.

Roosevelt habitat is often thick and dark, requiring archers to spend extra time looking from shadow to shadow to discover camouflaged elk.

The other obvious stumbling block to bowhunting Roosevelt elk is their habitat. They live in some of the most thick, nasty terrain possible. The vast amount of moisture received by the Pacific Northwest translates directly into jungley, temperate rainforest where visibility is highly limited, to put it mildly. Nonstop rains can also make bowhunting conditions miserable. This dense vegetation has created a secretive species of elk that offer completely different challenges than those presented by American elk. In fact, it is these conditions that make Roosevelt elk one of North America's hardest won archery trophies. Fighting clutching, tangled brush in a dripping, slippery setting is not everyone's idea of bowhunting fun. It's these challenges that make the Roosevelt as regionally revered as any eastern whitetail or even Rocky Mountain elk.

WHERE IT'S AT

Yet these are the conditions that prevail in the coastal ranges of extreme northwestern California (where tags are tightly controlled), through far western Oregon and Washington and north into British Columbia's Vancouver Island (where some of North America's biggest Roosevelt bulls come from, but limited tags mean hunts can cost upwards of $12,000 to $14,000). In more specific terms, Boone & Crockett accepts Roosevelt elk from areas found inside Del Norte, Humboldt and Trinity counties, and that portion of Siskiyou County west of Interstate Highway 5 in California; west of I-5 in Oregon and Washington; Vancouver Island, British Columbia; and from Afognak and Raspberry Islands in Alaska (Alaskan elk a result of a successful transplant from the Olympic Peninsula of Washington). Regionally, hunters may label elk close to but outside of these man-made boundaries Roosevelts, and while they may present all of the characteristics of the species, they must be entered in official records as Rocky Mountain elk.

ROOSEVELT INITIATION

Now, I'm certainly no expert on Roosevelts, but have bowhunted with some of the best Roosevelt hunters in the business, men who showed me the way and lead me to success in their backyard coverts. Those first hunts were eye openers. After all, I'd guided elk hunters something like 24 years, had tagged a dozen or so archery bulls myself during those years, three bettering 360 inches. I thought I knew a little something about bowhunting elk, but soon discovered the educa-

Trophy Roosevelt like this often require archery hunters to aggressively bugle while stalking through dense vegetation.

tion earned after decades of bowhunting Rocky Mountain elk was of little use in the rainforests of western Oregon and Washington.

My first couple days in the pursuit of my long-standing Roosevelt dream, in Oregon's renowned Coos County, were carried out alone. I had experts to point the way (experts who had invested in all the tedious, summer-long scouting) but was left to my own devices. It took me about three minutes to grasp what I was in for. I began that first morning with the gung-ho gusto Rocky Mountain elk had always rewarded. I was ready to stretch my legs, cover some ground, physically make something happen. I left the truck, following a defunct logging skid, looking for openings to invite a careful and distant look with binoculars. I was soon swallowed by the darkness of enveloping forest and the more I walked the thicker it seemed to become. It wasn't any kind of Rocky Mountain elk habitat I'd ever experienced, the darkest blacktimber of Colorado included.

CALLING ROOSEVELTS

I discovered sudden trails peeling off that razor ridge, pathways cut with time and the passing of untold thousands of elk hooves and showing recent elk sign, even fresh splashes of steaming urine. I unlimbered my bugling tube, cringed, and produced my first squealing call. I say cringed because I'd learned from hard experience that bugling to the average Rocky Mountain bull, even cow calling, was a sure way to literally blow my chances of success. But I was following instructions from my outfitter friend; an Oregon Roosevelt guru who guides archery hunters annually to percentages pushing 50-percent kill and 100-percent shooting, all in country that affords success numbers in the mere teens to the masses. Like Washington areas I would hunt later, the country was steep and densely inaccessible, but also public land well interspersed with roads of all descriptions and open to anyone willing to invest in an over-the-counter archery elk tag. I'd simply been conditioned to consider calling a sure way to lower already steep odds, as it was at home. It would be only the first of many assumptions that would eventually prove dead wrong.

This aspect of calling to Roosevelts came as the greatest surprise. It had always been my impression that Roosevelt elk simply weren't as talkative as Rocky Mountain elk, in fact, that they rarely call at all. This seems to be common Roosevelt lore and something I had heard related repeatedly as truth. In time I would discover that quite the opposite is true. In fact, calling is how the vast majority of bowhunting's better Roosevelt bulls are tagged. It's the nature of its habitat that likely creates this long-held myth. In those swallowing Coastal Range confines hearing elk talk is simply less likely; bugles simply do not carry far with all that thronged vegetation to soak them up. Too, population density seems to be lower than in Rocky Mountain haunts, meaning a lot of empty space in a seeming cornucopia of possibilities.

But then, too, I later bowhunted a crowded Washington island wildlife refuge where the Roosevelt elk as silent taciturn certainly proved the rule; a place where in a full week of bowhunting, despite seeing multitudes of trophy bulls, I never heard a peep from a single elk. It's always dangerous to speak in generalizations,

Contrary to popular myth, Roosevelt call openly and are highly susceptible to both bugling and cow calls.

but I would venture to say that Oregon bulls are more talkative than Washington bulls, based on my limited experience. This is likely a result of hunting pressure.

DAWNING PERCEPTIONS

I bugled on those preliminary days in Oregon because I was instructed to do so, but I did not believe in it. An hour into my first day of Roosevelt hunting I discovered the next pitfall to my approach. I tried the bugle intermittingly, moving along that passable trail, my only real option for unimpeded travel, but abruptly found myself out of road with several prime hours left of morning. Because I didn't know better, because I was determined to hold to the pretexts of Rocky Mountain elk hunting and cover some ground at all costs, I plunged into crispy, dusty forest, creating as much clamor as a herd of driven cattle.

My initiation as a Roosevelt elk hunter turned into an interesting one; interesting in a funny sort of way that is, because it little resembled the elk hunting I was so familiar with. In time I was at a loss as to how to proceed. I crashed through brush looking for openings that did not appear. I followed obvious trails that dead-ended in nasty blackberry brambles covered in ripping thorns. I pushed onward blindly, blowing on my bugle and wondering how it would be possible to get off a clean shot in that tangled forest even if a bull should respond to my calls. Obviously, there was more to this than I had once believed.

Back in camp my buddy and local expert, a man who has bowhunted and guided for Roosevelt elk a lifetime, smiled and nodded knowingly after listening to my morning exploits. Only after a couple days under his tutelage would I fully understand what that nod encompassed. Roosevelt hunting, unlike American elk at home, is not the physical dodge I'd attempted to make it. Roosevelt hunting is more a game of chess than the football scrimmage of Rocky Mountain hunting. It's still about covering ground, but doing so smartly. I should have stopped at that road end, turned around, and tried another spot, something that would have proven impossible that morning, considering my lack of knowledge regarding the lay of the land, having invested no prior scouting due to my reliance on local talent. It was becoming all too clear, though; Roosevelt must come to you if you are to succeed with regularity. In that jungle-like brush, going to them can prove essentially fruitless.

REAL HOMEBODIES

When my guide had shaken loose of clients I learned a new way of bowhunting elk. We covered ground in his truck, traveling a labyrinthine of logging roads, parking well back from landings or inconspicuous bends and stalking road edges to bugle over sudden clearcuts. We quietly trekked blocked logging skids, bugled at odd intervals, but nearly always turning back when that skid abruptly ceased. Being intimately familiar with his hunting ground, my friend also knew of secreted, fern-blanketed benches that traditionally harbored elk. Then we fought a half mile or more, choking on fern dust and tripping over hidden deadfalls, emerging to produce a couple bugles, only to retreat and try the next spot.

It became quite apparent that Roosevelt elk are more akin to whitetail in habit than nomadic American elk. Scouting is everything in this kind of elk hunting. The local experts spend endless hours each summer locating elk concentrations and particular bulls, glassing elk on clear cuts in an attempt to establish patterns, determining if new logging activity has created or destroyed a Roosevelt hotspot. In short, the kind of scouting that brings little reward while bowhunting Rocky Mountain elk. Unlike American elk in more wide-open country, Roosevelt elk are less apt to wander widely. Even with hunting pressure they seem more inclined to simply hunker down than seek greener pastures.

Scouting Roosevelt country typically revolves around logging activity, most notably clear-cut feeding grounds. Logging roads give you quick access to a huge expanse of country, long-range reconnaissance with powerful optics possible only on these open clear-cuts. The trick is in locating particular vantages that allow you to cover the greatest amount of ground quickly. Summertime scouting can also mean simply burning a lot of fuel, driving endlessly during cooler hours as time allows, taking notes on where elk are observed or creating new trails off steep hillsides accessing prime clear-cuts. Spring and early summer, before thick fern growth has taken a firm hold, is also a great time to take a hike and investigate a distant bench or ridgeline. The temporary lack of ground cover makes droppings and tracks easier to discern, and finding recently shed antlers can also give you clues to the presence of a trophy bull. Topographical maps reveal these potential hotspots far from roads, but it's still important to actually do some ground work and determine if elk are using those areas. When it comes right down to it, the most successful Roosevelt hunters never quit scouting. It becomes a full-time job.

It's this penchant for staying at home that gives the stand hunter an opening (something I've hinted at in Chapter 9). It would be something I will have to wait until later to test.

To this end we spent as much time in the truck as hiking, checking one pre-scouted elk pod after another. For the hunter used to stretching his legs to find elk-hunting success it can prove mentally taxing, perhaps "claustrophobic" is the best way to describe my feelings toward bowhunting in this manner. I wasn't entirely convinced that something, well, more proactive wasn't in order. I still stubbornly believed that leaving the truck well behind and covering as much ground as possible would do the trick, low population densities be damned. After all, following four days of concerted effort we had discovered only a single bugling bull (completely uninterested in our calls), approached seven or eight cows and a single spike in three separate encounters.

Successful Rocky Mountain elk hunting is a game of numbers. While dogging bugling bulls, it has been my general observation that six to eight encounters are required to earn each high-odds shot opportunity. On that Oregon hunt, on Roosevelt hunts to follow, we weren't racking up near those numbers and I was secretly beginning to form doubts regarding my friends approach.

RENEWED HOPE

But then late the forth evening, with the sun settled to invite a sudden coolness, we pulled off a well-groomed road to try just one more spot before hanging it up for the day, events unfolded that would ultimately show me that I'd been wrong yet again. My buddy tossed a bugle into a deep canyon head spilling into an open swatch of swamp ringed tightly with swallowing alders. Amazingly, a bull bugled in retort. My friend smiled and bugled again to the same results. "We're in business," my guide said, beaming. Just to prove it he bugled again, the bull answering immediately, but distance and impending darkness left me little convinced. As if reading my mind my guide offered, "Don't worry, he'll be here in the morning." As we loaded up in the very last alpenglow to see about dinner, another piercing bugle bounced down the hollow; a bugle that would make sleep that night quite impossible.

Those elk would have been long gone in any place I've bowhunted elk in

Author Patrick Meitin's first Roosevelt, a just-book five-by-five, was taken on public land during a rough week of hunting.

the Rocky Mountains, but with the first hint of morning light we could just make out distant tan grubs through binoculars, scattered across that grassy swamp. My reaction after so many frustrating days was to bail off the mountainside, fight through that dog-hair brush like a starving coyote. Instead we climbed back into the truck, turned around and drove down the road as if leaving our bull behind. At the bottom of the hill was a relatively passable trail that once served as log skid to the ancient clear-cut our elk occupied, direct access to our herd of talkative elk. I was reminded yet again that bowhunting smart beats physical determination when in Roosevelt country.

ROOSEVELT AGONY & ECSTASY

Our gentleman was talkative, even his cows chirping happily. After so many silent days, it was as if a supernatural circuit had been thrown. As we slipped forward a second bull bugled and we quickly set up to call, my pal fading back while I guarded an opening at the edge of the swamp. The three-point bull who showed at 40 yards was legal in this area of Oregon, but just barely. It was the last day and I wanted a Roosevelt badly but I'd glimpsed the herd bull and was gripped by greed.

But the small bull suddenly received our scent and rushed straight into our herd, stirring up trouble, a blunder that certainly would've sent New Mexico elk scattering. Instead the herd bull saw it as an infiltration, a challenge to his authority to govern his harem. The general melee remained intact, but it was easy to see that it wouldn't last. It was time to get aggressive, this much Rocky Mountain elk had taught me. I moved as quietly as possible while sprinting ahead in a low crouch, dodging behind cover and making time. The black-antlered five-by-five was marshalling his cows, prodding them toward swallowing cover. Once they made that jungle edge it was all over. I could see the bull through occasional alder gaps, fervently rounding up laggards, bugling and panting with an open mouth. I arrived at the edge of the herd, taking advantage of the temporary chaos. The range I popped from the bull's side with my laser rangefinder was discouraging but something Rocky Mountain elk had certainly prepared me for. I hesitated because my window of opportunity was a small one, something along the lines of a six-inch-wide slot between two hard firs.

Only later would I recall asking my outfitter friend, before venturing to Oregon, what kind of shot ranges to expect. He'd said anything from six to 60 yards; the six representing bulls responding to calls in the thick stuff, open clear-cuts making anything possible.

I snatched back the bow string, the bull paused in my tight shooting lane. I swept the proper pin onto the gap, double-checked everything before allowing the string to slip away. The arrow slipped through the gap cleanly and my insides twisted as the bright arrow arched in slow suspension, seemingly well high. But then it dropped in and piled through ribs with a watermelon thump and I was dancing spastically with pumping fists. My buddy appeared and I grabbed him in a bear hug, releasing all the frustrations of a mentally exhausting week.

Even then I was fully aware of how lucky I'd been. In the weeks to come that conviction would become more solidly established, bowhunting farther north, on Washington public land for bulls that despite ideal conditions (read wet and cold) refused to bugle or come to calls, who remained relatively visible (including some sure B&C contenders) but ultimately well out of reach. It was then I came to believe completely that Roosevelt elk just might be the toughest archery trophy in North America. The steep, jungley terrain is certainly part of this, the secretive nature of the animals developed in such a dark and obscuring place, but I'd also come to understand bowhunting Roosevelt elk requires as much mental fortitude as American elk require physical toughness.

No doubt about it, Roosevelt are different.

Chapter 12

Big Bull Minimums

I t seems all too obvious but bears repeating—elk are big. Six hundred to 700 pounds of mature Rocky Mountain bull equals three good-sized whitetail bucks. A Roosevelt bull will weigh, on average, even more. A big bull elk also has thicker hide, heavier bones and carries a whole lot more muscle than anything else regularly bowhunted in North America's Lower 48 (since few of us "regularly" hunt moose or bison). When I make a statement like that I don't have cows or raghorn bulls in mind. Those smaller elk aren't the hunk of pure tenacity a six-year or older bull elk represents. When bulls survive that long, reach maximum physical stature, they turn into a different animal. They're tougher, cling to life with the tenacity of a desert shrub. Hit well, they can prove surprisingly fragile. Hit marginally, they can turn into the toughest animal in North America, larger moose and bison included. Marginal hits mean shots that would have even a tough old whitetail buck looking for a bed within 300 yards, single-lung hits, neck and shoulder shots and especially paunch hits.

After all these years of guiding elk hunters and pursuing my own bowhunting success, I've seen my share of good and bad shot scenarios, fortunately keeping my own blunders to a minimum, though I've certainly lost a couple. I remember a B&C-quality, rump-shot bull that dropped dead after only 200 yards, leaving a blood trail behind a child could have followed. I've witnessed a seemingly perfect quartering hit turn into a seven-mile, all day trailing job with no reward to show when darkness fell. I've recovered some tough ones, even a couple gut-shot bulls, lost a couple I would've bet big money on immediately following the shot.

MAGNUM MENTALITY

I've said it often enough that it's become nearly hackneyed by my own use: I'd rather guide a fellow toting a .270 deer rifle he shoots well than the dude with a

Opposite page: This is the stuff that elk-hunting dreams are made of; a monstrous bull broadside at reasonable range. Are you prepared for the challenge?

You don't need a "magnum" bow set-up to cleanly tag an elk, though certain equipment choices help you succeed.

brand-new super magnum he's deathly afraid of. A certain segment of outdoor writers have put forth the proposition that elk should be hunted with nothing short of a .375 H&H Magnum; a viable Cape buffalo cartridge. The problem is few deer hunters have experience with such big, hard-kicking cartridges. This magnum mentality has also infiltrated our bowhunting ranks. I've witnessed all too many archers unable to fight a string back to anchor during the sapping excitement of a close encounter with a trophy bull. I've had as many spook nearby elk with wild, arm-sweeping draw cycles that covered a good portion of the compass. It's easy enough to understand where this heavy draw-weight mentality comes from. To be American is to believe bigger is better, more is best. Add the male ego to the mix and things quickly get out of hand; pulling heavy-duty draw weight worn like a badge of honor. The guy relating his draw weight puffs his chest out a bit as he tells about it.

A first-time or once-in-a-while elk hunter draws a tag and immediately believes he must pull an 80-pound bow. If you can confidently handle 80 pounds, that's wonderful, as there's no such thing as directing too much energy toward elk. I'd bet, though, that realistically, few archery hunters can actually handle such draw weight. Truth be known, with today's modern, more efficient compound bow designs you no longer actually need ultra-heavy poundage to get the job done. The majority of hunters draw 65 pounds because it creates more than enough energy to cleanly take the 150-pound whitetail or mule deer they bowhunt closer to home but is also quite adequate for bowhunting elk. And draw weight is only portion to the complete picture. I've killed nearly all of my elk with 70 pounds, a weight I find comfortable even on cold whitetail stands, but also necessary to get the smoothest release from modern, high letoff cams with my preferred finger release. I've guided more than one woman pulling 45 to 50 pounds (and shorter power stroke/draw length) who took bulls cleanly with a single shot.

BOOSTING ENERGY

That said; if you are currently wielding standard 55- to 60-pound whitetail energy, working up to a heavier draw weight is not a bad idea for the biggest bulls. This means adding 10 pounds to beginning draw weight over a three- or four-month period, during the course of a summer off-season, in other words. Beware that taking too big a bite in too short a time can lead to physical injury keeping you from practicing for weeks or months. Keep the ego in check and be patient. Like working to increase your bench-press maximum, work up slowly or risk serious injury.

More importantly, drawing a bow weight that you are not comfortable with can invite debilitating target panic. Target panic is the basic fear of missing, but can manifest itself in other forms as well. One of these is an uncontrollable urge to end discomfort, get rid of that string while holding back too much bow weight. Too, it's difficult to shoot accurately with quivering muscles. Bumping draw weight might also mean purchasing a new bow, purchasing one with a peak weight of 70 pounds, say, backing off the limb bolts to create an initial draw weight you can comfortably handle (one turn normally equals four pounds). After a couple weeks add a half turn to each limb bolt and start again.

While boosting draw weight is welcomed for big-bodied elk, don't handicap yourself by toting a bow you can't draw comfortably.

COMFORTABLE MAXIMUM

Comfortable shooting means pointing your bow directly at the target and smoothly pulling it straight back to full draw. It also means an ability to hold on target steadily for up to 30 seconds.

These are two important qualifiers, especially while bowhunting elk. Pointing your bow straight at the target and bringing it back in one fluid motion creates the least amount of attention-grabbing movement; certainly something that will give you an edge while shooting at a herd bull surrounded by milling cows. Being able to hold your bow at anchor, steadily, for 30 seconds or longer is also a boon. These scenarios crop up surprisingly often. Bowhunting elk is a dynamic pastime, especially while dogging bugling bulls or stalking.

Here are some examples: You draw on a walking bull and he suddenly stalls with his vitals behind a tree, but his head, and eyes, remain clear and able to take it all in. Letting down now is not an option unless you wish to alert your prize and send him packing. So you wait. A bull responding to a call comes in head on (always a risky shot). You have wisely achieved full draw before that bull cleared brush. Onward he marches, offering no shot but he's heart-poundingly close, in the wide open, needing only to turn slightly to give you a slam-dunk opportunity. So you wait.

In all likelihood your present whitetail or 3-D rig (as long as it is not candy-apple red!) likely provides ample elk energy. Yet, quality elk tags become more difficult to obtain every year. A tag in a prime area may be your one big shot at trophy antlers for years to come. Making the best of limited opportunities becomes important to success. Factors such as range, shot angle, tricky shooting obstacles,

Quality practice is important to elk hunting success. One of the best ways to become more proficient is shooting life-like 3-D targets.

all conspire to foil success. I'm not advocating taking chances or pushing the limits of your abilities. More energy doesn't turn a bad shot into a killing one, it simply gives you confidence to take a quartering shot, knowing your arrow will drive home, flattens trajectory to make a small shooting window more useful, delivers the goods with authority on longer shots that can arise in more open Southwest hotspots.

If you have already reached your maximum in regards to draw weight, leave well enough alone.

IT'S ABOUT ENERGY

In general, I'd call 60 to 65 foot pounds plenty of energy for big bull elk. I would call 70 to 75 a safer bet when the chips are down; especially on those tricky quartering shots. Today's modern compound bows make meeting these minimums nearly automatic. While certainly not taking in all the factors involved, the easiest way to measure potential effectiveness on game is by determining foot pounds of Kinetic energy. This is fairly simple, but does require a chronograph to determine arrow speed. The formula follows: Velocity squared (arrow speed multiplied by arrow speed) multiplied by arrow mass (finished weight, including point weight and all added accessories such as nock, insert, vanes/feathers and wraps), divided by 450,240.

A word of caution here: How you arrive at these numbers can make a huge difference between success and failure in worst-case scenarios. A lightweight arrow shot at blazing-fast speed can create the required numbers, but remember that such an arrow might not survive an impact with massive bone. Broadheads must also be up to snuff, made for penetration and dependability under the worst conditions. At the other extreme you might create the magic numbers by lobbing an extra-heavy arrow at slower speed. This handicaps you with a looping trajectory that can make threading an arrow through tight brush more difficult.

BALANCED EQUIPMENT

Day in and day out a more conservative setup—call it a middle-ground compromise—is most appealing for dealing with the widest variety of elk-hunting situations. What this means is a bow and arrow combination that gives you ample penetration on even less-than-ideal shot angles, like those dicey quartering shots again, while also providing the speed necessary to make the best of a longer shot or smaller gap in vegetation. If you know certainly that shot ranges in the country you hunt will average toward the shorter end, a heavier, slower arrow can certainly prove better for driving deeply into vitals, but I like to keep my options open. Short ranges often mean tight vegetation, and a flatter arrow simply leaves more options open when desperately seeking an elusive window of opportunity.

When it comes to bowhunting modern elk there really is no other arrow choice but carbon. Carbon is inherently tougher, less apt to break or splinter after impacts with unforgiving bone, and tracks broadheads most precisely following impact to provide the deepest possible penetration. By "track" I mean they recover more quickly from the flex of a hard impact, following the broadhead straight through the wound channel instead of slapping those walls to shed precious energy through friction. "Middle-ground" in the realm of modern carbon translates into shafts in the eight to 10 grains per inch (gpi) range, combined with a solid 100- to 125-grain broadhead. Overall, the toughest package at these weights generally include shafts with layered carbon construction, as well as those with protective camouflage outer layers. Aluminum provides the weight, but carbon simply offers a penetration and durability edge.

HEAVYWEIGHT PAYLOADS

Heavier gpi arrows certainly have their merits. Laser range finders make sure hits at longer ranges with even "slow" arrows easier. Is there a compound-toting archer who doesn't utilize a range finder today? If you don't own a laser range finder, get one, or you have no business taking shots farther than 35 yards. Carbon arrows in the 11- to 15-gpi class assures deep penetration, and also offer the most indestructible shafts possible, adding insurance when something goes terribly wrong. Hunting from water-holes, or calling in congested cover, can assure intimate shots, situations where heavier arrows shine. Heavier carbon normally involve thicker, more durable wall thickness, certainly welcomed for ruggedness, but camouflage or wood-grain finishes also tend to add to this mass (and toughness).

With the traditional bows I started with and find myself gravitated to more often as the years pass, a heavy carbon arrow (in relation to correct deflection/spine) is really your only viable option. Longbows and recurves simply can't muster the energy of even a conservative compound. Pulling too much traditional weight is a sure avenue to ruin. Heavy carbons and a razor-sharp, true cut-on-contact broadhead are the very best choice; as well as more careful shot selection and placement. Use woods if that is important to you, but know that they will not penetrate as deeply as modern carbon. Wood-grain carbons offer amazingly realistic graphics today's, fooling even the most snobbish observer...

Of course, arrow names and brands come and go, so using specific brands and labels isn't practical here. The only real important detail is the numbers, the gpi ratings in particular in relation to spine. Anything lighter may give you added speed, but sacrifices durability. In general, for elk in particular, I've come to prefer new-generation carbon owning lower outside diameters and thicker walls, the diameter of standard broadhead ferrules fitting snugly inside the shaft. The small diameters help buck a crosswind, penetrate deeper than anything currently on the market and are literally tough as nails. The snug interior ferrule fit also adds to reliability and precise broadhead alignment. It will be interesting to see how it will be possible to improve on this design, so far as the ultimate elk arrow is concerned.

TERMINAL TACKLE

Broadhead selection as it directly applies to bowhunting elk is sure to stir heated debate around any campfire. Every archer owns preconceived notions and preferences based on good or bad experiences. After witnessing everything good and bad possible in broadhead performance while guiding a couple decades of archery

Movement while drawing a bow can send wary bull elk packing. Choose a draw weight you can pull straight back smoothly.

hunters I've certainly developed some dogmatic notions. All I can really do is offer my personal biases and leave it at that. You don't have to agree with me.

With all due respect to the companies who manufacture them, while there are mechanical designs that will "get'er done," I outright skip them while bowhunting elk. When setting up a personal elk rig burning speed is not my goal, "burning speed" open to interpretation based on individual tuning skills, but in my definition includes any arrow exceeding 280 fps. There are simply too many rugged, straight-shooting fixed-blade heads to choose from. I've guided extensively for an outfitter (one of the most successful in New Mexico's Gila region) who flat-out prohibits mechanicals in his elk camps. Any long-time elk outfitter/guide can share a multitude of horror stories in regards to mechanical broadheads applied to elk, and negative experiences always loom larger than positive.

I'll choose a bullet-proof, cutting-tip replaceable blade with conservative cutting diameters (1- to 1 ⅛-inch) or a modern cut-on-contact design every time. I've killed at least two elk where a nail-tough cut-on-contact saved my butt on accidental lower-shoulder hits. Between them these hits averaged only eight inches of penetration, perhaps just enough to poke a hole in the heart wall and put the bull down. Sacrificing a single inch could have resulted in tragic results. Cut-on-contact replaceable-blade models have only recently appeared, razor inserts mounted at the nose to start penetration off right. High-tech heads with traditional cut-on-contact lines have also enjoyed a resurgence, engineered to tight tolerances and constructed of space-age materials to add accuracy and retain the toughness of classic one-piece-welded heads of old. I don't need to offer brand names and models here. Follow these guidelines and you'll seldom be disappointed.

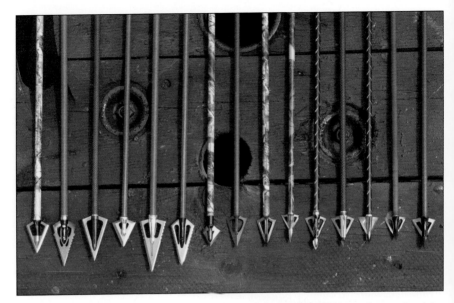

Broadheads designed for penetration and dependability are important to elk-hunting success. Cut-on-contact designs are normally best.

ROUGH & TUMBLE DEPENDABILITY

While this is primarily a discussion of energy and its relation to cleanly harvesting a very big animal, how you set up your elk rig can also make or break your hunt. And I guess, excusing the pun, that "break" is the key word here. Elk hunting is treacherous by nature. Exhausted hunters toss perfectly-tuned bows in pickup truck beds to bounce beside shovels and jacks and spare tires. Loose rock sends a hunter, and his bow, tumbling down a steep incline. An archer trips on a dark trail and drops his bow in order to catch himself and avoid injury. It's also difficult to ignore the fact that the nearest bow shop is likely located hours away, if the owner is not away bowhunting elk himself…

The elk rig should be assembled like the brick outhouse in tornado country; bulletproof and able to withstand prolonged abuse. Choose sights with highly-protected pins, preferably backed by fiber optics that make low-light shots (when the biggest bulls most often appear) feasible. Arrow rests should include solid lockdowns and rugged milled parts. Serve peeps in tightly and super glue them in place. Loc-Tite and super glue, in fact, are the elk hunter's best friends. Once my elk rig is tuned to perfection, I lock everything down permanently. I've ruined more perfectly good sights and rests with super glue than I can count, making them useful for only that single bow forever after, but I'm not one to baby my equipment. A bow is a tool, nothing more, and I would really rather not have to think about it when I'm far from civilization. When my shooting goes off I know it's me and not my equipment that's to blame.

Even so, I always carry spare parts; strings, cables, sights, sight pins, rests, peeps and so on. I also carry a compact portable bow press and assure it operates properly with my particular bow (parallel-limbed bows are making this more difficult all the time). I use a permanent marker to scribe important measurements right onto my bow square so I can see instantly if a string or cable has stretched. This includes not only nocking-point location, but brace height and where buss cables cross. I mark all important contact points with white correction fluid and ink a straight line across that patch of white. If something moves, I know it at a glance.

Too, while elk aren't the string-jumpers whitetails are, it still pays to have a silent bow. This is especially true of unnatural noise that occurs before you even get a shot off. Pad every conceivable arrow contact point on the riser shelf, the bottom of the pin guard, even the edges of your bow quiver where arrows are removed, with adhesive-backed foam or fleece to prevent metallic clicks. I don't even need to talk about bow silencing (which seems to be all the rage) other than to say take advantage of it all, from basic string silencers, to active stabilizers and limb, cable-slide and accessory dampeners.

GET WITH THE PROGRAM

Consistent success on trophy elk comes down to shooting well with your chosen equipment, and that often boils down to shooting well at longer ranges. Heavy hunting pressure, the special challenges of dogging bugling bulls surrounded by a multitude of cows, all add up to shots that can prove well beyond average in the whitetail woods. Extending your range should be part of preparing for any western elk hunt, while still adhering to a personal comfort zone, listening to your conscience or heeding a good or bad feeling before releasing any arrow. It's up to each archery hunter to determine his personal limitations but special practice can help you gain the confidence needed to become competent at longer ranges.

EXTENDING MAXIMUM RANGE

For the sake of argument, let's agree that maximum effective range should be determined by consistent five-out-of-five shot groups inside an eight-inch paper plate (six inches smaller than the average bull's vitals areas but allowing a good margin of error for factors such as wind, brush, low light and especially buck fever). Let's also assume that group size increases by 20-percent for every five yards of range added. Applying this logic means four-inch groups at 25 yards translate into about five inches at 30 yards, six and a half at 40 and eight at 50 yards, under ideal conditions. This theoretically keeps you in the vital area of any elk out to 50 yards. But say your 25-yard group is seven inches. At 30 yards you're facing nearly eight and a half inches, 11 inches at 40, 14 at 50. When applied to an actual elk kill zone it's easy to determine if your shooting is up to snuff for an assured kill at any range. Of course, there's no real way to measure the effect buck fever or target panic (fear of missing) has on actual bowhunting accuracy. When you find yourself "losing it" mentally you can expect to lose 50-percent or more of your effective range.

Laser range finders have definitely blurred the lines considerably. Without a range finder your ability to make accurate range judgments past 35 yards is

Quality practice includes learning to make quick decisions under pressure. Small-game hunting is one good way to hone those skills.

impaired greatly. Knowing the range absolutely makes longer shots easier, turns long-range shooting into a whole new ballgame. Laser technology is getting cheaper and more sophisticated with each passing season as optic companies compete for business. Scan modes and tilt compensation are now standard issue.

But the question remains. How far is far enough? As an elk guide most of my frustration stemmed from eastern whitetail hunters unable to take animals at average western ranges; say 40 to 50 yards. Consider that doubling your effective range essentially quadruples the square yardage covered around your position (wind direction aside). That instantly places considerably more elk within reach.

Still, while I have the ability to consistently direct arrows into the softball-sized center spot of my bag target at 70 yards, I very rarely take such shots at game. I know, though, a wounded animal needing a finisher at such range is not immune to my arrows. Too, being confident at 70 yards makes 50 a lot easier. The decision to shoot or hold off hinges directly on the animal itself. An animal moving or agitated isn't a candidate for a longer shot; while a bedded or relaxed animal permits such range, provided you are truly qualified. This means honestly reading each situation before making the decision to shoot. Self control is in order. If conditions aren't perfect, pass the shot. No matter how big the antlers!

HONING SHOOTING SKILLS

Extending effective range means first stepping well behind your accustomed shooting stake. This may seem basic enough, but most archers prefer to remain inside their comfort zone, avoiding failure or losing arrows. A large pile of sand, dirt bank, or wall of inexpensive straw quickly creates a confidence-boosting backstop to place your bag, block or 3-D target before while gaining proficiency. You shouldn't fear missing your target, and your neighbors certainly shouldn't fear stray arrows. Creating a large backstop alleviates apprehension, providing comfort when stepping back, and the inevitable stray shots that will follow in the beginning. You will miss. If you're not, you're not pushing yourself, not learning.

When you first begin extending yourself you'll quickly learn that small shooting flaws loom large. Loose groups at 20 yards turn into scattergun embarrassments at 50. The single most important advice I can give is to execute complete and thorough follow-through with each shot. As range grows longer so will anxiety. The normal reaction is to jerk the bow down to watch the arrow fly. This is a common pitfall. Strive to aim diligently from release until the arrow thumps the target. Attempt to keep your pin on target throughout the shot. Imagine you can direct your arrow in flight by concentrating hard enough. Of course, this is impossible, but encourages execution of proper follow-through.

And, of course, follow-through means little if your bow isn't properly tuned and you have glaring flaws in other areas of shooting form. Bad tuning, again, looms larger as you move away from the target. Other common shooting flaws include release-aid trigger punching, bow torque, equipment that doesn't fit properly and even bad eyesight. Strive for a surprise release, seek professional assistance at a local pro shop, have your eyes checked and keep eye-glass prescriptions updated.

Signs of sure torque are chronic left/right misses. Left misses can mean top-right bow cant at full draw; right misses choking or "palming" the handle on release. Install a wrist sling and use a proper loose grip, allowing the bow to balance in the web of your hand. If your bow doesn't want to sit up straight at full draw, install a stabilizer that forces it to do so. Side-mounted or off-set stabilizers are especially handy here, balancing sights or bow quivers that can cause a bow to list at full draw. Many bows are now equipped with rear mounts perfect for a stubby stabilizer

Competitive 3-D is one of the best ways to help the hunter better learn to convert under pressure.

Hit an elk well and they go down quickly. Wound one and you have a long trail on your hands. Good shooting is a must.

that alleviates front-heavy bows from pulling forward at full draw. Play with various options until your bow sits level in your hand effortlessly.

In the beginning evaluate your shooting critically to determine weaknesses. Prioritize each, working on only one weakness at a time. Only after one problem is under control should you move on the next. For example, recently my number-one problem was hurrying each shot. I spent a couple weeks working on slowing down and varying my shot rhythm. Only then did I begin working into a more repeatable, solid anchor. Afterwards I looked harder at hand placement and grip. Always work toward perfection in every aspect of shooting form. We're also talking quality practice, not quantity. Make each and every shot count, not something to be ticked off against a grand total. Borrowing from the Zen Buddhists; perfection is a path, not a destination.

Also spend the majority of your practice time shooting from longer ranges. This is a sure way to gain confidence. As I've hinted, becoming proficient at 60 or 70 yards makes lesser ranges chip shots. After closer pins are solidly sighted I find little reason to shoot at close range, other than warming up muscles before serious practice begins. If I can hold an eight-inch group at 70, when that big bull pauses broadside at 40, I know he's all mine.

SHOOTING RESPONSIBLY

Though laser range finders makes all this possible, precautions are still in order. As ranges stretch a steadier hand and a good measure of common sense are needed to assure the ranges your range finder provides are valid. Don't rely on a single range finder pop when readying for a long-range shot. Get a second or third opinion, or otherwise assure that the first range you received is correct and not a tree branch or grass stem surrounding your target.

Ranging obstacles are a major pitfall. Lasers don't discriminate between vegetation and animal hide. They hit the first thing they encounter and bounce back instantly. This makes ranging an elk in thronged oak brush or chest-high grass, for instance, dicey. Use a modern range finder's scan mode to your advantage in these situations, and exercise a certain amount of horse-sense. This makes old-fashioned, eye-ball range-judging skills as important as ever. If your range finder tells you 35 yards and your gut tells you that elk is more like 45, a warning light should go off. You need to give the range finder another try to insure you're not mistaken. Scan modes are a Godsend in tight situations, panning across your target until a viable range is acquired.

Long-range shooting comes with responsibilities. You can't afford anything but the most precisely-tuned equipment. You must commit the time necessary to practice longer and harder. But most of all, you must apply the discipline necessary when a shot just doesn't feel right. Purchasing the best in modern equipment makes longer shots possible. Getting yourself up to speed to shoot as well as this equipment is capable requires more dedication to detail and smart practice; a price that can pay huge when a bull of a lifetime steps into a shooting lane at a longer-than-average range.

Even the biggest bulls are not invincible. Straight shooting at longer-than-average distances is what it is all about.

So what is big? If you wish to take a Rocky Mountain bull that will "make book," to surpass Pope & Young's 260-inch minimum, look for these attributes: First, that bull will normally wear six points per side. There are 5x5 bulls that will occasionally make archery record-books, but 6x6s are much more common on those pages. Because brow tines can become easily confused, count back from the sword point for a faster count. The sword is always the forth point, and normally the longest and easiest to locate quickly. Look for an inside spread at least four inches outside each side of an average mature bull's 22-inch-wide shoulders. Finally, look for main beams at least a yard long. When walking broadside, antler tips should reach the end of his rib cage. While feeding, antler tips will reach the top of the shoulders. Of course, a 6x6 with exceptionally short tines could fall short, so make sure most of the tines are better than 10 inches.

Regarding Roosevelt elk, a 225-inch minimum doesn't seem like much to the bowhunter raised on Rocky Mountain bulls but is certainly a worthwhile prize. A record beater will basically look like a solid 5x5 with decent mass and tine length.

So what is really big? A Rocky Mountain bull 100 inches greater than P&Y minimum is a behemoth to most serious elk hunters. How do you tell a 350 to 360 bull from a younger 320 or 330? The difference is in the details, specifically mass and tine length. A 330 bull may wear an impressive frame, but not the score-boosting details of a behe-moth. Look for bases appearing difficult to reach around with both hands. Brows should nearly reach the nose tip. Pay special attention to the third point, normally the weakest tine on any elk rack. Exceptional thirds often mean everything else follows. Finally, look for deep "whale tails" reaching to the withers. A 6x6's fifth point and main beam create a rear fork, or whale tail. If deep forks are evident, you're normally looking at a behemoth. There's much made of 7x7 bulls when in fact most of the biggest bulls are 6x6s. Some 7x7s obviously qualify for behemoth status, but only if everything else described above follows.

While any book Roosevelt qualifies as a behemoth, being one of the most difficult of all bowhunting trophies to tag, a truly big bull is more difficult to define. While a Roosevelt that would pass Pope & Young Rocky Mountain minimums would qualify as a really big bull to most, the fact remains bowhunters regularly score on bulls bettering Boone & Crockett's 295-inch minimum. Minimum scores are most often established based on total listing numbers, so relative to the much more popular Rocky Mountain, really big in Roosevelt country can mean a bull that literally blows even B&C minimums away.

In the end, what constitutes a "trophy" is in the eye of the beholder. Don't allow arbitrary numbers to define your hunt. If it rattles your cage—be that a 4x5 bull scoring 195 inches, or something much larger—don't let anyone else's opinions dictate your pursuit of happiness.

I'd like all my shots at elk to be 20 yards, broadside, but when I've dogged a behemoth for days or weeks, I've trained extensively to convert on that opportunity if a bull pauses long enough at a range much longer. The most important aspect just might be an ability to think on your feet. Long, careful practice provides the confidence needed to make this easier.

MOST IMPORTANTLY

Once you've honed your shooting skills, the one bit of advice I'd drive home is to stay away from that shoulder! Perhaps it's 3-D archery and its scoring rings that bear no reality to the real world, but it seems too many archery hunters want to crowd that shoulder, looking for the "10-ring." Resist this urge. Dead center lungs is a bigger target, providing less chance of hitting that arrow-stopping shoulder. This means four to six inches behind the shoulder crease. Even a liver hit will cleanly kill an elk. There's simply no need to crowd heavy bone.

Shot angles are everything in bowhunting elk. We can't "break them down" as they are fond of relating in gun writing. Obviously, the broadside shot is what we are all looking for, offering the largest margin for error as well as the fewest large bones to deter an arrow. The problem comes when confronted by bulls angling even slightly. The old rule of thumb on quartering-away shots is to aim for the off-side, the opposite, leg. But before you do so you need to judge how much elk will have to be penetrated to get there, tossing in a realistic estimation of your equipment combination's abilities. If you have to think overly long on the matter, you're likely best advised to pass the shot. Remember, too, deflection from sturdy ribs can become as much of a factor as penetration, or lack of, on heavily-quartered shots.

Quartering-to and facing shots are the most controversial. An arrow that slips between the base of the neck and facing shoulder will certainly get the job done, but the potential for hitting bone is great. In general, much depends on how calm and confident you are when faced with such a shot, more importantly, the range. If you know without a doubt you can place your arrow just so (and have a thorough understanding of elk anatomy) I'd say go for it. If there are any qualms whatsoever, skip it. That goes for facing shots as well. They can be extremely deadly, but remember you are aiming for a softball-sized hole at best (that soft spot we all have at the junction of our neck and chest). Six inches one way or the other and your arrow finds nothing but unforgiving bone. Bulls responding to calls present this shot as often as not, tempting the frustrated hunter into making a rash decision. The decision to shoot or wait a better shot again depends on range, abilities and confidence. If the shot is beyond 20 yards, you should probably hold off. If you are shaking like a leaf, hold off. If you're experiencing any hesitation at all, hold off.

Big bulls are not the same beast as "average-sized" bulls or youngsters or cows. They're physically bigger, and worlds more tenacious. Based on toughness alone they are always more difficult to put down than young bulls or cows. It's true that your whitetail rig will typically get the job done, but when behemoth antlers are at stake why leave anything to chance? Setting up equipment for maximum yet realistic Kinetic energy punch gives you extra insurance when that long-awaited moment of truth arrives.

Chapter 13

Gearing Up

Whether bowhunting elk with a guide or on your own, operating in remote elk country requires a high degree of preparation. Just as importantly, it requires the right gear. Aside from a selection of elk calls and, of course, your basic bow and arrow setup, choosing the right gear keeps you bowhunting elk most efficiently. There seem to be two approaches in this direction; the minimalist line, and something quite the opposite. Some hunters seem inclined to bring it all, tossing in this and that to the point of sheer burden borne from a fear of forgetting or needing something. My own approach depends entirely on where I'm hunting, how far I will get from my truck or camp, and prevailing weather conditions most of all.

ACCESSIBLE FANNY-PACKS

While bowhunting elk in areas well interspersed with roads, when I know certainly I'll see my truck before lunchtime (or immediately after dark following evening hunts), I carry a compact, shoulder-harness-equipped fanny-pack (normally a Rancho Safari Catquiver which also serves my arrow quiver). In this I pack two knives (which saves pausing to sharpen a dulled edge in the middle of frantic field dressing), folding diamond sharpener, compact folding saw (for saw-

Getting lost can bring any elk hunt to a screeching halt. Today's quality GPS units make keeping your way easy.

ing off elk legs or creating hanging stubs for elk quarters beneath a shading tree), parachute cord (for hanging quarters in the cooling shade or tying an elk leg off while field dressing in a difficult spot while alone), game bags and a small can of black pepper (to deter egg-laying blowflies), camera, minimal first-aid items, spare

Opposite page: Choosing the right gear makes for a more efficient, thus a more enjoyable, elk hunt. This means more time hunting and less time fussing over camp and equipment.

bowstrings, broadheads, arrow nocks and Judo points/rubber blunts, a couple water bottles (one of these including a built-in water filter) and my lunch (a sandwich, apple and granola bars, for instance).

No matter where I'm bowhunting elk I always carry a GPS unit, compass and topographical maps (if for nothing else than to see where a herd of elk is headed), fire-starting necessities, spare batteries and a compact headlamp (because skinning an elk in the dark with even a compact flashlight clamped in your teeth literally sucks). I choose head-lamps/flashlights that accept the same batteries as my GPS unit, so power can be robbed from one or the other in emergencies. If rain is in the forecast I lash light-weight rain gear to the

During the average elk hunt it will rain. Quiet, high-quality rain gear is an important ingredient to successful elk hunting

outside with provided compression straps. In all, my entire keep-it-simple kit might weigh five to 10 pounds, allowing me to travel light.

LOADED DAY-PACKS

When elk take me into more remote or rugged country; places where I'm more likely to remain out an entire day, where if I manage to kill an elk it will most likely prove far from a road, when there's the real possibility of sleeping beneath the stars because I'm too tired to hike back 10-plus miles (or just because I'm into hot elk and the weather's fine), my pack becomes a bit more burdensome. Nasty weather conditions, especially in unpredictable high-altitude haunts, should also indicate a more careful approach, which always means more gear. The basic kit described above is still part of this program, but comfort and especially safety mean packing additional gear.

Any time help is far away it's smart to carry a compact first-aid kit. For those purposeful or unintentional nights out I pack a fleece vest or pullover (if I haven't started out with one as a layer in the cool of morning), added protection against night chill and doubling as a makeshift pillow, and paper-thin but super warm silk long-johns, which take up very little space. I always carry a spare pair of dry socks. A tightly-folded sheet of high-mill plastic is easily fashioned into water-shedding shelter, though more recently I invested in a waterproof, 1.5-pound one-man bivy. I've given up on thin space blankets, toting a feather-weight down "bicycling" bag that stuffs down to wine-bottle dimensions and includes a 40-degree comfort rating, warm enough to get me through even a frosty night if I sleep in layered clothing. My kit is completed by a compact, electronic-ignition backpacking stove powered by a butane/propane mix, tea bags, fuel bottle and folded stove fitting inside a lightweight titanium cup and a couple packages of lightweight dehydrated food and plenty of snacks.

I've spent many nights where darkness found me, alone in wild elk country, while toting a pack equipped this way. Total weight comes to something like 25 pounds maximum (including hunting gear to be discussed below), but keeps me relatively comfortable, and in worst-case scenarios, when weather turned rough, alive. I find this kind of hunting allows a brand of freedom difficult to come by

Every elk hunter must be prepared to deal with a large quantity of meat, and get the job done quickly. Daypack gear should reflect this need.

today, even therapeutic qualities that keep a harried man sane. The approach is best employed in areas where ready water is available, because toting what is needed into dry areas can essentially double pack weight and slow you down considerably. Thus, my filter-capped water bottle becomes highly important. Choose your fanny- or day-pack with care. Skip discount-store book bags disguised in camouflage, choosing instead something actually made for hunting. This should include contoured, heavily-padded shoulder straps, waist belt and back panels, plus a reasonable degree of weatherproof qualities. While a good number of packs are constructed of waterproof materials, few are actually 100-percent dependable because it's impossible (or simply too costly) to seam seal them. You can increase their reliability by spraying seams liberally with a silicon-based waterproofing agent. It goes without saying that a bowhunting pack should be shelled in something quiet like fleece, wool or synthetic suede. If extreme weather is an issue, stash gear inside Zip-Lok bags before slipping them in your pack.

ELK HUNTING OPTICS

Aside from the basic bow and arrow setup and loaded daypack, binoculars are the archer's most important piece of equipment. They are used to find distant elk while stalking or scouting, to size up a bull right below a tree stand in low light, and in the case of range finders, to determine the exact range before every bowhunting shot. Both come in myriad models and configurations, filling every bowhunting niche and budget. When it comes to serious elk hunting, though, higher-end models are worth their weight in gold. Buying the best you can possibly afford (even a bit more than you can afford) assures years of trouble-free use and improved performance.

High-quality, large-objective binos gather more light, reveal a bugling bull at the edge of legal shooting hours, are worlds more steady than the shirt-pocket models eastern stand hunters might have chosen in the past. What you choose depends mostly on personal preference, but also your primary mode of operation or habitat encountered most often while bowhunting elk. While waiting over water or dogging bulls over endless miles, something like an 8x32 might prove best suited. They're less burdensome, yet provide good light transmission at the dim edges of day. In more open country, or for classic spot-and-stalk hunting, the standard has become binoculars in the 10x40 or 10x42 class.

Even manufacturers whose product lines once consisted of little but budget-priced compacts have begun to introduce solid roof prism designs in the 8x40 to 10x42 category. I never thought I would see the day of $500 mid-range glass, or a $2,000 top end for that matter, but who could ever have envisioned $40,000 pickup trucks? Whether discussing binoculars or range finders, waterproof, shock-proof qualities are of utmost importance. Both will eventually become wet or be dropped. For years of trouble-free use, for dependability under the roughest conditions, sticking to mid to upper echelon glass saves you money in the long run. With optics you certainly get what you pay for.

DRESS FOR SUCCESS

Fall and elk hunting are synonymous to my mind, so when late August or September bowhunting seasons roll around, fall has arrived to my mind. This is a false premise, of course, because even September in most of the West is technically a summer month, complete with simmering heat. While frosty mornings hint of coming fall, soaring midday temperatures quickly dismisses that notion. This really hits home staggering to a waiting truck under a searing noontime sun or sweating up a steep ridge to circle a traveling elk herd. Hunting comfortably, and safely, during warm early seasons keeps you functioning longer, pushing farther.

It's said that clothing makes the man, but the right clothing especially makes the elk hunter. Warm early seasons are the only time cotton duds really make sense. There's certainly no shortage of cotton goods, and accounts for so many hypothermic hunters when true fall does arrive, or after a sudden thunderstorm. Cotton does wick body moisture, but also dries slowly. This can be welcomed when temperatures soar but a small breeze acts as an evaporative cooler. The same action that results in hypothermia during cold weather actually cools you off during warm days.

"Moisture management" has become the catch phrase in modern outdoor clothing. While cotton can act as air con-

Bowhunting elk is a highly physical dodge no matter where you hunt. Staying properly fueled and hydrated is extremely important.

ditioning, it can also leave you feeling wet and clammy, shivering after even a short thundershower. High-tech base layers are specifically designed to wick moisture off the skin, moving it outward where it can dry faster. The very best moisture management layers keep you feeling cool and dry even after sweating heavily; also warmer when wet. Many base layers now also include antimicrobial elements to retard human odors at the source. This is important several days into a physical elk hunt. The best are impregnated with silver to kill odor-causing bacteria on the skin, bonded or woven into the fabric fibers to last for years. Others include odor-filtering activated charcoal combined with anti-bacterial elements.

Of course, the West's high country means anything's possible. While warm weather prevails, August and September can also provide days with cold rain and even early snow. It pays to be prepared for anything. Layering is the key to comfort in fluctuating temperatures. Outer layers of soft fleece or wool make the quietest stalking gear, clothing that won't create game-spooking rustles. It also pays to keep a set of packable rain gear handy. Modern materials have made even 100-percent waterproof models lighter and bowhunting quiet.

REALISTIC SCENT CONTROL

I once would have excluded activated-charcoal, odor-eliminating clothing from any discussion regarding bowhunting early-season elk, because they simply proved too warm, especially while charging up and down steep mountains. This is no longer true, the major manufactures in this category of hunting duds now offering scent-containment clothing that breathes more readily to remain comfortable in hot weather, while also working to filter offending human odors before they reach the astute noses of your quarry. In modern elk hunting every little bit helps, and controlling your odor in the shifting, fickle breezes of broken elk country is certainly an advantage.

Included in this program as well are scent-elimination sprays, powders, soaps and underarm deodorants. When dealing with educated elk, adopting the scent-control obsessions of the average whitetail hunter reaps big rewards. Bathing regularly can be difficult in average elk terrain, but is worth the extra effort. A handy stream or stock tank serves in a pinch, but a portable solar shower is better. These black-backed bags hold up to five gallons of water, placed in a sunny area before departing for a morning hunt to enjoy sun-heated water on your return. Hung from a horizontal tree limb with a clean tarp beneath, it's the next best thing to your home shower. I generally shun camp trailers, refusing to be tied down to one, but that hot shower at the end of a sweaty day just might justify them completely.

ESSENTIAL HYDRATION

When it's warm and you're running hard, hydration should be constantly on your mind. Even mild dehydration prevents you from operating at peak performance, whereas severe cases can pose potential health hazards. Many modern daypacks include up to two water-bottle pouches for this very reason. As I've mentioned, my lightweight water-filtering bottle allows me to take advantage of questionable water sources when I need hydration on the fly, without worry of ingesting harmful bacteria or amoebas that can bring a screeching halt to any archery hunt. The latest thing is daypack-compatible hydration systems, stealth-conscience, no-slosh bladders with attached drink tubes for ready hydration on the go.

Water's a good thing, but when you're working hard, sweating freely, it's a good idea to fill your hydration containers with sports drinks. Essential ingredients such as potassium and sodium help reduce muscle fatigue and allow recovery from stress more quickly than water alone. When essential mineral and salt reserves are exhausted through heavy sweating, large quantities of water alone can actually cause stomach cramps, even vomiting that further exasperates dehydration and lethargy.

PREVENTATIVE MAINTENANCE

Early-season hunters should also think in terms of protection from all-day sun. Skin cancer aside, keeping UV rays off exposed skin simply reduces dehydration and painful sunburn. Don't be an idiot; applying sunscreen doesn't make you a sissy. A minimum 30 SPF-rated sunscreen slathered liberally to exposed skin, especially the nape, nose and ears, reduces potential problems. Thin cotton gloves and a wide-brim hat are also wise precautions.

It would be difficult to guess how many hunters in my guiding career I've seen end their hunt prematurely due to wrecked feet. Stone bruises and sprains and, more commonly, blisters of various dimensions, have accounted for these unfulfilled dreams. Healthy feet are as important to the elk hunter as a straight-shooting bow or quality optics. Without healthy feet you're simply not in the game.

A short stint in the world of week-long adventure racing showed me unequivocally that healthy feet separated finishing teams from dropouts. In wild, rough elk country you get there by walking and climbing and scrambling over long miles. You close the distance by putting one foot in front of the other.

THESE BOOTS WERE MADE FOR BOWHUNTING

Taking care of your feet means first choosing quality boots suited to the terrain you're bowhunting. This can mean heavy-duty ankle support in treacherous terrain, keeping feet dry in wet conditions, warm when it's cold, cool when it's hot. A good elk-hunting boot might represent some combination of all of these factors. Boots should provide support in areas you need it most; be that arches or ankles, and should protect your feet from sharp rock, day-long pounding under a heavy pack, or cactus spines. Too, the Southwest foothill boot may carry different criteria than those needed for trekking above timberline in Colorado high country, something else entirely for bowhunting Roosevelt elk in the wet Pacific Northwest.

A quality pair of hunting boots is an investment. Simply put, avoid discount "tennie-hiker" models for hardcore elk hunting. Also take care to get your boots fitted properly. If you are unsure of an exact boot size (including length *and* width) purchase your hunting boots only from sporting-goods outlets where trained

employees are on hand to assure a perfect fit. Remember, too, not every brand is alike in size and fit. For example, there's a particular brand that I order in size 13 D to get a perfect fit out of the box every time. Some other brands don't fit me quite so perfectly. Find a brand that works for you and stick with it.

I feel silly saying so because it seems blatantly obvious; but for God's sake, thoroughly break in hunting boots before venturing into the field and subjecting your feet to real punishment. This should be obvious, but the foot-sore clients I've alluded to earlier have normally failed to heed this advice, or did so only tentatively. Break-in doesn't mean a few rounds behind the lawnmower, or wearing them to the office a few days.

Blisters slow you down and can even put you out of the game. Carrying first aid supplies to deal with such contingencies is smart elk hunting.

I fill brand-new boots with warm water and leave them over night. Come morning I drain remaining water, don a heavy pair of socks, and wear them dry. This can require a couple days, but allows better conformation to my feet, and greatly speeds break-in. Once my new boots are completely dry I grease them thoroughly with a waterproofing/sealant. This prolongs life and assures stitches and seams will endure harsh treatment. Periodic cleaning and greasing is also a wise investment toward prolonged boot life.

AT THE BASE OF THE MATTER

Proper socks are another important element to healthy feet. Standard-issue cotton tube socks are a recipe for disaster, holding moisture that can cause blisters. Choose polypropylene, dual-density fleece or no-itch Merino wool, which provide required padding plus fast-wicking action. There are more good choices than ever, anything worthwhile typically setting you back from $15 to $25 per pair. This may seem excessive for a pair of socks, especially considering you'll need several pairs to carry you through a long elk hunt, but hard-working feet deserve no less.

Thin, tight-fitting liner socks are also a good idea if you are prone to blisters. Sheer silk or poly clings to feet and prevents heavier, padding socks from rubbing and chaffing. When socks become worn or saggy, replace them.

Under extremely wet conditions waterproof/breathable socks lined with Gore-Tex, or Dupont Seal Skinz socks, make a lot of sense. Both have served me well. Even waterproof boots can become flooded during a creek crossing or in heavy rains or dewy conditions when water runs down pant legs.

AVOIDING DISASTER

Keeping feet dry should be priority one by keeping outside water out and getting interior sweat moisture out. Choose boots with waterproof/breathable membranes that allow sweat to evaporate but keep moisture from seeping in. And always keep a spare pair of dry socks in your daypack, stashed inside a Zip-Lok bag, in case you find your feet wet and chaffing.

Blisters are the elk hunter's number one enemy. They can prove quite painful, even become infected to cause long-term problems. In fact, one of Teddy Roosevelt's sons died of blood poisoning on a prolonged hunting trip due to an infected blister.

Prevention is the best medicine. Savvy hunters carry adhesive-backed moleskin and apply it to feet immediately upon detecting a "hot spot." This means your boot or heavy sock rubs moleskin instead of skin. Duct tape can also serve in a pinch, applied directly to the skin over the offending area. When feet sweat heavily to make it difficult to keep moleskin in place, use cloth athletic tape, wrapping the area to keep it in place. Wrapping difficult areas such as heels, ankles, or the balls of your feet (all common hot spots) with tape can also prevent blisters. Tape or band-aids are also helpful for wrapping toes that show a proclivity to roll under adjacent digits or otherwise pinch (normally the result of boots that are too-tight or excessive socks, also long downhill descents). Wrap individual toes to prevent rubbing or to hold them in place. Keeping toenails properly trimmed can also prevent problems, cutting straight across to prevent "in-grown" toenail pain at the corners. Clean feet are also less apt to suffer problems. Wash your feet often and dry them well before donning clean socks.

If you do develop a blister, drain it only if it's causing discomfort, followed by washing the area well with soap and water; otherwise leave it alone. If a blister should break and turn raw, apply an antibiotic ointment and cover with a band-aid, then tape it over to prevent future abrasion and infection. One trick that is highly effective for protecting all types of wounds in the field is to first apply antibiotic ointment, then form a sparse bead of super glue around the wound area (leaving a quarter-inch margin), then adhere clean chamois leather over the affected area. This allows the wound to breathe and heal, while also keeping it clean and safe from further abrasion.

ELK HUNTING FUEL

A man's gotta eat. An elk hunter's gotta eat well. Long miles, rough terrain, the daily burden of toting a gear-filled pack and compound bow can quickly burn serious calories. Add high altitude and your body's furnace really kicks into over-

Camp life is one of the attractions of the average elk hunt. An efficient camp and good food give you more time to get much-needed sleep.

drive. The strain of backpacking into wilderness can put even more stress on your system. Arriving on that glassing vantage before good light arrives, reaching that bugling bull before he melts into swallowing cover, dogging a bull across endless canyons and ridges, means eating right, not just putting away empty calories.

Carbohydrates are slow-yield fuel that the body utilizes to provide long-term energy. Both weekend warriors and those going the distance through an entire elk season need ample carbohydrate fuel; starches and complex sugars found in potatoes, grains, breads, or pastas. Simple sugars provide instant pick-up, a necessary evil between meals, but provide no staying power. Fats and cholesterol are high-energy nutrients with two and a half times the energy of simple sugars, providing long-term energy, also a limited ability to repair damaged muscle tissue. But fats and cholesterol are bad for you, right? Not necessarily. When you're exerting yourself you need these components, or you're sure to physically "crash."

Proteins are important for maintenance and repair, repairing muscle damage after rigorous exercise, or skin after, say, sunburn. Proteins also contain some complex sugars for energy. Many grains contain proteins, but also legumes (beans), and especially meat. On prolonged backcountry trips, say a two-week wilderness hunt, a daily multi-vitamin helps keep mind and body sharp when not maintaining an ideal diet. That's the limit of my nutritional understanding, but it works for me. The details lay in where and how you're hunting.

TRUCK-CAMP VICTUALS

Even far from civilization a truck camp allows ice coolers full of good food. The only problems encountered are those of extensive preparation when hunting long and hard, and especially food spoilage on a prolonged hunt.

I normally pre-cook nutritious casseroles and stews and freeze them in storage containers when hunting out of my truck. This allows me delicious and nutritious meals such as green-chili pheasant enchiladas, hearty elk stew, pronghorn meatloaf, deer-meat lasagna, wild hog stir-fry—you name it. Cooking becomes no more difficult than dumping a thawed container of precooked food into a pot and warming it. Work out meals ahead of time, supplementing them with canned goods, bread or tortillas, for instance.

Camping wouldn't be the same without grilled meat. Again, start at home by placing steaks and chops in Zip-Loks, adding marinades or sauces before freezing, pulling them out of the cooler at lunch to thaw so they can go right on the fire when you return. (And of course, avoid cooking around smoky fire while wearing your scent-free hunting duds…)

Keeping cooler contents fresh, and especially frozen, requires extra attention. During high-altitude hunts when nighttime temperatures dip below freezing this can prove easy (open the cooler at night to re-freeze, close it by day to maintain what you've gained). Warmer elk hunts at lower elevations present more challenges. I use a huge 150-quart cooler, dividing it with a smaller "picnic" cooler nested inside. One side of the dividing cooler holds frozen foods beneath dry ice covered with layered newspaper or bath-towel insulation. The other side keeps

In elk hunting you get there by putting one foot in front of the other. Quality, comfortable hiking boots make the elk hunter.

Camping with friends and family, and campfires, are part of elk hunting's allure. Changing into street clothes while in camp keeps hunting duds fresh.

fruits and vegetables fresh but unfrozen or bruised from dry-ice burn. The clean picnic cooler is kept full of cube ice. This ice remains longer, which is great for cold drinks after a sweaty day of chasing elk, and the dry and cube ice feed on one another to prolong life.

Ice also lasts longer if coolers are religiously kept in shade. Use old sleeping bags to wrap coolers during warm hunts, keeping heat out and cold in. Store canned drinks such as soda and beer in separate coolers, ice added from the nearest country store as needed. Remember, adding warm drinks to fresh ice melts it more quickly.

WILDERNESS FARE

Backcountry hunts offer a completely different set of challenges. Any number of foil-pouched dehydrated foods are available that can actually prove quite delicious if you avoid suspect exotic fare. They are extremely lightweight, convenient, and for the most part, nutritious. Many lack fat content, though. One of my favorite wilderness elk spots is conspicuously void of ready drinking water, so the need for hydrating water (which must be packed in if it's not raining daily) makes dehydrated food packets impractical. In such cases military MREs (Meals Ready To Eat) are handy, and require no additional hydration. They provide energy-producing fat, and are slightly constipative, eliminating the possibility of stress dysentery during a taxing hunt.

There are a good number of inexpensive and lightweight victual alternatives to be found in the local grocery as well. Carbs are easily gained from instant mashed potatoes and rice, and oriental soup-noodle blocks. Instant oatmeal, cream of wheat and grits make a quick, filling breakfast. Add dried fruit and nuts to improve taste and nutrition. There are a good number of foil-packaged "noodles/rice & sauce" concoctions available today and most taste great. Look for selections that require adding only water for less complicated preparation. A stick of butter or small bottle of olive oil is worth the extra weight (wrapped in Zip-Loks against leakage), adding energy-giving fat and flavor.

Meat is more problematic in the backcountry. Nitrate-cured meats aren't exactly spoil-proof, but do last longer under reasonable conditions; especially if you can place them in a stream or spring to keep them cooler. These include bacon (the grease also welcomed for frying a Judo-bagged rabbit, game meat, or mountain trout), smoked sausages (not brats or Italian), and ham. On prolonged trips or during extremely warm periods choose canned ham, chipped beef, chunk chicken, salmon and foil packs of tuna, if only to add to a "rice and sauce" packet to form a complete meal while also boosting calories.

Snacks are important when on the trail. You need the calories to keep you going, and you can't exactly stop to prepare a meal when you begin to fade. Nut-laden candy bars, trail mix, dried fruit and nuts are all good quick-fuel choices. Also consider sports bars. They are normally nutritionally well balanced and worth the extra cost. Sardines and kipper snacks make super fuel, not only high-energy food that's easy to pack, but good for you in general. Jerky is also power-packed. Make your own at home from last year's deer or elk or buy the factory stuff. Eaten during the day instead of candy, jerky will keep you going longer.

Don't count on water being safe to drink from any open source, even in pristine wilderness set-

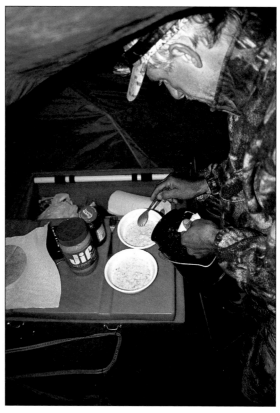

Elk hunting in rough country burns serious fuel. Eating right is just as important as being in good shape.

tings. This is especially true if beavers are present, creating the high-odds presence of giardia, or "beaver fever." Chemical tablets or a couple drops of chlorine bleach per gallon of water will suffice, but can taste awful. I prefer a backpacking filter pump for providing large quantities of camp water. They are easily found in any well-stocked sporting goods store or catalog. Drink plenty of fluids. Between hunts drink until you feel you'll burst. It's easy to get dehydrated while bowhunting elk, making you sluggish, even terribly sick.

Personally, I can do without enough sleep for several days running, but never food. I can remember several occasions when long hours stacked into days, tough terrain, early wake-ups and late nights, and poor food choices, combined to leave me feeling drained and defeated. It can keep you closer to the truck, make you surrender on a hard-won tag, even make you grumpy. Sometimes I must force myself to eat after a tough day, when nothing but sleep seems appropriate, but fuel is a must. Eating well lessens the strain of hunting hard and keeps you in the game.

THE HUNTIN' TRUCK

A common oversight is vehicle maintenance and preparation prior to an elk hunt. Getting stuck is highly common in elk country, as well as flat tires. Unimproved roads that traverse the best elk country can be rough on a vehicle, long uphill pulls in four-wheel-drive putting strain on a drive-train normally not experienced via city or highway driving, sudden ruts and rocks testing suspension like nothing else. Minor breakdowns such as a burst radiator hose, broken fan belt or busted shock absorber can loom large when the nearest mechanic or parts store is hours away.

If you hunt elk long enough eventually you will get stuck, especially if it's raining. I've stuck more trucks than I can recount, and have become exceptionally talented at getting out of tight spots. In nearly all these cases a rescue party certainly wasn't forthcoming. I was on my own. One of the most indispensable tools for un-sticking a truck is a "high-lift" jack. These are becoming more difficult to locate these days, but can

Anything's possible during a long elk hunt. Carrying tools for vehicle emergencies keeps you in the game.

often be found at most independent parts stores or farm-supply outlets. They are used to jack a truck corner high enough to stuff supporting rocks under a mired tire, to jack rocks into mushy ground until a solid base is created beneath, simply to lift a flat tire off the ground in a tricky situation involving uneven or soft ground. Believe me, the factory jack that came with your modern vehicle won't get the job done under these circumstances, designed to lift a tire off the ground just high enough to remove it and replace your spare on flat pavement.

A heavy-duty hand winch, or "come-along" in ranch speak, and plenty of heavy-duty tow straps can also get you out of tight spots. Models equipped with a "block and tackle" arrangement offer an amazing amount of pulling power when attached to a nearby tree. Of course, a bumper-mounted winch offers the most sure-fire insurance against un-sticking a mired vehicle, but is difficult to justify for once-a-year use. Always carry a long-handled shovel. Simply removing mud or sand from behind or in front of truck tires can sometimes allow you to drive right out. When sunk down to your frame, digging is your only hope of freeing a heavy truck without hiring a costly tow truck.

Every truck comes equipped with a spare tire, but when far from civilization, a second spare is a wise move. Get a single flat and a trip to town is in order, time taken away from your elk hunt. Once your single spare is on the vehicle, you're really sticking your neck out to continue hunting, because another flat means you're stranded. I've long carried a portable air compressor, or cans of "fix-a-flat" tire sealer/inflator, and a tire-plugging kit. This precaution has gotten me out of some tight jams, and a tire-plug repair actually proves surprisingly reliable. Too, crawl under your truck and assure yourself your hanging spare is actually holding air. I've witnessed too many spares, after a year of neglect, lose pressure for

Mother Nature can be cruel. High-quality, dependable camping gear keeps you dry and warm when weather turns nasty.

Essential Fanny/Daypack Gear Checklist

Binoculars
Hunting Licenses & Tags
High-Energy Snack Foods
Rain Gear
GPS/Maps/Compass
Surveyor's Tape (for marking trail, downed game)
First-Aid Kit (or assemble your own in Zip-Lok bag)
Compact Flashlight & Headlamp (LED models prolong battery life)
Extra Batteries (choose GPS unit/flashlights that use the same batteries)
Two Knives (extra sharp)
Diamond Sharpening Steel (folding)
Folding Bone/Wood Saw
Water Bottle (preferably with purification filter lid)
Parachute Cord (for making shelter, hanging elk meat)
Waterproof Matches & Cigarette Lighter (placed in Zip-Lok bag)
Tinder Material & Candle (for starting fire with wet wood; waxed-soaked
   cardboard)
Toilet Paper (in Zip-Lok, also works to help start a fire)
Camera (extra film/memory card)
Sunscreen (minimum SPF 30)
Insect Repellent (scent-free brand)
Game Bags (enough to cover four elk quarters, plus black pepper when warm)
Two Plastic Lawn Bags (keep gear dry in rain, pack camp meat, make-shift
   raingear)
Spare Bow Gear (broadhead blades, nocks, small-game points, etc.)

no apparent reason, only to be discovered when it was needed badly.

Jumper cables are a bare-minimum precaution against a dead battery. We've all done it; in the excitement of a hunt we run off and leave our headlights on, only to return to a dead truck hours later. If you're lucky another hunter will be along to offer a boost. For a better guarantee you'll get your truck started on your own, look into a self-contained booster unit. These plug into your cigarette lighter to charge the unit while driving. They then hold a charge that can be used when needed; even to charge cell phones and digital cameras.

Before every prolonged elk hunt I take my truck into a mechanic to replace major belts and hoses and change all fluids; whether they need it or not. This is cheap insurance against a time-consuming and potentially expensive backcountry breakdown. I also assure my battery is fresh and reliable before starting out (and anchored securely), and time tire purchases to coincide with hunting season, starting my elk hunts with brand-new rubber all around. It's always wise to toss in enough oil to refill your crank case, and a couple gallons of antifreeze. You

A clean, well-lighted place (borrowing from Hemingway) makes for a more enjoyable elk hunting experience. Dry tents and bedding are paramount.

never know when an unseen rock or minor accident will punch a hole in your oil pan or radiator. Having spare fluids on hand could allow you to cripple into the nearest town for repairs.

Perhaps I've spent too much time trapping fur, alone in remote areas with questionable vehicles, but years later, even after acquiring more reliable transportation I always take to wild places expecting the worst. I've spent entirely too much time walking endless miles to find a phone, wasting precious hunting time getting a vehicle dislodged from a mud bog or into town after a breakdown.

CAMP REHEARSAL

Prevention also means carefully inspecting your camping gear. Nothing is worse than returning to a leaky tent and wet bedding at the end of an exhausting day of elk hunting. Set up your entire camp in the backyard (the kids will think this is great fun), inspecting tents for rips and tears, even spraying them down with a garden hose to test for leaks. Adding a layer of waterproofing spray won't hurt a thing even if it isn't leaking. Assure stoves and lanterns are operating properly and sleeping pads are reliably holding air. Pour over your camp trailer to assure stoves and refrigerators are receiving propane, and that improperly-drained water pipes have not burst during cold winter weather. After you have arrived in wild elk country is no time to discover problems. Summer weekend scouting trips can also be used to ferret out problems with camping gear, assuring no troubles or inconveniences once your hunt begins.

Gearing up for an impending elk hunt is part of the fun, expending nervous energy while assuring you spend your elk hunt hunting, not dealing with unforeseen problems. Start gathering your gear well before season and everything is sure to go off without a hitch.

Getting Into Shape

My rural lifestyle and geographic location allow me to lead an extremely active and healthy existence. My home also sits at relatively high altitude (6,500 feet above sea level). Even during those endless summer months when I spend more time behind the computer than outside (shamefully sucking down cigars to release nervous energy) I spend nearly every evening just prior to sundown making the rounds on my 30-target, "backyard" 3-D range. The course starts essentially right off the front porch and continues in a 1.5-mile loop of canyon country and gentle hills. I shoot to unwind and clear my mind at the end of those tedious days, enjoying the fresh air, watching the Labs "hunt" out-of-season quail and dove, as much as shooting my bow. I also have ready access to nearby mountains that rear to 10,500 feet, if I feel like taking a break on weekends and going for a strenuous hike. And yes, I fully understand what a lucky man I am. Not everyone is in the position to care-take a sprawling ranch.

But this could change soon enough. The ranch is for sale and I've acquired a wife, a woman I love and will follow anywhere. She's a quality engineer and must go where her work takes her, work that is seldom located in picturesque mountain communities. So soon enough I could become just another average denizen of the dreaded 'burbs; living at low elevation, far removed from healthy mountains and trout streams, working to keep in shape on tedious pavement and indoor exercise contraptions. And you can bet that's exactly what I will do. If you are an archery hunter and an elk hunter most especially, what other choice is there really? This will require more work; will no longer prove as "automatic" as it presently is.

BETTER ELK HUNTING THROUGH HEALTHIER LIVING

Dedicating yourself to physical fitness promotes a healthier lifestyle, a higher quality of life in general, but also means you're not playing catch-up when you

Opposite page: No matter your age, being in the best shape you can be before an elk hunt not only makes you more efficient, but makes your time afield a quality experience.

draw a coveted elk tag, during the average mountain hunt in general. I guess I'd have to admit a certain amount of contempt for self-proclaimed "archery hunters" who let themselves go physically. I perceive it as a lack of commitment to a way of life that means everything to me, something that drives and defines me. But I also understand why it is so. Being saddled with a demanding wife and children and a mortgage understandably shifts priorities.

As a long-time outfitter/guide in elk country I've seen the direct results of too much work and not enough play. One of the greatest challenges of that dodge was working around clients' physical (and mental) handicaps; something that—again being brutally honest—eventually encouraged me to abandon it completely. It's never fun to feel you're forcing someone to do something they'd obviously just assume skip, only going through the motions to save face or because of the cash investment. Others simply refused to try at all, leaving me to wonder why they bothered. There are much cheaper options for relaxation than an outfitted elk camp.

But there were notable exceptions, people who even though they held down demanding jobs, had large families and myriad responsibilities, arrived from their East Coast or California or Midwest sea-level homes ready to enthusiastically attack steep mountains and ridges, push beyond their physical limit to make something happen in often treacherous elk country, all without complaint and a wide smile across their faces. These hunters make a guide's job easy and fun. More importantly, they're having fun; getting the most from their hard-earned elk hunt. More revealing are my hardcore bowhunting buddies, people like Kansas-resident Keith Jabben or West Texan Steven Tisdale or Californian Jerry Gentellalli, who despite hectic work schedules and low-elevation residencies arrive in my mountains able to match me step for step when traveling in rough and remote country.

In order to reach elk country in the best possible shape it helps to think like an athlete. This means goal setting, "training" and proper time management. Time management enables you to achieve your fitness goals well before a hunt. Training means striving to increase endurance, and running or jogging is the cheapest way to this end. Your neighborhood high school running track is a good place to begin.

THE FOUR-DAY A WEEK ENDURANCE WORKOUT

This need not consume every free moment. In fact, you can get into top-notch shape by investing only a couple hours every other day, reducing your "training" to only four days a week through higher-quality sessions. Sports fitness expert Ben Wisbey, coach and sports scientist for FitSense Australia and Endurance Sports Training, breaks these sessions into a long run; "tempo" session; "VO2max" intervals; and a recovery run with "strides." Each of these sessions includes a different focus, and is important to your overall endurance improvement. It's one of the best solutions to elk-hunting fitness I have come across.

The long run is extremely important to improving aerobic endurance (strengthening the cardiovascular system; heart, lungs, and blood vessels and their ability

Opposite page: Plenty of hard work well before your elk hunt makes it that much easier later; especially as archery hunters age.

High altitude, long hours, running to cut off a traveling bull, these are the conditions you will encounter while elk hunting.

to deliver oxygen to the body), so does not need to be high intensity. This is best conducted (when possible) over undulating terrain so that you get the added benefit of strength development with the intended aerobic elements. Start with a stretching warm-up, followed by 10 minutes of relaxed jogging. The intensity should gradually be elevated to a moderate pace, not too taxing but not too easy, simply moderate and sustainable. Strive to build up to a 60- to 90-minute workout session, including 10 minutes of warm-up and cool-down (falling back into the relaxed pace of warm-up). At what intervals you increase running duration (and mileage) depends on your starting point, escalating more quickly if you're already in reasonable shape, over a period of months if you're starting from the bottom. A 10- to 15-percent increase per week should suffice thereafter. For example, start with a single mile, setting a goal of three miles by month's end.

The tempo session is key to improving your anaerobic threshold (breaking down and rebuilding, strengthening muscle), endurance economy and strength, while also improving aerobic endurance. This session should be run at approximately your anaerobic threshold—a pace that is uncomfortable and difficult but not impossible, sustained for a 30- to 60-minute period (depending on your current conditioning). This session is best run on flat or only slightly undulating ground, on grass or dirt where possible to avoid impact injury. Start and finish with the usual 10-minute warm-up and cool-downs, but the main portion of the run should include numerous hard pushes ranging in duration from five to 10 minutes, with "resting" low-intensity jogging between at a ratio of two to one. Also when beginning, make your ratios a bit easier than you think you can actually handle, getting a better feel for your realistic abilities so you can adjust them accordingly.

V02max intervals aim to improve the maximum amount of oxygen that your body can utilize when stressed. Boosting VO2max capacity allows your body to produce more energy aerobically, thus operating more efficiently at high intensities. A 10-minute warm-up is especially important here, preparing your muscles for the high-intensity efforts to follow. The basic premise is to complete three 500- to 600-yard sprints, each followed by a 90-second slow recovery jog. As you become better conditioned, strive for five 1,000-yard dashes, following with two-minute recovery jogs. As a good rule of thumb, when the quality of your efforts drops, stop the session and finish your 10-minute cool-down jog.

Recovery runs with strides is your easy training day, but still highly important. The aim is to provide active aerobic recovery training so that you can freshen up while still getting some light conditioning. This means a slow jog for 20 to 25 minutes, followed by two to four 50- to 80-yard fast runs on flat grass. These are not sprints; but a fast jog that can be completed in 10 or 20 seconds, followed by a leisurely walk-back recovery between each short run. You should finish this session feeling better than you started, so the idea is to avoid pushing too hard. Complete the session with an easy 10-minute jog.

These sessions are conducted every other day, with an off day between each session that allows your body to repair itself and make training more productive. It also leaves important time open to shoot your bow between training days. It's also best to plan your training structure around the long run, because it's the most time consuming. This most often indicates a weekend day.

TAKE THOSE HILLS

"Hill" training has also become popular with winning professional runners, and can shorten workout times. This helps develop power and muscle elasticity, encourages improved coordination and promotes strength endurance. Five- to

10-second sprints up short hills improve anaerobic energy production, while longer hills (150 to 200 yards) develop strength endurance. Downhill runs or those across undulating terrain help develop better coordination, something certainly welcome in rugged mountain terrain.

SLOW & STEADY

A recent Spanish study suggested that longer, low-intensity runs also provide benefits. Researchers monitored eight well-trained runners during a six-month period, recording heart rates (how much time they spent in various VO2 zones, measured one through three; low-intensity, moderate intensity and high intensity). These runners spent 71-percent of their time training in zone one, only eight-percent in zone three. Yet, they enjoyed improved performance (endurance) during long-distance races.

This involves development of slow-twitch verses fast-twitch muscles fibers, the technical details I'll spare you from. Slow-twitch muscles, endurance muscles, generate aerobic energy by allowing plentiful supplies of oxygen to reach the working muscles and numerous mitochondria. Mitochondria turn food (primarily carbohydrates) into energy required for muscular action. Development of slow-twitch muscles also increases capillary density, another enhancement to efficiently transporting oxygen. Slow-twitch muscles are best developed through longer, low-intensity exercise. That said, fast-twitch muscles are important in implementing lactate energy production, and reducing lactate threshold (sore muscles caused by excess lactic acid after exercise). This, of course, is a greatly simplified version of a very complicated process.

In a nutshell, developing your endurance capacity relies on a number of adaptations: Enhancing the already high oxidative capacities of slow-twitch fibers and improving the capacity of fast-twitch fibers to contribute to endurance activity. This makes the case for Wisbey's mixed program that I have discussed above.

WHAT ABOUT AGING ARCHERY HUNTERS?

Exercise experts were once certain that once you reach the age of 35 aerobic capacity began to steadily decline, slow at first, but picking up momentum as men reached their mid-40s, then plunging out of control at about the age of 60. More recently exercise scientists have begun to realize that much of the decline in performance accompanying aging is actually the result of disuse and not the aging process itself. In fact, recent studies show that people who exercise regularly often don't experience significant drop-offs in performance until they reach their middle 40s or early 50s, or later. In addition, the eventual downturns are usually far smaller than expected.

In a study conducted by Ball State University, Muncie, Indiana, eight inactive men showed characteristic declines in fitness; including a 15-percent per decade loss of aerobic capacity and a 12-beat per minute regression of maximal heart rate, in addition to downturns in general agility. Eighteen runners who trained only moderately lost only nine-percent of aerobic capacity per decade. More to the point, 11 individuals who continued to train intensively suffered no significant loss of VO2max or maximal heart rate. Of course, in this study of elite athletes, "old" was defined as mid-40s, but few of us muster elite status and the point is that exercise is important no matter your age.

Aging hunters might consider twice-a-week interval sessions on a treadmill, striving to push through quarter-mile stretches with no more than 1-minute recoveries between, since intensity is a more powerful producer of fitness in older men than mileage. Injury prevention and accelerated recovery can be achieved by cutting back on the miles while slightly increasing average training intensity. Added recovery time should also be considered part of growing older. The treadmill makes the most sense here because they are a little easier on aging legs and joints.

Fitness experts also suggest older men maintain training volume by engaging in low-impact "cross-training" such as aqua-running, swimming, cycling, ski machines, stair-steppers and weight training. Such workouts typically produce less muscle-tissue and joint damage, compared to running, and helps preserve important VO2max. Strength training is particularly important for hunters over the age of 50 when atrophy of muscle and skeletal tissues begins to become an issue. The old adage of "use it or lose it" couldn't be more apt than exercise in relation to age. Of course, as age increases, always consult a doctor before embarking on any program of strenuous exercise.

EMPLOY AN EXPERT

If you have the money, or an inner city existence leaves few options, consider joining a gym, even hiring a professional fitness trainer. The best in the business should have little challenge tailoring an exercise program that helps you quickly achieve your goals to become a more physical elk hunter. A word of caution: As many fitness trainers are "muscle heads," a heavy emphasis is often placed on upper-body weight training, body building if you will. Toning muscles never hurt anyone, but remember that bulk serves little purpose in vertical elk habitat; as well as the aspect that such workouts also own the potential of keeping you sore enough that shooting your bow becomes uncomfortable. Muscle discomfort can quickly lead to mentally-debilitating target panic and poor shooting.

THE MENTAL EDGE

To my mind, mental toughness is just as important as physical conditioning in the taxing world of modern elk hunting. Studies of elite athletes have shown that mental imagery is an integral part of their success. It's clear that creating, or recreating, an all-sensory experience can have positive effects on physical performance and psychological functioning. This becomes most important when faced with the almost overwhelming pressure of shooting a bow (an involved mental process) at a trophy bull elk (something you want badly, almost more than anything at that very moment).

Imagery can help develop a mental blueprint for performance under pressure by building confidence and reducing performance anxiety. The very young are naturally imaginative, regularly engaging the intuitive (for lack of a better term) right hemisphere of the brain. Unfortunately, systematic education, behaviors

The thin air of high altitude elk habitat makes physical conditioning even more important than in nearly any other bowhunting endeavor.

highly valued by adults, focus largely on logical and analytical processes which engage the brain's left hemisphere. The problem is that without constant practice the brain's imagery center reacts in much the same way as unused muscles (toward) atrophy. Although imagery can be applied to very dynamic situations, learning to do so on demand requires a quiet, relaxed, non-competitive setting. Begin this learning process by relaxing, closing your eyes and concentrating only on deep rhythmical breathing. With practice detailed mental imagery comes easier.

This is more than visualization, which is not the same animal. Imagery involves far more detail; including feelings of movement, sound, emotions and even smells. The elk hunter does more than see his arrow sinking into vitals. He attempts to hear the bull's hooves crunch atop gravel as he advances, the bull's grunting breath, the sound of wind through pine boughs, the smell of that bull traveling on a head-on breeze and into his nostrils. The subsequent sounds of the bow going off and the feel of the riser jumping in his hand are also portion. The sense of control as the correct pin is placed just so, the arrow released, a feeling of determination, even the nervous energy involved helps to stimulate all of the senses. The next step is to develop vividness, promote overall clarity. The final stage involves control.

As you are rehearsing what you are going to do, it's important to have control over your images. Imagery can be destructive as well as helpful. Seeing yourself crumbling, missing the easy shot, is hardly helpful. The wonderful thing about imagery is that even if you have missed easy shots at game before it provides an opportunity to correct past errors. This stage should incorporate a desired outcome. You should feel the movement and see a positive result. If you do began imaging negative outcomes, imagine a sudden and literal STOP sign, then work to redirect your thoughts by recalling a previous success and replicating this in your mind, with yourself in the role of successful performer.

AVOIDING CHOKE

Performance anxiety as it relates to bowhunting can take on many forms. "Buck fever" is one of these, as is any form of target panic. Making the difficult shot, keeping it together under pressure, is about controlling anxiety and sometimes even working to channel it positively. Anxiety is a natural reaction to threats around us, part of our hardwired "fight or flight" response. It is man's primitive and automatic response for survival from perceived harm or attack. In the case of pulling it off on a big bull, there is a threat posed to our ego and sense of self esteem; psychological factors that, unfortunately, can prove just as frightening to our minds as real physical harm. Essentially, when the demands of performing exceed one's perceived ability (natural doubts), anxiety is the inevitable result.

There's certainly nothing damaging about the stress associated with bowhunting. In fact, if this stress were removed, few of us would continue hunting. In fact, stress can be a very positive influence that leads us to tackle the challenges that make life far more rewarding. While bowhunting provides challenge and stimulation, it also provides considerable uncertainty. As a bull approaches your position, when a stalk is at a critical juncture, at that precise moment when the archer releases an arrow, the outcome is unknown. Buck fever is inevitably linked to this inherent uncertainty. Conversely, bowhunting brings us such joy because it is a theatre of unpredictability. The more important the "trophy" the greater the pressure, and the more likely you are to feel stress. I guess, too, there is an additional factor in the expectation of success. I see this in guided hunters most tangibly; the need for a return on their considerable investment, the wife at home who wasn't so keen on the idea of such an expensive vacation and the "told-you-so" demoralization sure to follow an unsuccessful hunt, from heckling peers. This is pressure that can cause you to choke at the moment of truth.

Again, professional sports trainers suggest many techniques for controlling performance anxiety, most of them impractical for on-the-fly use in the field. Of these, breathing exercises have proven most helpful to me; whether being pressured during an important 3-D competition, or faced with the biggest bull elk of my life. Start by inhaling slowly, deeply and evenly through your nose only. Hold that breath momentarily and gently exhale through your mouth; just enough to move a candle flame but not extinguish it. Take a breath and allow your face and neck to relax as you breathe out. Take a second breath and allow your shoulders and arms to relax as you breathe out. Next your chest, stomach and back; then your legs and feet; finally concentrate on allowing your entire body to relax while breathing out. Continue the exercise as long as is needed—or time allows! Each time you breathe out silently say the word "relax" or "calm." Call it silly if you will, but I can tell you without reservations it works wonders, helping my 3-D results immensely.

THE INNER VOICE

I've also found it important, on occasion, to talk to myself sternly (if silently) when faced with an impending shot at game, even when only the possibility of a shot is present. Sometimes I simply have to remind myself of important steps in the shooting sequence; especially shooting form, most notably to slow down. Sometimes when your mind is reeling from pressure, you have to remind yourself of the obvious. The mind under pressure commonly loses it's ability to accurately account for passing time. Everything seems to occur in a blur, when actually nothing at all has changed.

LEARNING FROM MISTAKES

Finally, don't allow a single failure (a missed shot in particular) to put you into a defeated funk. Develop the ability to forgive yourself. Move on, leaving the past behind. For this reason alone, I find 3-D extremely healthy for bowhunting mental health. No one likes losing or missing a target but it's easy to give up on an entire tournament due to a single missed shot. The attitude of dropping a single shot becomes "Well, that's it. I just blew the entire thing. I'm out." This is a cop-out. Mental fortitude requires more effort but allows you to carry on. Use that same miss to instead gain increased determination, saying something to the effect of, "Okay, I missed. No problem, I just have to bear down and shoot all 10s from here on out."

In the real world of bowhunting, after a miss on a fine bull elk, one healthy approach would be to say to yourself, "Thank God I got that out of the way. The next one's all mine." Much more productive than to allow self doubt to creep into your thoughts. It takes willpower. Positive mental imagery is a tool to create that will.

The importance of physical conditioning preceding a high-country elk hunt is blatantly obvious. Perhaps more than any other form of blood sport, bowhunting modern elk is a completely physical dodge. Even the seemingly simple pastime of guarding water or hanging a stand over a fence break or well-worn trail comes only after initial scouting (physically covering ground), the best of these sites just as likely to involve a moderately taxing access hike. Too, the elk hunter living near sea level, far removed from the elk's lofty haunts, will be forced to acclimate to a sudden increase in altitude, complete with "thinner," oxygen-deprived air, something getting into shape simply leaves your system better prepared for, abbreviating the process considerably. Days spent elk hunting are long, nights all too short, sleep deprivation constantly in play. Then when you are successful, there's suddenly the problem of 300 pounds of meat to remove quickly, no doubt from some hellish place, because few elk show the courtesy of falling near a handy road. Again, physical conditioning helps you cope.

Just as importantly is mental toughness. Conquering rugged elk country requires a "can-do," "never-say-die" attitude. When your legs ache and sleeping through the third alarm snooze button seems all too inviting, it's mental fortitude that

Mentally keeping it together during high-pressure shots at trophy bulls makes all the difference to success. Strengthen your mental muscle as you would your body.

keeps you pushing. When that behemoth bull steps into a shooting lane, pausing well within your maximum effective range, you had better bet that it's mental control that determines the ultimate outcome of your hunt.

These are the factors that make modern elk hunting so popular, what keeps veterans coming back for more, what makes elk the most sought after game in the entire West.

Are you up to the challenge?

Epilogue

t's customary at this point to paint a rosy picture of the future. I certainly wish that were possible, but in reality I can't even begin to guess what's in store for the future of elk hunting. The word that comes to mind is uncertainty. What has changed most about modern elk hunting is the uncertainty of hunting at all today or at least in places where the biggest bulls roam, even when seemingly harmless archery equipment is included. I haven't managed to draw a first-choice New Mexico tag in something like eight years, and I live in the middle of some of the best elk ground in the entire West, a resident privy (supposedly) to 78-percent of available tags. And yes, there is an element of sour grapes at play, because as I write this I've received my freshest rejection notice emblazoned with the tell-tale bear-head state seal. I've drawn some elk tags recently, sure, but these were consolation prizes compared to the units I really wanted to hunt. All this while friends from around the nation, non-residents paying $688 more than I do for a tag, draw quality tags on a semi-regular basis; or at least conspicuously more often than I do. There are no secrets left in elk hunting, so far as big bulls and high-odds success are concerned. We live in an information age and if it produces, especially if there are outsized bulls at stake, everyone understandably wants in on the action.

I've pretty much given up on the possibility of ever seeing an Arizona or Nevada elk tag, because I refuse to be exhorted for the price of an expensive hunting license, required to buy bonus points, that I will inevitably burn in the end. Should current odds prevail I could have more then $2,000 invested before drawing my first Arizona elk permit. Of course the Arizona situation was created by a lawsuit visited on the state by a single self-serving outfitter applying Wal-Mart mentality to the once folksy business of hunting, looking to provide his considerable and well-heeled client base an edge in obtaining what have become the most coveted tags in elkdom. These folks don't care that they have made it more costly for Joe Average to hunt elk in the Grand Canyon State, so long as they get their tag.

There seems no end to man's greed, and in the end this does not bode well

Opposite page: If we are to keep the elk hunting spirit alive we must fight to preserve wild places from the greed of man. Make your voice heard, become a joiner.

for elk hunting, public-lands hunting in particular. Politics have become so polarized in this nation that it's all or nothing to one extreme or the other. The right wants our land, the left our guns (which will eventually mean our hunting rights) and there seem to be fewer clearer heads in charge as each decade passes.

Threats to elk welfare abound from every front; public-lands grazing, powerful mining and logging interests, especially land development. The latter, perhaps, concerns me most of all (though public-lands ranchers have politically positioned themselves to control an amazing amount of game-management policy today—typically not to the betterment of elk welfare). Take a look around the next time you're in elk country. Once empty valleys and pristine mountainsides are filled and covered with vacation-home sprawl and retirement dreams fulfilled. The baby boomers have arrived, and they don't want to suffer through another single year in urban hells such as Detroit or Milwaukee or Hartford or Van Ives, where the money is made, socked away carefully for their eventual escape to paradise; to a place without crime and drugs and runaway property taxes—yet. I think of a plethora of elk meadows near home now filled with high-dollar homes and suddenly void of elk.

The public-lands grazing issue remains a double-edged sword. Leasees slowly destroy elk habitat through blatant overgrazing (it's not their land after all, and there are few incentives to curb abuses) and lowered elk carrying capacity (all the while subsidized by the American taxpayer), demand more elk are killed to maintain a dying lifestyle in an atmosphere of an ever-more-demanding world market. Yet to put them out of business is to invite still more land development in the heart of elk country. You can't blame the cattleman, really. Their backs are against the wall and they own something valuable and highly desired. It's easy to understand why they cash in and move to more viable cattle country, like eastern Oklahoma or Georgia, increased moisture directly inverting carrying capacity ratios—one cow-calf unit per 40 acres turning into 40 cows per acre.

Public-lands ranching interests and a willing, money-hungry Game & Fish Department have conspired to transform what was arguably the best elk hunting on Earth—New Mexico's Gila region—into something increasingly mediocre.

Elk management could easily be boiled down to a quality verses quantity argument. Quality elk mean fewer tags and less hunting pressure which directly improves age class structure by allowing more bulls to grow to full potential (to grow bigger antlers in plain speak). Everyone wants bigger antlers and higher success rates. Still, quantity gives more hunters an opportunity to participate, and no matter what a game agency PR department relates in way of creating increased opportunity for the good of "We The People," in reality it's simply the revenue they covet to fund their top-heavy bureaucracies. The common consensus seems to be that overall hunter numbers are plummeting, but this is difficult to swallow where once you secured an archery elk tag for the asking, today you wait years between hunts in those same areas.

I think of a pair of enthusiastic teenage boys (one from a decidedly non-hunting family, another parentless and being raised by his 70-year old grandmother) I've recently introduced to archery. They call regularly, begging to come out and shoot holes in my 3-D targets. I take them to summer weekend tournaments whenever possible. They cost me plenty in entry fees and ever-stouter bows and arrows and points and feathers they seem to go through like so much popcorn. I'm glad to do this because I remember all too well what it's like to be their age and bitten hard by the archery bug. They're addicted in every sense of the word. More recently they've expressed a burning desire to graduate to live targets. They even went to the trouble of taking hunter's safety classes; no small feat in a little town far removed from cities where such classes are offered only sporadically. They literally have deer in their backyards but missed an early application deadline and will have to wait an entire year to give it a try. I only hope they can manage to draw a tag when that time comes. The industry talks exhaustively about the future of bowhunting; but how's a young archer to get his start in this ridiculous atmosphere?

There are still big bulls out there no doubt, potential world records in the future, but increasingly I worry that these bulls will soon be reserved for only the privileged classes, those with the means to pay the price of admission to heavily-managed Indian reservations or exclusive private lands. Or simply invest in the correct number of preference points in every single key trophy elk unit in the West each and every year to increase their odds of hunting. It's always fascinated me that an Indian reservation comprising a very small portion of prime elk habitat can manage to produce so many more big bulls than surrounding public lands. Is there something magic about a five-strand barbed-wire fence?

After talking to a good number of the game managers responsible for maintaining these elk meccas, it has become apparent this country's government agencies have regulated themselves into complete ineffectiveness. Controlled burns and forest thinning that create grass, the construction of a needed watering site, to name but a few management factors, cannot be performed without the input of five government agencies and a very high stack of completed Environmental Impact Studies.

A game and fish department attempting to do the right thing is subjected to lawsuits and court injunctions from special interest groups of all kinds, forced to allot thinly-spread funds to support a federally-imposed Endangered Species Act that does nothing to create better elk (or any kind of) hunting. There's little left over for game, for elk. Did you know, for instance, that the U.S. Fish & Wildlife spends more money annually on the management of non-native wild horses and burros than it does on all game species combined? These monies came directly out of your pocket, the hunter's pocket, cash derived from Pitman-Robertson and Johnson-Dingle taxes tacked onto the top of every sale of hunting-related equipment. The backpackers, the bird-watchers, the anti-hunting tree-huggers who also enjoy our public lands, contribute nothing. If it were up to me, unless you are contributing, you would have no say in how land or game is managed. Yet these people who would happily take away your hunting rights are extremely vocal; and listened to, and taken seriously.

These are truths that should enrage the hunter, should have us storming state and national capitols demanding justice, but complacency has become a national pastime. Hunters in general have traditionally been poorly organized and this is why insane anti-hunting views become accepted public opinion, when in fact, few educated people would share such beliefs if provided an informed counterview. Our very nature works against us, quiet individualists who are not joiners or inclined to participate in group activities or the public forum.

It's time for that to change if we care anything for the future of our sport. Become a joiner. There are some good groups out their doing some very important things, making a difference. These would include foremost for our discussion here, the Rocky Mountain Elk Foundation, but also the Boone & Crockett Club and Safari Club International. The Professional Bowhunters Society is also notable, a traditional-archery-based organization but true to everything that is good about bowhunting in general. I would like to see the Pope & Young Club used more effectively but they seem more intent on maintaining their elitist private boys club than promoting bowhunting rights. Perhaps the new batch of directors waiting in the wings will bring about that change (at least they talk a good spiel). Think what you will of the National Rifle Association, but they are a politically powerful group fighting for our guns rights, the first front. And don't believe for a moment anti-gun advocates will not come after your bows, and overall hunting rights, with time.

Perhaps more importantly, attend state game commission meetings and make your desires heard. Only recently, Arizona game legislators succumbing to pressures from public-lands ranchers and the predictable greed for additional funds, proposed increasing elk-license quotas in that state. Short-sighted hunters looked upon it as an opportunity to secure a long-awaited elk tag. More savvy hunters were unwilling to sacrifice the state's longstanding and successful elk management program, something that is obviously working wonderfully. They circulated petitions, initiated a letter-writing campaign and arrived at key game commission meetings to make it clear they were not in favor of these potentially disastrous measures. Hunters won that first fight, but unfortunately when the subject raised its ugly head once again it was rammed through despite noisy opposition.

And it's time to look at ourselves more closely. I'm venturing into dangerous waters here, but if we wish to maintain our primitive status, our special bowhunting seasons, it's time to take a hard look at our equipment and how it directly affects success and our impact on the elk resource. There will always be those who prefer rifle hunting, and game will continue to be managed with a huge emphasis on that larger contingency. We gained our special seasons on the premise of major handicap and low impact. It will not go unnoticed should we began posting the same success numbers as rifle hunters. We will ultimately be punished for it. While it's simple human nature to stride ever forward in technological advancements, where will it all end? Will we be able to shoot an elk cleanly at 150 yards in the year 2050 (if we are still able to archery hunt at all)? Will there come a time when spending money will replace practice and skill in achieving bowhunting success?

It's now possible to competently shoot farther, gain proficiency more quickly and certainly with less practice. This is what has made archery seasons so appealing to a greater number of nimrods, archers who hunt for the more appealing seasons and not the love of archery. It also offers a possible explanation as to why even archery elk tags have become so hard won. I'm as guilty as anyone; possibly more so, because I'm a direct participant in the apparatus of promoting everything new and more efficient in archery. The time I spend bowhunting has become ever-more precious and I want to succeed as badly as the next guy. But I've started to worry. The subject represents another Catch-22: We need new archery hunters, added voices in our fight to keep what we have, but I foresee the possibility of our sport being loved to death. And yes, this worry is partially born of self interest, another undeniable human trait.

There's also the aspect of the public's perception of us as hunters. ATVs have taken the place of old-fashion Shank's Mare, gadgets and gizmos the place of hard-won woods lore. Early conservationist and avid archery hunter Aldo Leopold lamented of this trend as early as the early 1930s, a time when laser rangefinders and GPS units and all the paraphernalia we seem to find necessary could not even have been fathomed. We have an image to uphold, a responsibility to show the masses that we are upright, responsible citizens, and depicting elk hunting as a conquest, an all-out war, is not an attitude the non-hunting public is likely to embrace. It's these non-hunting citizens who will ultimately decide our fate. Creating a good impression wherever possible has never been more important to our survival.

But all's not gloom and doom. There are still plenty of places where elk flourish and even continue to expand, where the music of bugling bulls still rings through hollows and bounces off rough canyon walls, where it is possible to get away from the contrived living of modern life. More states than not are doing the right thing management-wise, improving their elk resource year by year. There are still wild places where securing an archery elk tag every year is possible, places to fulfill the primal need to pursue what is arguably the most majestic big game animal on the entire planet. These places may require more effort and fortitude to find success, but this is not a daunting prospect to most of us, even welcomed for those who love bowhunting elk; the simple pursuit, as much as the success.

Continued and growing interest in bowhunting elk will undoubtedly create savvier quarry, more difficult hunting conditions, so perhaps this factor alone will outpace the advancements in modern archery equipment. But I can assure you that elk will still remain as popular as ever. Success will depend on continuing to adapt, keeping an open mind to new techniques and approaches. For those of us who couldn't imagine a year without elk in it, we will happily adopt the inevitable new ways, forever maintaining the beautiful obsession that is bowhunting modern elk.

• GUESTS •

• GUESTS •

• GUESTS •

• Guests •

· Guests ·

• GUESTS •

• GUESTS •

• GUESTS •

• GUESTS •

• GUESTS •

• GUESTS •

• GUESTS •

• GUESTS •

· GUESTS ·

• GUESTS •

• G U E S T S •

• Guests •

• GUESTS •

• GUESTS •

· GUESTS ·

• GUESTS •

• GUESTS •

• GUESTS •

• GUESTS •

• GUESTS •

• GUESTS •

· GUESTS ·

• GUESTS •

• GUESTS •

• GUESTS •

• GUESTS •

• GUESTS •

• GUESTS •

· GUESTS ·

• GUESTS •

• Guests •

• GUESTS •

• GUESTS •

• Guests •

• GUESTS •

• GUESTS •

• GUESTS •

• GUESTS •

• GUESTS •

• GUESTS •

• GUESTS •

• GUESTS •

· GUESTS ·

• Guests •

• GUESTS •

• GUESTS •

• GUESTS •

• G U E S T S •

• GUESTS •

• GUESTS •

• GUESTS •

• G U E S T S •

• GUESTS •

• GUESTS •

• GUESTS •

· GUESTS ·

· GUESTS ·

· GUESTS ·

• GUESTS •

• GUESTS •

· Guests ·

• GUESTS •

• GUESTS •

• GUESTS •

• GUESTS •

• GUESTS •

• GUESTS •

• GUESTS •

_____   _____

_____

_____   _____

_____

_____

_____   _____

_____

_____   _____

_____

_____

• GUESTS •

• GUESTS •

• GUESTS •

• GUESTS •

• GUESTS •

• Guests •

· GUESTS ·

• GUESTS •

_____

_____

_____

_____

_____

_____

_____

_____

_____

_____

_____

_____

_____

_____

• GUESTS •

• GUESTS •

• GUESTS •

• GUESTS •

• GUESTS •

• GUESTS •

• GUESTS •

• GUESTS •

• GUESTS •

• GUESTS •

• GUESTS •

• GUESTS •

• GUESTS •

• GUESTS •

PETER PAUPER PRESS
Fine Books and Gifts Since 1928

OUR COMPANY

In 1928, at the age of twenty-two, Peter Beilenson began printing books on a small press in the basement of his parents' home in Larchmont, New York. Peter—and later, his wife, Edna—sought to create fine books that sold at "prices even a pauper could afford."

Today, still family owned and operated, Peter Pauper Press continues to honor our founders' legacy—and our customers' expectations—of beauty, quality, and value.

Designed by David Cole Wheeler

Copyright © 2011
Peter Pauper Press, Inc.
202 Mamaroneck Avenue
White Plains, NY 10601
All rights reserved
ISBN 978-1-4413-0559-6
Printed in China
14 13 12 11

Visit us at www.peterpauper.com